CAREER
OPPORTUNITIES
IN PHOTOGRAPHY

CAREER OPPORTUNITIES IN PHOTOGRAPHY

GEORGE GILBERT

With

PAMELA FEHL

Checkmark Books

An imprint of Infobase Publishing

Career Opportunities in Photography

Checkmark Books
An imprint of Infobase Publishing
132 West 31st Street
New York NY 10001

Library of Congress Cataloging-in-Publication Data
Gilbert, George, 1922–
    Career opportunities in photography / George Gilbert with Pamela Fehl.
        p. cm.
    Includes index.
    ISBN 0-8160-5678-1 (hc : alk. paper) ISBN 0-8160-5679-X (pb : alk. paper)
    1. Photography—Vocational guidance. I. Fehl, Pamela. II. Title.
    TR154.G53 2006
    770′.23—dc22   2005021495

Checkmark Books are available at special discounts when purchased in bulk quantities for businesses, associations, institutions, or sales promotions. Please call our Special Sales Department in New York at (212) 967-8800 or (800) 322-8755.

You can find Facts On File on the World Wide Web at http://www.factsonfile.com

Cover design by Nora Wertz

Printed in the United States of America

VB Hermitage 10 9 8 7 6 5 4 3 2 1

This book is printed on acid-free paper.

CONTENTS

INDUSTRY OUTLOOK

Photography has evolved tremendously over the years to become a truly global industry, due in particular to the development of digital cameras and photographic design software. Now, more people than ever before are capable of taking pictures, manipulating and enhancing the images digitally, and transmitting them within seconds, via the Internet, to people based anywhere in the world. These technological advances are simultaneously a blessing and a curse for professional photographers. The boon is that digital photography and computer design software enable professional photographers to transport their equipment and set up shoots even in the most remote locations while still maintaining consistent contact with clients to secure approvals and report on work progress. Digital photography also saves photographers time and money in film. If they work solely in digital, they no longer have to purchase film nor do they have to handle the film processing. The downfall, though, is that with the proliferation of digital cameras and photographic design software in the marketplace, many more people have access to the equipment and are usurping the work. While they may not be professionally trained, nothing prevents them from hanging a shingle outside their doorway advertising their photographic services. Unfortunately, digital technology enables a wider range of people to create, store, and access their photographs without need of the professional photographer. On the other hand, companies and individuals who recognize quality and appreciate highly skilled and experienced photographers will continue to need and commission professionals to help them with their projects.

The photography field has always attracted more people than there are jobs to fill, and competition for those jobs is expected to remain fierce through 2012, according to the Department of Labor. Photographers are generally freelancers with entrepreneurial spirits; more than half are self-employed and manage their own businesses. The outlook is bright for those individuals who are not only technically proficient, creative, and talented but also extremely flexible, adaptable to change, and able to keep abreast of technological developments in the field. Individuals who have work-related backgrounds and who are savvy business owners are usually the most sought-after and the most successful in the industry.

In 2002, photographers held about 130,000 jobs. Many are self-employed and own their own commercial studios or portrait studios. While many work on a contract basis, with portraits and projects varying, still others may also create photographic images for stock photography agencies. Photographers may be salaried employees of advertising agencies, magazine and book publishers, newspapers, or television networks, or they may be contracted for individual projects. Most photographers run their own businesses in large metropolitan areas. The *Occupational Outlook Handbook* predicts that employment in the photography field will grow about as fast as the average, by about 10 to 20 percent, for all occupations through the year 2012. Of all the disciplines, portrait photographers will most likely fare the best, as demand for their services will grow as the population increases. Commercial photographers who work digitally may also have greater success in finding work; they will be able to secure projects with magazines, journals, and newspapers that are increasingly publishing electronic versions for consumers.

Industry outlooks for the major media that hire photographers to create photographic images are as follows:

Advertising & Public Relations

Industry Overview: There are 47,000 advertising and public relations organizations in the United States, with one in five agencies being public relations firms. Of the advertising agencies that exist, four out of seven are full-service houses, meaning they offer copywriting services and the creation of artwork, graphics, and photographic images for advertisements. Once the advertisements are completed, test-marketed, and approved, these agencies place the ads on television, radio, and the Internet, and in newspapers, magazines, and other periodicals. Many of the largest agencies, such as Ogilvy & Mather, J. Walter Thompson, Grey Global, Young & Rubicam, OMD, and others, have offices around the world and receive a great deal of revenue from abroad.

Employment: In 2002, the advertising and public relations industry employed 442,000 workers, with an additional 56,000 contracted as self-employed workers. The majority of advertising and public relations agencies are located in large cities and states. New York and California offer the most opportunities for work; these two states alone account for one in five firms and one in four employees in the entire industry. Some agencies may be small shops, with merely a handful of employees; others may have thousands of employees throughout the world. More than half of all advertising and public relations agencies, however, have small staff structures, with less than 20 employees. Most employees are between the ages of 25 and 54, which means that prior work experience and training that is specific to the industry are important prerequisites.

Outlook: Keen competition for jobs in the advertising and public relations industry is expected because, as with all *glamour* industries, there is an overabundance of candidates compared to the number of positions available. The industry is expanding slightly faster, however, than other industries, and a 19 percent growth in employment is projected from 2002 through 2012, which is a 3 percent increase over all industries combined. Advertising and public relations services are directly linked to the economy, and as things improve, more money will become available for promoting and advertising products and services. The creation of new media outlets and expansion of current outlets also offers greater opportunities for employment, as skilled workers will be needed to create Internet content and photographic images. The flipside of this potential growth, unfortunately, is that nonprint media (i.e., Internet, radio) has the potential to also preclude the need for employees. Also, legislation can directly and adversely impact agencies that work with clients whose products are controversial or affect public health and safety, such as alcohol, tobacco, etc. Laws prohibiting advertisements for cigarettes or alcoholic beverages, for example, can decrease business for agencies that work in these areas. Layoffs are another inherent part of the advertising and public relations industry. When clients move their business to other agencies, or slash their budgets, agencies are directly affected and must lay off workers in order to survive. People who enter this business understand this is just part of the terrain.

Publishing

Industry Overview: Publishing companies produce books, magazines, newspapers, directories, greeting cards, calendars, software, and other literature in a variety of formats, from print and audio to CD-ROM and other electronic media. Job hunters will find that the best opportunities for employment in the publishing industry are at newspapers. Of all publishing businesses combined, it is a known fact that newspapers employ the most workers. These days, large corporations such as Gannett own most of the newspapers in America. Many companies are also *clustering* newspapers, which means they're buying several newspapers that are circulated within the same region, thereby easing production costs and increasing efficiency, particularly because the newspapers can be printed at, and distributed from, the same printing plants. Clustering can also create more jobs and money for advertisers, who can now place advertisements in numerous publications at one time.

A few large corporations, such as the Hearst Corporation and Time Warner, also own most of the book publishing companies in this country, many of which are based in New York City. This is not to say that New York City is the only place to find work in book publishing. Some midsize and small publishing companies across the country, particularly those that specialize in certain subjects, are also thriving. But because they are smaller, it will mean a fiercer competition to secure work. Textbooks, technical, scientific, and professional books comprise almost half of the book publishing industry's revenue, with adult trade (i.e., bookstore books, such as paperback, juvenile, religious, reference books, etc.) comprising the other half.

Magazines or periodicals are usually either run as small shops or fall under the umbrella of large media conglomerates that publish scores of magazines, again such as the Hearst Corporation. Magazines can be geared for *trade,* or business-to-business, or strictly for consumers. Trade magazines are targeted specifically to certain industries, professions, or services, and consumer magazines are for a wider and more general audience.

Employment: In 2002, the publishing industry provided nearly 714,000 salaried jobs, with an additional 39,000 self-employed workers. (Note: These numbers do not take into account the freelance contributors to the publications, such as writers, journalists, photographers, and artists.)

Outlook: As with advertising, the publishing industry is a glamour business that always features more job applicants than there are jobs to fill. Competition for work is perpetually keen. The Bureau of Labor Statistics predicts a 1 percent drop in wage and salary employment in publishing (save for software) from the 2002 through 2012 period, compared to the projected 16 percent growth for all industries in that same time frame. As the demand for more information arises, however, publishing companies will have to hire skilled workers to meet those needs. People will continue to want to be informed by newspapers, magazines, and books that have been produced in diverse media. Much content is now on the Internet, and e-books are particularly on the rise and predicted to grow through 2012. The economy also drives the publishing industry. The consequence of a depressed economy is that advertisers reduce their advertising budgets, local and state governments reduce their budgets for school and library books, and publishers search for ways to save money, by also cutting budgets and laying off employees.

Internet news sites are on the rise because each year, the number of people who are able to easily access the Internet steadily increases. While newspaper subscriptions have been declining over the years, mergers and clusters are increasing the efficiency of newspaper production. They are also helping to expand the reach and scope of writers and photographers, whose work can often be published in numerous publications at one time. Newspaper mergers are expected to decline through 2012, and as technology improves and newspaper production becomes more efficient, even less people will be needed to produce a newspaper. This impacts the production and administration side of the business more so than it does the creative side. Writers and photographers will still be needed to generate content and to help share the news with readers. And while newspaper mergers may decline, magazine mergers are projected to continue. The high school and college student population is also expected to increase through 2012, leading to increased demand for textbooks. As new discoveries and experiments emerge, technical and scientific books and journals will be needed to share information with the general public. The Federal Communications Commission (FCC) is expected to lighten its rules in regard to banning ownership of TV stations and newspapers in the same market. Should this happen, employees may be mandated to work in both the print and broadcast mediums. For photographers, this might mean learning to use video cameras.

Broadcasting

Industry Overview: The broadcasting industry is composed of radio and TV stations and networks that create their own original content or are licensed and legally permitted to broadcast (or "air") taped television and radio programs. Networks are responsible for literally *networking* the shows. They use satellite signals to transmit from broadcast studios to local stations or cable distributors. Cable television lines, satellite distribution systems, or transmission tower airwaves then carry the broadcast signals to TV and radio antennae. If they are within the range of the signal, people can see and listen to a variety of programs, such as movies, national and local news, talk shows, concerts, plays, musicals, live performances, sports programs and competitions, advertisements, and more. Most stations produce their news programs, as well as some other programs, in their own studios. The motion picture industry produces a great deal of filmed or taped programming for radio and television sta-

tions and networks. Television is moving in the digital television (DTV) direction, which enables the transmission of higher-resolution pictures and better-quality sound, or high-definition television (HDTV). By 2007, the FCC aims to have all stations cease analog signal broadcasting. Almost half of all TV stations are already complying with FCC regulations by broadcasting digital HDTV signals. HDTV does not require the specialized hardware that was needed for analog transmissions, thus stations are replacing all of that equipment with less-specialized computers, which has software that achieves the same results. Digital cameras, HDTV cameras, and computer-editing equipment and servers are the tools of choice.

Employment: About 334,000 wage and salary jobs were provided by the broadcasting industry in 2002. More than half of all the jobs were in organizations with at least 100 employees. Most jobs are located in larger cities, although broadcasting stations can be found across the United States.

Outlook: Employment growth in the broadcasting industry is expected to be slow, increasing by less than 9 percent between 2002 and 2012. Industry consolidation, the creation of new technologies, and competition with media outlets will account for the sluggishness. Consolidation of broadcast stations into major networks means corporations will need fewer employees. They will streamline their staff structures and increase efficiency by running many stations, for example, from only one office. New technologies will also reduce the need for specialized staff. And Internet media outlets, such as video-on-demand services, also constrain job growth in the broadcasting industry. Applicants with prior work experience and degrees in broadcasting, photojournalism, or related fields will have better odds of securing employment in this field.

HOW TO USE THIS BOOK

The 62 job descriptions provide basic information about the photography industry and specific information about various branches of photography and related careers. Unlike employees in many other industries, photographers do not always follow clear career paths. They often work on a freelance or self-employed basis, and those on staff are not necessarily promoted in a structured, hierarchical manner. Skills and techniques acquired and honed in one particular discipline can often be transferred to other photographic branches, and versatile, reliable photographers can often build their career by taking on work outside their primary specialty. Photographers tend to be independent workers, and their career ladders are often shaped by their personal interests, creativity, and entrepreneurial spirit.

Career Opportunities in Photography is an excellent starting point to begin your research into jobs in this industry. The information presented here comes from interviews with working professionals and industry experts, statistics made available by the United States Department of Labor (specifically, the Bureau of Labor Statistics and the *Occupational Outlook Handbook*), surveys conducted by industry associations and numerous other sources such as trade magazines, books, and Web sites.

The careers covered here have been grouped into nine categories: Business and Industrial Photography; Cinematography and Videography; Commercial Photography, Advertising, and Publicity; Event and Travel Photography; Fine Arts and Education; Medical and Scientific Photography; News Media and Entertainment Photography; Photography Business and Related Jobs; and Portrait Photography. These groupings have been made to aid the reader in his or her research, but keep in mind that while some successful photographers specialize in a single field, others may build a career by working in multiple categories.

Each job article includes the following elements:

Career Profile

The career profile section provides a brief summary of the job duties, any alternate title or titles that may exist, the salary range, employment and advancement opportunities, prerequisites (which include education, training, work experience, and special skills and personality traits), and, if they apply, licensing or certification requirements.

Career Ladder

The career ladder indicates the job that can lead to the title profiled and the next job up. The top job listed is usually the

senior-level position, the middle job is frequently the job profiled, and the bottom job is the entry-level position. In some instances, the job profiled is a senior-level position and may be listed at the top. Senior photographers often advance by growing their businesses and branching out into other disciplines, as well as teaching and writing. Career ladders are not hard-and-fast career paths but only representative of those that are common or likely.

Position Description

This section provides a more in-depth look at the job. This description covers a typical working day and the work environment for workers in the specific career under discussion. It notes the kind of schedule these workers may have, what employer expectations will be, what their various tasks and responsibilities will be, what difficulties they might face, and how the job relates to photography jobs and industries.

Salaries

Salary ranges were ascertained from working professionals, trade associations and organizations, and the U.S. Department of Labor. Some specialized jobs are not singled out in government reports. Information for such jobs has been based on other sources, such as information from professionals and industry surveys, or it has been extrapolated by looking at related jobs and expectations for growth and earnings in key related industries. Salary ranges reflect annual wages, flat day or project rates, or hourly rates. Factors that can impact salaries are also mentioned, (i.e., years of experience, educational background, technical expertise, type of clientele, type of product, how the work will be used, geographical location, size of budget, overtime, rush jobs, and more). Tips about how certain artists enhance their incomes are also included.

Employment Prospects

Employment prospects are rated poor, fair, good, or excellent based upon discussions with professionals who are currently working in the jobs and those who have experience in the field, as well as the U.S. Department of Labor's *Occupational Outlook Handbook,* which predicts expected industry growth through the year 2012. Factors that can impact employment prospects include the economy, technological advances, whether the job is in an exciting or glamorous environment and therefore highly competitive, as well as the prospective employee's background and initiative.

Advancement Prospects

Discussed here are advancement *possibilities.* Career paths in photography can come in different manners, and so opportunities for advancement exist in a variety of forms. The information is, again, based on discussions with professional photographers, industry experts, and research gathered from various organizations and publications. While most staff employees require some management expertise, a solid understanding of photography and new and emerging technologies is generally necessary for advancement of any kind in this industry.

Education and Training

Four-year college degrees are often recommended for the jobs listed in this book, but they are not always required. A bachelor's degree provides an overall, well-rounded education that serves as a solid basis for working in any branch of photography. For some fields, advanced degrees are required. The types of courses individuals should take, as well as any additional training—such as computer image software or digital photography—are also mentioned in this section.

Experience, Skills, and Personality Traits

Work backgrounds, special skills, and personality traits that are important to being successful, comfortable, and happy in this particular field are covered. Freelance employees share an independent-minded and entrepreneurial spirit. Staff employees will, perhaps, prefer more structured environments. Most photographers will be required to deal directly with clients, subjects, and the public on a regular basis, so personality is a big factor in achieving success. This section will help you determine where you fit best in the industry.

Unions and Associations

Membership to trade associations and other professional organizations can enhance photographers' careers by offering them workshops, conferences, educational opportunities, and networking targeted to their specialization. Some branches of photography require workers to belong to unions. Union membership assures members of set wages and working conditions. The associations discussed in this section are suggestions based on recommendations from working professionals and research. To learn more and find other organizations and those that may be based near you, use an Internet search engine and visit association Web sites.

Tips for Entry

Each career profile ends with three to five tips that shed light on important steps a prospective employee can take to get a foot in the door. Professional photographers shared this advice based on their personal experiences, as well as what they know to be the protocol for entry, whether it is an apprenticeship or internship, networking, creating a stellar portfolio, or a combination of all.

Other Resources in This Book

Appendixes: The appendixes provide listings of schools and associations that specialize in photography. Separate appendixes cover two-year programs, four-year programs, graduate programs, and more. Also included are directories of associations and organizations, industry periodicals, and useful Web sites.

Bibliography: For further information or research, the books listed here can be helpful.

BUSINESS AND INDUSTRIAL PHOTOGRAPHY

AERIAL PHOTOGRAPHER

CAREER PROFILE

Duties: Takes aerial photographs for architects, builders, landscapers, state departments, national parks, realtors, estate owners, newspapers, magazines, and others; arranges for airplanes and pilots or flies own plane; scouts locations; reviews flight plans; creates estimates and handles accounts receivable and payable

Alternate Title(s): None

Salary Range: $50,000 to $200,000

Employment Prospects: Excellent

Advancement Prospects: Excellent

Best Geographical Location(s): Massachusetts, Connecticut, New York (upstate), New Jersey, Maryland, Virginia, Florida, Michigan, Colorado, Nevada, California, New Mexico, Arizona, and Washington, D.C.

Prerequisites:

Education or Training—Four-year degree, with specialization in photography; flight training; on-the-job sky photography training

Experience—Prior assignments of high- and low-level flying, including cliffside approaches, obscured forest settings, and weak light conditions

Special Skills and Personality Traits—Good with heights and comfortable in small aircraft; flexible attitude; good eye for detail; solid grasp of lighting; strong communication skills

Special Requirements—Commercial pilot's license required for those photographers who fly their own plane; Federal Aviation Administration certification

CAREER LADDER

```
┌─────────────────────────────────────┐
│       Aerial Photographer            │
└─────────────────────────────────────┘

┌─────────────────────────────────────┐
│ Commercial Photographer / Pilot /    │
│ Radio or Television Weather Briefer  │
└─────────────────────────────────────┘

┌─────────────────────────────────────┐
│      Assistant Photographer          │
└─────────────────────────────────────┘
```

Position Description

The widening range of oil prospecting, growing environmental monitoring, and the government's need for updated data on rivers, lakes, and even golf courses or resorts located on waterways has created an increased demand for Aerial Photographers. Through their photographs, Aerial Photographers help specialists observe targeted areas during droughts and floods, as well as pinpoint damages from storms and related environmental changes.

Aerial Photographers survey environmental conditions and conduct research work for cartographers and scientists studying lakes. Real estate agencies appraising land also hire Aerial Photographers. Advertisers and publishers retain Aerial Photographers for a wide variety of products and messages. Some Aerial Photographers have experience covering the weather for radio or television news stations. Another avenue Aerial Photographers pursue is photographing airplanes in flight for airline companies and others. Sometimes they work from helicopters. They might also take aerial photographs for the purpose of creating art. They publish their work in books and magazines and post them on their Web sites.

From the air, all focus is at infinity, and all exposures are at 1,000th or higher speeds. Aerial Photographers capture images at oblique (slant) and orthographic (vertical) angles. Technological advances have made things easier and more convenient for Aerial Photographers. Many use digital cameras, gyro-stabilizing devices, and vibration-reduction lenses and later edit the images using Adobe Photoshop. Small, portable printers that plug right into cameras, operating independently of computers, are also invaluable tools.

If piloting the plane, Aerial Photographers need to be mindful that they act first as pilot and second as photographer. Getting caught up in photographing images can distract from the primary and serious job of flying the plane. If working with a pilot, Aerial Photographers communicate to the pilot, usually through headphones, when they spot areas they want to photograph. They take at least several backup photographs because there is never an assurance that just one will come out accurately.

Salaries

Aerial Photographers' annual salaries can range from $50,000 to $200,000 or more, depending on the time of year, region, business specialization, and government requirements. Independent Aerial Photographers who own their own planes must factor into their earnings costs for maintaining their plane to Federal Aviation Administration specifications, plus license and registration upkeep. If they are renting aircraft and hiring pilots, they must factor this in, also. Aerial Photographers who are pilots and own their plane can enhance their salaries by renting their services to other photographers.

Employment Prospects

Although there are no statistics specific to the employment of Aerial Photographers, a parallel can be drawn by reviewing the job prospects for cartographers, surveyors, photogrammetrists, and surveying technicians. These specialists often work closely with Aerial Photographers, thus it is reasonable to extrapolate that as they secure work, so, too, will Aerial Photographers. According to the *Occupational Outlook Handbook (OOH)*, employment of surveyors, cartographers, photogrammetrists, and surveying technicians is expected to grow by 10 to 20 percent through the year 2012.

The *OOH* further explains that in 2002, federal, state, and local governmental agencies provided one of six jobs for these specialists. The U.S. Geological Survey, the Bureau of Land Management, the Army Corps of Engineers, the Forest Service, the National Oceanic and Atmospheric Administration, the National Imagery and Mapping Agency, and the Federal Emergency Management Agency are the major federal government employers. Local and state groups such as highway departments, urban planning and redevelopment agencies, as well as construction firms, mining and oil and gas extraction companies, and utilities also employ cartographers, surveyors, and the like.

Advancement Prospects

Aerial Photographers are typically well-seasoned professionals and are at the senior-level in the industry. They can always advance by expanding their studio's services, branching out into other media (such as video), and hiring more staff. They can also write for books, magazines, and Web sites and lecture or teach.

Education and Training

Aerial Photographers should have a college education, often at a four-year liberal arts or art college, with a specialization in photography. If planning to fly his or her own plane, the Aerial Photographer must pursue flight training and can do so either during college or any time thereafter. Several years of photography experience in a commercial studio is required.

Special Requirements

Aerial Photographers who fly their own airplanes or helicopters must possess a valid commercial pilot's license. A small aircraft can be a primary tool in this industry, though it is not by any means a requirement. Many successful Aerial Photographers do not own their own aircrafts and instead hire pilots for their shoots. Aerial Photographers who pursue the license must pass the Federal Aviation Administration's (FAA) medical examination, as well as meet FAA flight-time requirements, which can take years to accumulate. Additionally, airplanes and helicopters must be licensed by the FAA.

Experience, Skills, and Personality Traits

Aerial Photographers are comfortable with heights and at ease in small planes and helicopters. They have a good appreciation of natural light; they understand how to work with it and how to time their photographs to best capture the images they seek. They are patient, flexible, detail-oriented, and have strong communication skills. Successful Aerial Photographers know how to work with challenging conditions, such as weather, and how to solve problems quickly and intelligently. They are technologically adept and have digital camera and Adobe Photoshop experience.

Unions and Associations

The Professional Aerial Photographers Association (PAPA) provides members with educational newsletters and conferences, annual print competitions, and networking opportunities. Through PAPA, Aerial Photographers can also participate in Web forums and online chats, sign up for stock evaluations and representation, access historical photograph resources, and more.

Tips for Entry

1. Check your local phone book for Aerial Photographer listings and keep an eye on bulletin boards at your

local airport. Call photographers, introduce yourself, and see if you can set up a meeting. Bring a list of questions to the meeting so you can reap as much information as possible while you are there.

2. Offer unpaid assistance to a pilot in order to learn more about flying and photography. See if you can get a ride on a flight to an actual aerial photography destination.

3. Read as much as you can about aerial photography. Immerse yourself in books and magazines. You can also find innumerable resources on the Web; just key in *aerial photography* in an Internet search engine.

CONSTRUCTION PHOTOGRAPHER

CAREER PROFILE

Duties: Records site progress for builders, architects, contractors, and others; takes notes on what is being photographed and angle of view (i.e., 18th floor interior, east to west); creates estimates; handles billing; creates prints and digital images; may appear as witness in court cases between builders and subcontractors, with photographs used as evidence of work progress and specific work being done

Alternate Title(s): Architectural Photographer, Building Photographer

Salary Range: $35,000 to $60,000+

Employment Prospects: Fair

Advancement Prospects: Fair

Best Geographical Location(s): Major cities with ongoing construction needs, such as New York, Boston, Washington, D.C., Atlanta, Chicago, Dallas, Denver, Las Vegas, Miami (and other parts of Florida), Seattle, Portland, San Francisco, and Los Angeles

Prerequisites

Education or Training—Two- or four-year degree in photography; digital camera and design software training

Experience—Minimum, several years of experience as a commercial photographer; some experience in or familiarity with construction and building equipment and materials helpful

Special Skills and Personality Traits—Technologically adept; comfortable with heights; physically fit; focused, able to concentrate amid extreme noise and disruption; versatile communicator, able to work with variety of professionals, from construction crew to building owners; organized; decisive

CAREER LADDER

```
┌─────────────────────────────────┐
│   Construction Photographer     │
└─────────────────────────────────┘

┌─────────────────────────────────┐
│   Commercial Photographer       │
└─────────────────────────────────┘

┌─────────────────────────────────┐
│   Photographer's Assistant      │
└─────────────────────────────────┘
```

Position Description

The Construction Photographer is the visual diarist of the construction of any private, industrial, governmental, or other building project for technical or legal considerations. Depending on the photography assignment, he or she may maintain a photographic project history from the first shovel to break ground to the final ribbon-cutting ceremony. In some cases, Construction Photographers are hired to photograph interiors, to document floor-by-floor progress of office and apartment buildings.

Such photographs provide construction management with visual support of worksite progress. The architect tracks construction details and monitors the brick-and-mortar progress, from delivery of wet cement to placement of door and window apertures. The Construction Photographer photographs workers installing heating, air-conditioning, and water and sewage flow systems. Most of the work typically takes place during business hours on weekdays. Construction Photographers may work after hours or on weekends for special once-only moments, such as groundbreaking ceremonies, the removal of hoists, and the "topping-off" parties, celebrated when the tops of large buildings and skyscrapers are completed.

A Construction Photographer's primary tools are small, handheld digital cameras with all-weather imaging capability that work even in difficult lighting conditions or in corners of the construction site. The photographer works from notes provided by the on-site offices as requested by responsible project participants, ranging from the insurance company, the bank, the architect's quality-control manager, and others. Construction Photographers may photograph at the site daily, weekly, monthly, or at any other time frame as required. They photograph in some kind of sequence, to visually match the progress of the construction. Each photographer sets this up differently. For instance, each time visiting the site, the photographer may photograph the outside of the building first, then photograph three floors, shooting every third floor until reaching the top, then starting from the bottom for the next sequence.

When Construction Photographers arrive at the site, they check in with the construction manager and safety manager for a status report on the building's progress and any particular work or blasting that they should be aware of. Photographers may request ladders from the field tool room for higher views or for security assistance before ascending to aim cameras where girders meet the sky. They work closely with the quality-control team members to confirm size of wood and steel before riveting or concrete deliveries. Construction Photographers keep timed records and data on the number of exposures they make and special listings of unusual features to e-mail or fax to the photography project manager. They also keep track of job-related expenses and maintain receipts for authorized expenses.

Construction Photographers obey all safety rules, such as donning a hard hat and wearing an orange outer vest so construction workers, tracker and truck drivers, and other operators of large equipment can easily see them. Photographers must also keep their wits about then when on a site, always keeping aware of any calls or horns signaling blasting or work breaks.

When builders have disputes with subcontractors, they may ask Construction Photographers to appear in court as witnesses to the work being done. The photographers will document the work that has been accomplished and what needs to be addressed. Builders also use photographs to assure people financing the work that the work they have paid for has been completed.

Salaries

Construction Photographers can earn annual salaries ranging from $35,000 to $60,000 or more for their technical skills and their commitment to traveling to construction sites and working in all-weather conditions. Some may earn higher wages based on their years of experience, special skills, or the nature of the project they are covering. Large and smaller companies offer periodic salary growth for staff photographers, often slightly in advance of the changing cost-of-living index.

Employment Prospects

The construction industry is a vital American growth industry. Most commercial construction projects require photographers on site, so demand is steady and openings can be numerous. The building industry is reaching new growth heights in construction of major downtown, waterside, and new industrial parks, private-home communities, and resort cities. New commercial zones with funding underway have been established from private, state, and federal government upgrading of older facilities. Other major construction projects that are on the rise are new or renovated prisons, the replacement and extension of schools in high-density inner cities, and the modernization of office and service facilities.

Advancement Prospects

There is no specific job to which Construction Photographers can advance. They can explore photographing different aspects of buildings. They can move into architectural photography and other disciplines.

Education and Training

An associate's or bachelor's degree in photography is usually recommended for work as a Construction Photographer. Digital camera and design software training is required.

Experience, Skills, and Personality Traits

A background in construction or building trades, with some knowledge of architecture, is helpful in this field. Construction photographers should be decisive and self-confident, with natural flexibility for moving from close-up details to overall views. They are competent, extroverted, and unfazed by weather, noise, massive equipment, and heights. Construction Photographers must be physically fit and mentally equipped to handle working outdoors in buildings that, for the most part, are not enclosed. Climbing stairs and walking planks at extreme heights is a big part of this job. Construction Photographers must be prepared with proper safety equipment: protective pants, jackets, boots, hard hats, safety harnesses if needed, and more. They stay tuned into their environment and have extremely good communication skills. As they move about the sites, they always make sure that where they plan to head is safe and won't disrupt the work.

Unions and Associations

There are no associations or unions specifically dedicated to Construction Photographers. Primary associations Construction Photographers can join for educational resources and other benefits include Professional Photographers of America, Advertising Photographers of America, and American Society of Media Photographers.

Tips for Entry

1. Check your community for ongoing construction of major buildings. Visit the streetside trailer office and see if you can speak with the project managers. Ask when the Construction Photographer will next be on site.

2. If the Construction Photographer is based locally, call and ask if you can set up a meeting and the possibility of volunteering to assist, or trail, for a day on the site.

3. Look through local phone directories and do a Google search for local Construction Photographers. Contact them and set up meetings.

4. Contact local commercial photographers to ask if they make periodic photos of building projects. Ask about summer or freelance work opportunities.

INDUSTRIAL PHOTOGRAPHER

CAREER PROFILE

Duties: Photographs various aspects of industries, such as machinery, equipment, and products, for training manuals, company literature, annual reports, publicity, equipment records, and so on; creates portraits of industry executives and staff; travels and works on location at factories and power plants; handles invoicing clients and accounts receivable and payable

Alternate Title(s): None

Salary Range: $40,000 to $100,000+

Employment Prospects: Fair

Advancement Prospects: Good

Best Geographical Location(s): New England, Washington, D.C., Florida, Nevada, California, and Michigan

Prerequisites:

Education or Training—Two- or four-year degree in photography; training in design software

Experience—Two to three years of experience as a photographer with commercial studio; several years of experience as an apprentice or assistant photographer

Special Skills and Personality Traits—Self-starter; detail- and deadline-oriented; familiarity with the industries, machinery, equipment, and processes being photographed; diplomatic; patient and flexible; organized; able to travel and work on location at various sites

CAREER LADDER

```
┌─────────────────────────────────┐
│     Industrial Photographer      │
└─────────────────────────────────┘

┌─────────────────────────────────┐
│    Commercial Photographer /     │
│       Press Photographer         │
└─────────────────────────────────┘

┌─────────────────────────────────┐
│     Photographer's Assistant     │
└─────────────────────────────────┘
```

Position Description

Industrial Photographers take photographs of different aspects of industries for company reports and records. They work on location at factories, mines, power plants, tankers, and other sites. They photograph machinery and equipment, products and people, and sometimes even the architecture of the buildings. They work closely with industry executives, foremen, and factory workers to coordinate shoot schedules and prepare for any challenges.

Advertising, communications, and public relations offices of the industries hire Industrial Photographers to generate the images needed for employee training manuals, annual reports, posters, advertisements, brochures, and Web sites. Like commercial photographers, the Industrial Photographer's job is to turn the mundane into special images that will engage viewers. They may create portraits of industry executives and staff or take extreme close-ups of machinery. They may take shots of warehouse interiors or be called upon for rooftop overviews of a plant's parking lot.

Depending on the project, Industrial Photographers will either work alone or hire an assistant to help carry and set up camera equipment and lights.

Industrial Photographers also meet with on-site safety managers to discuss safety issues. They discuss logistical issues regarding upcoming shoots. For instance, areas of factories that are not well lit will require supplemental lighting. Industrial Photographers need to learn all of this in advance, otherwise a day's shoot can be ruined. For larger products, such as factory equipment, battery-operated lighting gear is inadequate. One of the issues Industrial Photographers will discuss with on-site safety managers will be how best to wire for the shoot. Sometimes taping a cable down to the floor is sufficient, other times taping overhead to avoid heavy traffic sites, especially those used by cars, which can create a hazard, is a better option. In cases where there is no other way, wires are left visible in the shots, to be later retouched out using Adobe Photoshop.

Photographers who choose to enter the industrial photography field should go out of their way to learn about general safety practices as well as any specific safety issues that pertain to the types of products and equipment they will be photographing. For instance, if factory employees are working with hazardous materials near a planned shoot location, photographers need to be sure they don't set up lights and create flashes that could distract workers and cause dangerous situations. They need to check all of this out in advance and come up with appropriate plans for each shoot.

Industrial Photographers should have their own safety equipment, including footwear appropriate to the site, clothing that won't become entangled in machinery, a hard hat and safety goggles, a safety harness, if applicable, flashlights, and so on. This equipment is not always available at the site, and photographers need to be prepared to protect themselves and any creative staff they have hired for the project. If working in particularly dusty environments (i.e., a construction site or steel mill), photographers also need to take special care to protect their cameras and gear.

Salaries
According to many experts in the photography field, Industrial Photography is typically the highest paying of all of the disciplines. The annual income for Industrial Photographers can range from $40,000 to $100,000, depending upon years of experience, types of industry, and geographical location. Most Industrial Photographers work freelance and are usually paid by the hour. Staff Industrial Photographers who work for corporations will enjoy steady salaries and such benefits as paid vacations, health insurance, profit-sharing options, pension programs, and possibly even company cars. Industrial Photographers who are willing to contract for work overseas may earn higher wages.

Employment Prospects
As with many photography disciplines, the Industrial Photography field is highly competitive. Most Industrial Photographers secure work through classified ads in print and online publications, as well as through word of mouth. The *Occupational Outlook Handbook* predicts that employment of photographers overall will grow by only 10 to 20 percent through 2012, so the industrial photography field will remain a challenging one to enter. Industrial Photographers

who diversify their job hunt by simultaneously pursuing all avenues, from networking and advertising to self-promotions and direct mailings, will have greater chances of securing commissions. Trade associations such as Professional Photographers of America also offer photographer members access to employment listings and work referrals.

Advancement Prospects
Staff Industrial Photographers can advance to become department heads if they work for large corporations with large creative or photography departments. Freelance Industrial Photographers, on the other hand, are usually at the top of the career ladder. They can advance by branching out into other industries, adding more photographers to their staff, and enhancing their services. They can also broaden their scope by teaching at technical schools and universities, writing articles and columns for trade publications and Web sites, and participating in panel discussions and lecture circuits hosted by trade associations.

Education and Training
A two- or four-year degree in photography, with training in technical photography, design software, and small-business management, is a solid foundation for Industrial Photographers. Prior on-the-job training as an apprentice or assistant to an Industrial Photographer, with exposure to safety practices within industrial settings (i.e., factories, mines, power plants, etc.), is also extremely valuable.

Experience, Skills, and Personality Traits
Industrial Photographers have prior commercial photography experience and are adept at dealing with diverse people to meet deadlines. They are flexible and professional, always prepared for a variety of minor emergencies with equipment, appointment schedules, personality conflicts, and other potential stressors. Industrial Photographers must be fast thinkers with excellent communication skills. They know how to diplomatically offer helpful suggestions to prevent or solve problems, and they know how to stay on track to meet deadlines and clients' needs. Industrial Photographers must also be able to work with a variety of cameras and equipment in a wide variety of environments. Many factories and corporations have strict schedules and rules. To succeed in this field, photographers must be punctual, responsible, and capable of adhering to the rules and regulations.

Unions and Associations
Industrial Photographers join the International Industrial Photographers Association and Professional Photographers of America for educational workshops, employment referrals, and networking opportunities. They may also become

associate members of trade associations that are dedicated to the industries they cover.

Tips for Entry

1. Promote your business by advertising in publications prospective clients read. Some photographers secure work by advertising in trade publications, such as *The Blue Book of Building and Construction.*
2. Contact labor unions to find out if they need photography services for upcoming annual reports, company brochures, or even their Web sites. Put together a portfolio of work that matches the clients you plan to see and set up meetings to pitch your services.
3. Subscribe to mailing lists, such as Adbase, that are targeted to specific industries. Hire a graphic designer to create a postcard or brochure promoting your business. Schedule regular promotional mailings throughout the year. You may want to do this biannually or quarterly, whichever works best for your schedule and budget.

INSURANCE AND LEGAL PHOTOGRAPHER

CAREER PROFILE

Duties: Provides photographs for insurance and legal documentation and business transactions, such as real estate sales, accidents, personal injury suits, estate matters, and other matters; may appear in court as an expert witness

Alternate Title(s): Business Photographer, Personal Injury Photographer

Salary ranges: $40,000 to $65,000+

Employment Prospects: Fair

Advancement Prospects: Good

Best Geographical Location(s): Major cities and communities with extensive real estate development or housing turnover

Prerequisites:

Education or Training—Bachelor's degree in photography recommended

Experience—Several years of experience as a freelance or staff photographer; prior portrait photography or photojournalism experience helpful

Special Skills and Personality Traits—Digital camera expertise; knowledge of color-enhancement programs and design software (i.e., Adobe Photoshop and Illustrator); deadline-oriented and organized; diplomatic; excellent communication and people skills, particularly if photographing for personal injury or medical malpractice suits

CAREER LADDER

```
┌─────────────────────────────────────┐
│  Insurance and Legal Photographer    │
└─────────────────────────────────────┘

┌─────────────────────────────────────┐
│      Freelance Photographer          │
└─────────────────────────────────────┘

┌─────────────────────────────────────┐
│     Photographer's Assistant         │
└─────────────────────────────────────┘
```

Position Description

Insurance and Legal Photographers provide photographs that support claims of such things as property damage due to storms, floods, and fires or poor construction materials or design flaws; personal injury and medical malpractice; not-at-fault automobile accidents; and other legal matters. Home and car owners, individuals who have been physically injured or scarred, as well as insurance providers, lawyers, builders, building owners, and others hire Insurance and Legal Photographers when they need visual evidence to substantiate their cases in court trials.

Photographs often lead to uncontested claims. Insurance and Legal Photographers can help property owners, estate heirs, and others secure recourse on losses. Their photographs assist in showing the location and extent of damage to homes, such as the conditions of roofs, drainage pipes, windows, stairways and steps, porch construction, foundations, beams, and more. Insurance and Legal Photographers also help owners create timelogs of their homes, providing a series of photographs from the date of purchase onward. They help document excessive wear, paint deterioration, termite damage, molding and hardware details at the time of acquisition, and other relevant conditions. Their photographs may also help establish arson as a source of a fire and may equally prove accidental fires from overloaded electrical connections. Insurance and Legal Photographers also photograph landscape and structural details when designs, materials, or construction differ from what was originally commissioned and agreed upon.

In addition to photographing evidence to support legal claims, Insurance and Legal Photographers may also appear in court to testify about the photographs. Professional photographers themselves may even need to file suits on occasion and will require expert testimony. For example, a professional photographer hired an Insurance and Legal Photographer to testify to the worth of damaged slides. The case concerned the loss of 50 slides made during unusual and unrepeatable trips into Brazil's jungle. The slides were color close-ups of rare vegetation that were to be delivered to and explored by a drug company. The slides were organized and stacked in photo trays on a tabletop and left over a weekend in a locked room. During that weekend, a slow leak from the ceiling caused irreparable damage to the slides. In the courtroom, the Insurance and Legal Photographer testified to the stock value and future worth of these images. This testimony led to a settlement that included full compensation for the travel expenses to Brazil, the estimated value of the 50 slides, and compensation for the losses.

Insurance and Legal Photographers keep detailed records of the photographs they create and retain negatives, digital files, and clear prints for their clients. They may be called upon to provide enlargements for presentations in courtrooms, corporate meetings, and school auditoriums. They travel and work in all conditions—outside at accident scenes, inside homes documenting damages, and in their studios photographing individuals.

Salaries

Insurance and Legal Photographers can earn salaries ranging from $40,000 to $65,000 or more. They are contracted for service on a day-to-day, per-photograph basis or on a monthly fee basis. Photographers' salaries may be augmented when their photographs become critical evidence in court cases and they are called into courtrooms to testify about the details surrounding the photographs. Because they are freelancers and their time is valuable, they typically negotiate their rates in advance of their court-appearance dates.

Employment Prospects

Most Insurance and Legal Photographers work independently. The field is small and employment prospects are only fair because there are more photographers than there are jobs to fill. Insurance and Legal Photographers who are well networked through law firms and insurance agencies will have greater opportunities to find work.

Advancement Prospects

Established Insurance and Legal Photographers can advance by increasing clientele, expanding services and raising fees,

or adding staff and growing the studio. They may also enhance their careers by speaking at conferences, teaching workshops, and writing articles for trade and mass publication. They may also create agreements with insurance brokers and law firms to be the exclusive photographers for their clients. Other creative advancement options include establishing studio space within the insurance or law firms' offices, helping to increase the client base while reducing overhead costs. A selling point is that photography prior to property loss is like health care prior to illness. Each step provides individuals with a more stable base to operate from, with increased likelihood of faster resolution when issues arise.

Education and Training

A four-year degree in photography, with business coursework, is usually a solid foundation for most Insurance and Legal Photographers. Familiarity with law and real estate practices and business management is also helpful in this industry. On-the-job training in a commercial or portrait studio, with regular use of digital cameras and design software, is recommended.

Experience, Skills, and Personality Traits

While it is by no means necessary, Insurance and Legal Photographers who have a basic understanding of and appreciation for the elements of law may connect better with their clients. They will understand the cases better, the purpose of the photographs will be clearer, and their communication will be facilitated with claimants, insurance agencies, real estate agencies, builders, building owners, contractors, and law firms. Three or more years of prior experience as a professional photographer in a portrait or wedding studio is beneficial, particularly when photographing individuals who have been injured in accidents or during medical procedures. To do this kind of work, Insurance and Legal Photographers must be organized and deadline-oriented. They often work on an on-call, as-needed basis and must be prepared to photograph the details of accidents thoroughly but quickly. If working with individuals, Insurance and Legal Photographers must have diplomacy, tact, and sensitivity. They must know how to make people feel comfortable and safe, as well as provide them with clean, appropriate studio spaces for their photography sessions.

Unions and Associations

There are no unions or associations specifically committed to insurance and legal photography. Insurance and Legal Photographers can join the Professional Photographers of America for access to educational conferences and workshops, industry-related publications, discounts from various service providers, networking opportunities, and business management advice.

Tips for Entry

1. Contact those lawyers you may know in the family or through friends. Ask them whom they hire when they need photographic services. Contact these photographers and set up an informational interview to discuss their experiences in the field and to learn of any recommendations they may have for you.

2. Contact insurance brokers, law firms, and real estate agencies to find out if they hire photographers and if they are currently in need of one. Set up informational interviews and network as much as possible.

3. If you are a freelance photographer and aiming to expand into this business, advertise your services at real estate, law firm, and insurance offices, in their publications and on their Web sites, and in newspapers and magazines.

INTERIOR DESIGN PHOTOGRAPHER

CAREER PROFILE

Duties: Photographs furniture, lights, and accessories as arranged in interior designers' studios or in photography studios; also works on location inside homes, office buildings, museums, historic buildings, and hotels to photograph kitchens, living rooms, bathrooms, conference rooms, fitness facilities, and so on; creates photographs for print advertisements in furniture showrooms, at trade shows, and in public areas

Alternate Title(s): Architectural Photographer, Commercial Photographer, Lifestyle Photographer

Salary Range: $15,000 to $50,000+

Employment Prospects: Good

Advancement Prospects: Fair

Best Geographical Location(s): Major cities and suburban areas

Prerequisites:

  Education or Training—Four-year degree in photography, with coursework in graphic design, interior design, and art history; trained in digital photography and photography design software (i.e., Adobe Photoshop and Illustrator)

  Experience—Several years of experience as a photographer's assistant in a commercial photography studio, preferably one with interior design clients

  Special Skills and Personality Traits—Excellent eye for detail; knowledgeable about design; strong communication skills; flexible attitude; able to travel to various locations

CAREER LADDER

```
┌─────────────────────────────────────┐
│   Interior Design Photographer       │
└─────────────────────────────────────┘

┌─────────────────────────────────────┐
│      Commercial Photographer         │
└─────────────────────────────────────┘

┌─────────────────────────────────────┐
│      Photographer's Assistant        │
└─────────────────────────────────────┘
```

Position Description

Interior Design Photographers photograph interiors of homes, office buildings, historic buildings, museums, hotels, and more for a variety of clients. Magazines may hire them to create photographs to accompany articles for publication. Hotels may hire Interior Design Photographers to take photographs of accommodations and various on-site facilities for publication in promotional literature and on Web sites. Furniture stores hire them to photograph chairs, tables, bureaus, beds, and interiors of stores for flyers, posters, and advertisements in magazines and newspapers. They may also work with architectural firms, photographing interiors for portfolios and Web sites. Interior designers themselves may commission photographers to photograph their design work either for specific clients or for their own promotional purposes. Interior designers' clients can range from *Home* and *House Beautiful* magazines to the Hilton and Hyatt Hotels, from stores such as IKEA and Levitz to those like Anthropologie and Macy's.

Interior Design Photographers meet with clients to discuss their specific needs and negotiate contract terms.

They learn how the photographs will be used and to whom the photographs are targeted. They usually visit locations prior to the shoot so they can see the colors that are involved, the sizes of the objects or rooms being photographed, and the lighting at different times of the day. This helps them determine the specific types of lenses, flashes, and filters they will need, and it also helps save them time during the shoot because they can predetermine composition and framing. They may hire assistants to help transport cameras and photographic equipment to and from locations, set up and breakdown sets, and assist with film developing and processing.

Interior Design Photographers usually offer a menu of services beyond interior design as a means to broaden their earnings potential in the marketplace. Typically, they are also architectural photographers, capturing exteriors, facades, gardens, and landscapes. They may specialize in fine art, too, or become specialists in photographing just chairs or tables. They may exhibit their work in fine arts galleries, museums, educational institutions, and historical societies, and they may participate in design photography competitions.

Salaries

Interior Design Photographers can earn annual salaries ranging from $15,000 to $50,000 or more. Most are freelance, and those who work for large publications, broadcast networks, successful interior designers, and long-established architectural firms often secure the highest wages. According to the Department of Labor's *Occupational Outlook Handbook,* salaried photographers (of all disciplines combined) earned median annual earnings of $24,040 in 2002, with the highest 10 percent earning more than $49,920. Interior Design Photographers can enhance their salaries by entering and, hopefully, winning photography competitions with large cash prizes, exhibiting and selling their work in art galleries, and licensing their work.

Employment Prospects

There are no statistics currently available that pertain to employment prospects for Interior Design Photographers. Parallels can be drawn, however, to predictions for interior designers and architects. The *Occupational Outlook Handbook* cites that the employment of architects and designers will grow by about 10 to 20 percent, as fast as the average for all occupations, through 2012, indicating a potential parallel increase in demand for Interior Design Photographers. Interior Design Photographers will also find greater opportunities for employment as more interior design magazines and publications are introduced to the market. Of added benefit is the growing focus of the media on home renovation and "make-over" projects. Experienced Interior Design Photographers can find work with lifestyle television shows and broadcast networks dedicated to interior design, decor, and architecture.

Advancement Prospects

Interior Design Photographers are normally freelancers who run their own businesses. They can advance by expanding into new areas of interior design and architecture. If they specialize in interiors of smaller homes, they can segue into luxury homes and estates. They can also grow their businesses by adding photographers with different specialties to their staff and opening studios in new locations. Interior Design Photographers can write articles for magazines and newspapers. They can also become columnists and teach in technical and art schools. Some Interior Design Photographers secure grants from public organizations, such as the National Endowment for the Arts, corporate or private foundations, or individuals to pursue photographic projects and research and publish articles and books in the field.

Education and Training

A four-year degree in photography, with coursework in graphic and interior design and architecture, is recommended for this position. Many Interior Design Photographers have a master's of fine arts degree in photography. Most are trained in digital photography and design software programs.

Experience, Skills, and Personality Traits

Interior Design Photographers usually have at least several years of experience as freelance commercial photographers. Some may have backgrounds in real estate, architectural, fine arts, or construction photography. They have an excellent eye for color, composition, and light and are adept at both digital and film photography. Interior Design Photographers work with a variety of clients and must have strong verbal and written communication skills. A strong appreciation for design and architectural form is required. Most important, Interior Design Photographers know how to tell a story and convey a feeling about the rooms and objects they photograph.

Unions and Associations

Interior Design Photographers may join the American Society of Media Photographers, Advertising Photographers of America, and Professional Photographers of America for portfolio critiques, photography competitions, educational publications and workshops, employment referrals, and other membership benefits. They may also join the American Society of Interior Designers and the American Institute of Architects for access to trade publications, trade conferences and shows, and professional networking opportunities.

Tips for Entry

1. Keep up with industry news and issues and learn about upcoming employment opportunities by regularly reading trade publications. Read design magazines such as *Architectural Digest, Architecture Week, Home, Interiors and Sources, Frame,* and *Metropolis* and e-zines such as *designboom* (http://www.design boom.com).

2. Secure an assistant position or internship with a commercial photography studio or a studio that specializes in fine arts photography. This is an excellent foundation for interior design photography and will give you the chance to hone your skills and see firsthand how the business works.

3. Network. This is an industry that thrives on word of mouth. Attend the events, conferences, trade shows, and workshops that interior designers and architects attend.

4. Create a list of interior design and architectural magazines. Familiarize yourself with the styles of photographs published. Contact the art directors of these magazines to find out how they secure photography and if they have need of assistants on any upcoming shoots. Volunteer for a day or two, if you must, to get the exposure.

REAL ESTATE PHOTOGRAPHER

CAREER PROFILE

Duties: Photographs homes, office buildings, recreation centers, small malls, churches, ponds, lakes, clusters of trees, or shorelines for real estate brokers introducing new communities or regenerated older neighborhoods; creates "virtual tours" of interiors and exteriors of buildings using specific digital equipment and photo design software

Alternate Title(s): None

Salary Range: $50,000 to $75,000

Employment Prospects: Fair

Advancement Prospects: Limited

Best Geographical Location(s): Major urban areas, new suburban communities, and resort areas generating new development

Prerequisites:

Education or Training—Bachelor's degree in photography

Experience—Two to three years of experience as a commercial photographer

Special Skills and Personality Traits—Skilled in digital photography and photographic design software (i.e., Adobe Photoshop); basic understanding of the real estate business and practices; reliable; deadline-oriented; strong communication skills; flexible; able to travel to sites

CAREER LADDER

```
┌─────────────────────────────────┐
│    Real Estate Photographer     │
└─────────────────────────────────┘

┌─────────────────────────────────┐
│     Commercial Photographer     │
└─────────────────────────────────┘

┌─────────────────────────────────┐
│    Photographer's Assistant /   │
│        Studio Assistant         │
└─────────────────────────────────┘
```

Position Description

Real Estate Photographers photograph homes, buildings, and their surrounding areas for real estate agencies to promote to prospective buyers. They discuss with the agencies the features they should highlight in the photographs, such as two-car garages, driveways, side yards and backyards, front and back paths, entranceways, home interiors, gardens and sheds, trees and other outdoor foliage, and so on. Real Estate Photographers often visit the locations twice, the first time to take test photos and the second time for the actual shoot. The "scouting" visit entails taking photos of various aspects of homes and buildings at different angles (some even aerial) and at different times during the day to check for lighting and other conditions. They share the test photos with real estate agents for review and selection of the fea-

tures, objects, angles, and preferred time of day to feature in the final photographs. They may even photograph nearby conveniences and attractions, such as schools, libraries, post offices, supermarkets, malls, salons, restaurants, or cafés. When they return for the actual shoot, they may bring an assistant to help set up equipment and lights. Real estate agencies print the photographs in magazine and newspaper advertisements, as well as with Web site listings.

Digital photography has both enhanced the Real Estate Photographer's work and diminished it. More people than ever before are equipped, though not necessarily adequately skilled and trained, to take photographs for immediate posting, thanks to digital cameras. Digital technology has truly benefited Real Estate Photographers, however, in the three-dimensional or panoramic photography arena. A growing number of real estate Web sites offer virtual tours of home and building interiors and exteriors, featuring 360-degree photography. Real Estate Photographers are able to capture panoramic views by using such equipment as an EGG Photo 360° Pack First, which consists of a lightweight lens and software. When viewers click onto images that have been created with EGG or other such technology, they can drag the mouse through the photo and span 360-degrees vertically and horizontally. They can see the buildings surrounding a home, stroll the street, then look straight up at the sky. Real estate agents can also e-mail links to the images for prospective buyers to view.

Real Estate Photographers use photographic design software such as Adobe Photoshop and Illustrator to correct color and enhance images. If the weather was less than ideal on the day of the shoot, they can make the sky blue, add billowing clouds, or add or remove light. They can erase distracting shadows or crop out adjacent houses or trees blocking certain selling points of the home or building that is for sale.

Self-employed Real Estate Photographers are responsible for maintaining their businesses and studios. They handle promoting and marketing their services by continually researching prospective clients, creating direct-mail pieces, sending out e-newsletters, networking, and scheduling meetings. They handle accounts receivables and payables, or they hire a bookkeeper and accountant to oversee money management. They purchase and maintain their photographic equipment and accessories, as well as all business and office equipment and supplies. They also secure permissions and releases to photograph at certain sites, when applicable.

Salaries

Real Estate Photographers can earn salaries ranging from $50,000 to $75,000 or more. Income levels will depend upon real estate agencies' budgets, geographical locations in which the photographer works, and his or her years of experience in the field. Real Estate Photographers can increase their earnings by providing 360-degree photographic services. Not all real estate agencies are offering the panoramic viewing options on their Web sites, and those that are have been willing to pay higher wages for this service.

Employment Prospects

Employment opportunities for Real Estate Photographers will fluctuate, depending upon the economy and the housing market. According to the *Occupational Outlook Handbook,* employment of real estate brokers and sales agents as well as related workers is frequently sensitive to swings in the economy, especially interest rates. When economic activity declines and interest rates rise, fewer people are interested in buying homes and property, thus employment opportunities in real estate simultaneously decline. Most photographers offer real estate photography as one service among many

others in their commercial studio work. Real Estate Photographers will continue to experience some job opportunities due to the growing population and increased need for housing. While some real estate brokers and property managers may try their hand at digital photography, many others will continue to rely on Real Estate Photographers to create images and virtual tours of properties that are up for sale.

Advancement Prospects

Real Estate Photographers are freelancers who advance according to their own interests and self-initiative. Photographers working in smaller communities may choose to move their business into larger or more affluent areas. They may also expand by growing their client base, offering architectural, aerial, or environmental photography services, and adding more photographers to their studios to widen and enhance their services.

Education and Training

A two- or four-year degree in photography from either a technical school or liberal arts college is sufficient educational background for Real Estate Photographers. Training in digital photography, photographic design software, and three-dimensional photographic equipment and software is critical in this field.

Experience, Skills, and Personality Traits

Real Estate Photographers have at least several years of prior experience in commercial photography. Some may have construction or architectural photography experience. They are accustomed to taking outdoor and indoor shots and have a solid knowledge of lighting for all times of day and night. Real estate photography is an on-location job, thus Real Estate Photographers must be extremely organized, detail-oriented, able to follow directions, and prepared with everything they need to shoot at short notice, if needed. They have excellent communication skills, are reliable, and able to meet deadlines.

Unions and Associations

There are no unions dedicated specifically to real estate photography. The Professional Photographers of America is a valuable association offering multiple benefits and information, along with its monthly publication *Professional Photographer.* Real Estate Photographers can also join Advertising Photographers of America for educational and networking opportunities.

Tips for Entry

1. Peruse the Internet for real estate brokers in your area. Visit their Web sites and look through the photographs and tours to get an idea of how things are done.

2. Contact the real estate brokers to see if they use photography services. Set up an informational meeting. Put together a portfolio of images of interiors and exteriors of homes and buildings.
3. Check the Internet and your local yellow pages for Real Estate Photographers. Visit their Web sites to familiarize yourself with their work. Contact them to see if they need any assistance.
4. Check the Internet for aerial photographers who may also provide real estate photography. See if you can register as a passenger on a real estate photography mission. This will give you a chance to be exposed firsthand to another aspect of real estate photography.

SURVEILLANCE PHOTOGRAPHER

CAREER PROFILE

Duties: Takes photographs of business projects and proposals, building inspections and renovations, for lawyers, property owners, private individuals, police departments, private investigators, and others; adheres to local and federal laws when photographing subjects, as photos may be used in criminal investigations or as evidence for court cases

Alternate Title(s): Private Investigator

Salary Ranges: $20,000 to $50,000+

Employment Prospects: Good

Advancement Prospects: Fair

Best Geographical Location(s): All major cities, and resort cities, and affluent suburbs

Prerequisites:

Education or Training—Four-year degree in photography recommended; training in digital photography and photographic techniques and printing processes

Experience—Several years of experience as an event photographer; daily newspaper, publicity, or press photography experience useful

Special Skills and Personality Traits—Analytical; patient; observant; persistent; tenacious; self-starter; independent worker; detail-oriented; excellent written and verbal communication skills; ethical and professional

CAREER LADDER

```
┌─────────────────────────────────┐
│   Surveillance Photographer      │
└─────────────────────────────────┘

┌─────────────────────────────────┐
│   Freelance Photographer /       │
│   Uniformed Photographer         │
└─────────────────────────────────┘

┌─────────────────────────────────┐
│   Photographer's Assistant       │
└─────────────────────────────────┘
```

Position Description

Surveillance Photographers take photographs of people, places, and activities for lawyers, police departments and private investigators, and property owners and insurance companies. Their photographs are used as evidence to help build cases to be tried in criminal and civil courts. They photograph building and home structures for tenants claiming unsafe conditions and demanding repairs. Property owners may also hire Surveillance Photographers when they are considering purchasing and building in certain areas. They will have Surveillance Photographers photograph sight lines and traffic flow. Surveillance photographs may also play a large role in divorce cases, providing evidence for courts in states where infidelity is a basis for divorce proceedings. The husband or wife usually hires a private investigator, who is also sometimes a Surveillance Photographer, to follow the alleged cheating spouse to covert meeting spots and photographically

document the trysts. Surveillance Photographers may also be employed by law-enforcement agencies to track and document the movements of suspected criminals.

Surveillance Photographers may or may not use hidden cameras to capture interior shots, depending upon local and state laws regarding privacy. For their images to be accepted as evidence during courtroom trials, they must operate within the boundaries of the law. Otherwise, their work is futile. For instance, a couple's innocuous meeting outside in a parking lot may be a completely different type of "meeting" behind closed doors. Surveillance Photographers might use hidden cameras inside the rooms to document indoor activities, but they must first understand the legal ramifications and the rights of those involved.

Insurance companies hire Surveillance Photographers when they suspect disability claims frauds. Surveillance Photographers will follow the claimants, aiming to photographically capture them doing an activity that, if truly disabled, they would be incapable of doing. For instance, a man who claims a severe back injury may be photographically tracked playing golf, something he could not do if he truly experienced this injury. The Surveillance Photographer will photograph the man carrying the golf bag from his home to his car. He will follow the car to the golf course and using a telephoto lens, take photographs, with date stamps, of the man bending down to place the tee into the ground and swinging the club.

Surveillance Photographers use photographic equipment similar to that of sports and press photographers. They rely on long telephoto lenses, fast film, and light tripods for portability. They also use a variety of sequence cameras to accurately capture activities every step of the way at hotel entrances, restaurants, parking lots, and other locations.

Salaries

Surveillance Photographers may earn annual salaries ranging from $20,000 to $50,000 or more. Photographers new to the field will earn lower salaries until they build up clientele and establish their names in the business. They are usually independents who work from their own homes or offices. They will be responsible for covering their business expenses, such as photographic equipment and film, rent, utilities, office equipment and supplies, and medical insurance. Surveillance Photographers may also be employed full time or as contractors for private investigation firms, where they may enjoy employment benefits such as bonuses, paid vacation and sick leave, and pension plans. They may enhance their salaries by appearing as expert witnesses in court cases.

Employment Prospects

Surveillance Photographers should have good opportunities to find work, particularly with the public's increased interest in security and protection and heightened litigation. While there are no employment statistics available for Surveillance Photographers, the U.S. Department of Labor predicts that employment of private detectives and investigators will grow faster than the average for all occupations through 2012. More Surveillance Photographers will also be needed to help lawyers working on civil litigation and criminal defense.

Advancement Prospects

Staff Surveillance Photographers can advance to become heads of photography departments, delegating work, hiring, managing and overseeing staff, and creating department budgets. With years of experience, a steadily growing clientele, and appropriate training, they can start their own private investigation firms and hire more Surveillance Photographers to cover assignments. They can write articles and books, lecture at association meetings, and teach.

Education and Training

Surveillance Photographers usually have four-year degrees in photography or bachelor's of science degrees in criminal justice. Training in digital photography and particularly in surveillance photography is recommended. Surveillance Photographers stay educated about new technology in the field by reading magazines and Web sites and taking continuing education courses. They also keep abreast of local and state laws either by establishing consistent and reliable sources at local police precincts or reputable law firms.

Experience, Skills, and Personality Traits

Surveillance Photographers usually have a background in the detective field, in private investigation work, or in press or sports photography. They are independent, ethical workers who have a solid knowledge of local laws and always follow those laws in their work. They research their assignments and pay close attention to all details from beginning to end. They are observant and analytical. Much of the job is following people and waiting for the right moments to start taking pictures, which can sometimes take hours or days. Patience and persistence are key characteristics of individuals in this position. They must also have physical stamina and mental acuity. Surveillance Photographers have excellent communication skills and are able to speak the language of their clients, whether it is law, real estate, or insurance. They have strong negotiation skills, understand industry practices, and make sure they clearly understand what is expected of them for each assignment.

Unions and Associations

There are no associations or unions dedicated solely to Surveillance Photographers. They can join the Professional Photographers of America for educational resources and networking opportunities, such as annual conventions, where new surveillance photography equipment is demonstrated.

Tips for Entry

1. Contact law firms in your area to see if they use Surveillance Photographers in their legal services. Ask if this has helped them in their cases and if they have any current needs for photography help.
2. Contact and meet with private investigators or insurance brokers in your area. Ask if they use freelance Surveillance Photographers, in which types of areas, and if they have any need of photography services.
3. Check online as well as in the public library for publications read by lawyers, private investigators, and insurance industry brokers. Look in the classifieds sections for employment listings, as well as for Surveillance Photographer advertisements. Contact other Surveillance Photographers to set up informational meetings and learn more about the field from them firsthand.

UNIFORMED PHOTOGRAPHER

CAREER PROFILE

Duties: Photographs traffic accidents, scenes of crimes and fires, police department events, fire department events, parades, awards ceremonies, charity events, precincts, squads, firehouses, police stations, and so on for documentation and reports, archival records, as well as public safety campaigns and promotional literature

Alternate Title(s): Crime Scene Photographer, Fire Department Photographer, Forensic Photographer, Police Photographer

Salary Range: $30,000 to $60,000+

Employment Prospects: Good

Advancement Prospects: Fair

Best Geographical Location(s): Major urban areas

Prerequisites:

Education or Training—Two-year degree may suffice; education and training requirements vary depending upon the organization (e.g., military photographers must attend boot camp and train to be soldiers first)

Experience—Experience in college as a sports or yearbook photographer helpful; prior professional photography experience beneficial

Special Skills and Personality Traits—Strong interest in the agency's mission; able to adhere to rules and regulations; able to work in structured environment; team player; thick-skinned; hard worker; physically and mentally fit

CAREER LADDER

```
┌─────────────────────────────┐
│     Senior Photographer     │
└─────────────────────────────┘

┌─────────────────────────────┐
│    Uniformed Photographer   │
└─────────────────────────────┘

┌─────────────────────────────┐
│  Policeman, Fireman, Soldier │
└─────────────────────────────┘
```

Position Description

Uniformed Photographers work for city, state, and federal agencies, such as police departments, fire departments, the army, the navy, the Federal Bureau of Investigation, and many others. When they sign up for their jobs, they commit first and foremost to the main mission of these agencies, which is to serve and protect the people of our nation. For instance, a photographer in the army is trained to be a soldier first. After passing rigorous physical and classroom tests, photography instruction follows. During times of war, the military photographer will have a camera for documentation purposes but will also be armed and expected to fight.

Uniformed Photographers cover many of the same subjects and disciplines that non-agency and nonmilitary photographers cover, such as advertising, portraits, publicity, and more. They photograph graduations and awards ceremonies. They create portraits of individuals and take group shots. When people receive medals or promotions, Uniformed Photographers are there to document the events. Their photographs are also used in public education campaigns about prevention and safety. For example, a photograph of the scene of a car accident caused by a drunk driver may be part of a public service announcement to help promote safe, sober driving.

Uniformed Photographers will also document equipment by photographing parts for groups such as NASA. This helps especially when new equipment is being tested and something fails to work; engineers and scientists can analyze the photographs and come to conclusions about what caused the failure and what can be done to prevent it in the future. Uniformed Photographers' images are also used for insurance claims and forensic evidence. Those who work in forensics will photographically document crime scenes for use as evidence in court. In addition to accidents, they will photograph fingerprint and footprint recordings as people who have been arrested are processed. They will also photograph injuries that were caused by assaults or accidents.

The subjects Uniformed Photographers cover will depend upon the agencies they work for, and the agencies will often work together on cases. For instance, fire department photographers will document buildings and homes where fires have occurred and where arson or foul play is suspected, and the police department will collaborate with the fire department in their investigations of possible crimes. Police photographers photograph crime scenes, and military photographers may also document war crimes for national and international investigations.

Salaries

Salaries will vary depending upon the type of agency that employs the Uniformed Photographer. Earnings are regulated by Congress, state legislators, or union contracts, which dictate conditions, promotions, and health and retirement benefits. Salaries are often based upon the rank, years of service, and performance record. Uniformed Photographers may not be able to resell their work in the secondary market according to the rules and regulations of their employer.

Employment Prospects

Uniformed Photographers have good opportunities to find work in various city, state, and federal agencies. First-time applicants trying to enter the field must be committed to attending classes, studying and passing tests, and devoting time to physical training. According to the U.S. Department of Labor's *Occupational Outlook Handbook,* employment of firefighters is expected to grow about as fast as the average for all jobs through 2012. Employment of police detectives and related occupations is expected to grow faster than average for this same time frame, due to the public's increased concern about security and protection. Uniformed Photographers normally work day or evening shifts, which can be during business hours, weekends, and holidays.

Advancement Prospects

Uniformed Photographers can advance to take on more responsibilities in the field. They can become senior photographers, overseeing the photography department staff and managing more complicated projects. Through specialized education and training, they can move into crime-scene investigative work. Depending upon their employment contracts with the agencies, they can write articles and teach others how to do this type of work. Military photographers can often transfer their experience to successful careers in civilian photography jobs.

Education and Training

A two-year degree in photography may be sufficient background for Uniformed Photographers. A bachelor's of science degree in criminal justice can be beneficial. Some police departments require a bachelor's degree. Further education and training is mandated by agencies and will be specific to those agencies' missions. Uniformed Photographers will be educated by agencies in such areas as hazardous materials, crime scene investigation, and emergency medical procedures such as first aid and cardiopulmonary resuscitation. They will have to pass interviews, entrance exams, assessment tests, and will also be expected to pass physical examinations and medical tests for acceptance into the field.

Experience, Skills, and Personality Traits

Uniformed Photographers must be organized, detail-oriented, and able to follow strict rules and regulations while conducting their work. Because they will be documenting crime and fire scenes or scenes of war crimes, they must be tactful and respectful, particularly if victims, families, and witnesses are still on these scenes. Uniformed Photographers must also be able to pay careful attention to details because the smallest details can have a tremendous impact on a case. They must be thorough in their work and have a good understanding of what it is they should be photographing and why. They must be well versed in photographic techniques and be meticulous in how they approach photographing images and recording dates and events.

They must also be knowledgeable about the agencies' methods. Those who photograph homicide scenes must understand anatomy, as well as have an ability to do their job effectively and efficiently while witnessing disturbing sights in uncomfortable environments. A thick skin and a stomach for the business help.

Professionalism and discretion are also key characteristics of Uniformed Photographers. They interact with a range of professionals, both internally and within other organizations, so excellent verbal and written communication skills are important. Physical and mental fitness are also crucial in this field. Above all, individuals who receive the greatest rewards from this type of work are those who are dedicated to and passionate about serving and protecting the public.

Unions and Associations

Fire photographers can belong to the International Fire Photographers Association (http://www.ifpaonline.com) for membership publications, educational resources, and photography contests. Forensic photographers can join Evidence Photographers International Council, Inc. (http://www.epic-photo.org) for educational workshops, industry ion as possible about the agency and the employment4

24   CAREER OPPORTUNITIES IN PHOTOGRAPHY

news, and employment referrals. All Uniformed Photographers can become members of the National Press Photographers Association and Professional Photographers of America for career-enhancing benefits.

Tips for Entry

1. Do your research on this field before you sign up for a job. You need to be sure you are committed to the service the agency provides and that you can abide by its rules and regulations before you sign on the dotted line. The commitment may be asking for more than you may be able to give, so you must be sure the work and the organization fits your skills, interests, and moral character. Use an Internet search to find out as much information as possible about the agency and the employment requirements. You will also find useful information on PoliceCareer.com (http://www.policecareer.com) and Fire Fighting Careers (http://www.firecareers.net).

2. Check in with local police and fire departments to learn more about the hiring programs and prerequisites.

3. See if you can speak with photographers who are working in the field you are considering. Set up an informational meeting and bring a list of questions with you about the job. Learn as much as you can from them about the pros and cons of this kind of work. Ask them what they wish they had known before taking the job.

CINEMATOGRAPHY AND VIDEOGRAPHY

CINEMATOGRAPHER

CAREER PROFILE

Duties: Establishes the mood of a film by translating the narrative aspects of a script into visual form; responsible for framing every shot of the film, as well as the lighting, color level, and exposure

Alternate Title(s): Director of Photography

Salary Range: $14,710 to $65,070+

Employment Prospects: Good

Advancement Prospects: Good

Best Geographical Location(s): Major cities, such as Boston, Chicago, Hollywood, Los Angeles, New York, and San Francisco

Prerequisites:

Education or Training—Bachelor's degree in photography or cinematography; coursework in art, literature, and theater recommended

Experience—Several years of experience as a camera operator or assistant cinematographer required

Special Skills and Personality Traits—Artistic; technical and scientific; energetic, with stamina for long work days/nights; strong communication and interpersonal skills; leadership and management abilities; good visual eye; passionate about literature and theater

CAREER LADDER

```
+-----------------------------------+
|         Cinematographer           |
+-----------------------------------+

+-----------------------------------+
|    Assistant Cinematographer      |
+-----------------------------------+

+-----------------------------------+
|         Camera Operator           |
+-----------------------------------+
```

Position Description

Cinematographers are responsible for translating scripts into visual stories for films and television programs. They work closely with movie and TV directors to determine the look and feel of movies and shows by choosing camera angles, lighting, and composition to match the action and dialogue. They also survey locations. Before the shoot, Cinematographers read scripts and make notes throughout regarding photography suggestions and potential issues. They meet in advance with directors to discuss the scenes and all aspects of filming that will best capture and convey the story. Together, they decide upon all photographic aspects of the project, including camera movements, framing, filters, effects, and more. Every decision is crucial to the end result; the slightest nuance can change the entire feeling and mood. For example, Cinematographers can

change the mood of a scene by deciding to film the actors in close-up or panning in from a long shot. They can intensify scenes, such as a brewing fight, by moving the camera around the actors at various angles and speeds. To achieve their goals, Cinematographers and directors must have good rapport and clear communication.

In addition to setting the artistic direction of the film, Cinematographers are also responsible for selecting the camera crew and directing and overseeing their work. Their technical expertise in photography is heavily relied upon in this role, as there are countless ways to visually capture scenes. The smaller, independent film-production studios will not necessarily have the budgets for large and specialized production crews, so job titles with "slashes" may dominate. For example, Cinematographers may also operate cameras, thereby becoming Cinematographers/camera operators. Assistant camera operators test the cameras to make sure they are working properly and help set the camera's focus and film exposure, change filters and lenses, load film, track film stock, create camera reports, and sometimes even do screen tests of actors for the directors. Cinematographers often get their initial exposure to film projects by working in these roles. Cinematographers signal the beginning and ending of filming. At the end of the shoot, they review the completed film and make adjustments to best suit the film.

Cinematographers who work on a freelance basis must also manage their businesses. They will be responsible for purchasing and maintaining all of their photography equipment and film, advertising and promoting their services, networking, setting prices and contract terms, invoicing clients, overseeing accounts receivables and payables, hiring and managing staff, stocking office supplies, fielding phone and e-mail inquiries, and making sure their Web site is current and functioning.

Salaries
According to the Department of Labor, Cinematographers' salaries can vary widely, from $14,710 to beyond $65,070, depending upon the employers they work for and the projects they work on. Naturally, well-established and successful Cinematographers with excellent reputations in the industry will command the highest wages, some more than $1 million per year. Most Cinematographers are freelance or union workers (i.e., the International Alliance of Theatrical Stage Employees, Moving Picture Technicians, Artists and Allied Crafts of the United States, Its Territories and Canada, or IATSE). Those who work for major film-production studios with multimillion-dollar budgets often receive higher wages than those who are commissioned by small, independent studios. Minimum day rates for Cinematographers, as established by IATSE, are determined according to the type of film being shot. Cinematographers earn more for location shoots ($670 per day) compared to feature film shoots ($520 per day), with provisions for holiday and overtime work. Freelancers need to factor into their yearly earnings costs for health insurance and photography equipment, both of which they will have to pay for themselves.

Employment Prospects
Cinematography is fiercely competitive. Film and television production studios, large and small, often seek experienced Cinematographers with names in the business. This is a hard field to enter, and any foot in the door, whether by volunteer work or as an intern, is considered a good start. The *Occupational Outlook Handbook* predicts that employment of Cinematographers will grow about as fast as the average, or by 10 to 20 percent, for all occupations through 2012. The entertainment market, particularly motion-picture production and distribution, is expected to continue expanding, thus creating more job opportunities in the cinematography and camera-operator arenas. Interactive productions are also on the rise for computer and Internet services. Cinematographers will be needed for music videos, sports features, and other entertainment segments for Web sites and various television and film projects. The U.S. Department of Labor cites that 25 percent of all camera operators, including Cinematographers, are freelancers, which means 75 percent are salaried employees and most likely union members. Joining a union, such as IATSE, may provide wider access to job opportunities and employment benefits. Some Cinematographers also secure agents to represent them and to secure projects.

Advancement Prospects
For many, Cinematographer is the top job in the career ladder, one achieved only after numerous years of training and working on various projects. Once they have reached a level of expertise and success in the field, Cinematographers can advance by taking on more complicated projects and being hired for multimillion-dollar projects with higher profiles. Cinematographers can broaden their scope and share their knowledge by teaching at film and liberal arts schools, writing books and articles, and participating in lecture circuits. They can also advance by delving into other areas of film and television production or by starting their own production studios.

Education and Training
A bachelor's degree in cinematography, photography, liberal arts, or film studies is recommended. Coursework in English composition and literature provides essential exposure to narrative development. Cinematographers also learn the basics of lighting and composition through art and photography courses and camera operation and video production in broadcast journalism and media classes. While not required, a master's degree in film can further enhance one's career in the industry. The School of Visual Arts in New York City, New York University, and the University of Southern California are just some of the well-established schools with acclaimed film and fine arts programs. The New York Film Academy also offers students an excellent taste of what filmmaking is like through intensive six-week courses, in which students create three short films.

Experience, Skills, and Personality Traits
Film and television production studios usually require Cinematographers to have at least several film projects under their belts, working as camera operators, assistant cinematographers, or Cinematographers. Successful Cinematographers are artistic and creative, with strong hand-eye coordination and the ability to intuit the best ways to trans-

late a script visually. They have strong communication and management skills and are able to juggle tasks and meet deadlines. Long days and hours may be required, so they must have stamina and a certain degree of physical fitness. Freelance Cinematographers need to be entrepreneurial to survive in the industry. They must know how to manage every aspect of their businesses, including creating and negotiating contracts, securing permissions and releases, sending out invoices and paying bills, maintaining camera and office equipment, and more. Cinematographers must also stay curious and up-to-date on what's going on in the field. Technology changes constantly, and they need to stay tuned into the newest developments and train in the latest creations. Cinematographers must be technically savvy and extremely comfortable with the technology. The job requires patience, flexibility, diplomacy, the ability to work in all conditions, both inside and outside, and solid leadership skills.

Unions and Associations

Many film studios commission only those Cinematographers who are union members. Cinematographers can join the International Alliance of Theatrical Stage Employees, Moving Picture Technicians, Artists and Allied Crafts of the United States, Its Territories and Canada (IATSE) for fair wages and work conditions, as well as a variety of professional benefits. The American Society of Cinematographers and the International Cinematographers Guild provide members with access to industry newsletters and books, professional networking opportunities, educational forums, and more. Cinematographer members can also learn technical tips, news of awards and upcoming projects, and read interviews with fellow members on the Web sites. Cinematography.com also offers useful resources, such as e-chat information, product information, software and videos, and online forums.

Tips for Entry

1. Get an internship in a film, television, or documentary production studio. You can find internships through postings at your school, on your city's film commission Web site, or directly at the studios with whom you're interested in working. You'll get on-the-job training and valuable connections to other crew members for future networking and job referrals.

2. The best entry into this field is via the film-festival route. Create a short film and submit it to a festival. One industry expert says that if your film is shown and receives recognition, you'll have both of your feet in the door.

3. Study the various filmmaking styles that are out there by watching great films. *Rebecca* (1940, George Barnes), *The Diary of Anne Frank* (1959, William C. Mellor), *Close Encounters of the Third Kind* (1977, Vilmos Zsigmond), *Apocalypse Now* (1979, Vittorio Storaro), *Schindler's List* (1993, Janusz Kaminski), *Titanic* (1997, Russell Carpenter), and *The Lord of the Rings: The Fellowship of the Ring* (2001, Andrew Lesnie) are just some of the films that have won an Academy Award for Best Cinematography. Also watch the documentary *Visions of Light: The Art of Cinematography* (1993), directed by Arnold Glassman, Todd McCarthy, and Stuart Samuels, which is an excellent introduction to some of the finest cinematography in the history of film.

4. Use a 16-millimeter camera, a camcorder, or a digital camera to experiment with lighting and composition. Volunteer at your school to record activities or events for the media center or journalism department. Check with your school's media center, journalism department, or even the drama club about reporting on and recording school events.

5. Immerse yourself in the industry by reading trade publications and keeping up with the news in the field. Read magazines such as *American Cinematographer, Daily Variety, Hollywood Reporter,* and *Cinefex.* You can also find educational articles on their Web sites.

TELEVISION CAMERA OPERATOR

CAREER PROFILE

Duties: Works with specific cameras to convey images for television shows, news, sporting events, music performances, and more; follows action closely and chooses shot angles and directions; takes direction from producers and photography directors, as well as from *shot lists;* works with cameras that are stationary or above stages in cranes; may travel and work outdoors; may participate in editing work

Alternate Title(s): Cameraman, Cameraperson

Salary Ranges: $14,710 to $65,070+

Employment Prospects: Good

Advancement Prospects: Good

Best Geographical Location(s): Major cities with broadcast networks

Prerequisites:

Education or Training—Two- or four-year degree in communications, photography, or film and video production; on-the-job training in television camera work or training at a vocational or technical school

Experience—Several years of experience as an apprentice cameraman at a television or cable station

Special Skills and Personality Traits—Strong interest in photography, video, and film; exceptional eye for detail; able to visually track movement to keep viewers engaged; observant; meticulous; technical and artistic ability; skilled at staying calm and focused in pressurized environment; flexible; able to work odd hours and weekends if needed

CAREER LADDER

```
┌─────────────────────────────┐
│    Chief Camera Operator     │
└─────────────────────────────┘

┌─────────────────────────────┐
│     TV Camera Operator       │
└─────────────────────────────┘

┌─────────────────────────────┐
│   Remote Camera Operator     │
└─────────────────────────────┘
```

Position Description

Television Camera Operators work on programs that are aired on television and cable stations. They also work for independent production companies. They may work on live television shows or videos for television shows, documentaries, or cartoons. Television Camera Operators usually specialize in specific cameras and film. They work closely with a team that typically includes photography directors, producers, editors, grips, focus pullers, clapper loaders, and lighting cameramen.

Camera operators may work in a variety of roles, depending upon the show and how the studio or stage is set up. Television shows that are recorded with live studio audiences are usually shot in studios or theaters with multiple electronic cameras to capture different angles. There are periods when the network's TV cameras are on standby while the network is linked to overseas networks or switched to local programming. Cameras may be mounted on tracks, enabling camera operators to shoot scenes from different directions and angles. Some camera operators, particularly those covering sports, sit on cranes, with crane operators moving them into position so they can follow the action. Camera operators who operate steadicams, a special type of mobile camera, move around as necessary to get the shot they need. They wear it mounted to a harness and move about with the action. Some may also capture the action from moving vehicles. Studio camera operators, on the other hand, usually work at a fixed position. News camera operators or electronic news gathering operators are part of a reporting team and frequently travel to the sites where news is taking place. They use lightweight cameras in their work.

Camera operators follow a *shot list,* which is literally a list of shots they need to take, with the specific times they need to take them. Camera operators have the freedom to choose the angles and distances. They may start one shot with an extreme close-up, then zoom out to a wide-angle view. While they are working, they put themselves into the viewer's seat and imagine the visual flow that will make sense. They listen carefully to show dialogue and match the shots to the action.

Salaries

Television Camera Operators earned annual salaries ranging from as low as $14,710 to more than $65,070 in 2002, according to the U.S. Department of Labor's *Occupational Outlook Handbook.* The range for the middle 50 percent was $20,610 to $51,000. One in five camera operators is self-employed. These freelancers have to allot money from their earnings to purchase and maintain their own photographic equipment and supplies, as well as business expenses and health insurance. As with most freelance fields, earnings will fluctuate each year. Most camera operators belong to a union, which can help secure more work and higher wages.

Employment Prospects

There are Television Camera Operator jobs to be had, but competition is fierce as many flock to this field. The U.S. Department of Labor predicts that employment of camera operators and editors will grow by about 10 to 20 percent, or as fast as the average for all occupations, through 2012. More jobs will be available for Television Camera Operators due to rapid expansion in the entertainment field as well as in the Internet arena. Television Camera Operators often bring a wide variety of educational backgrounds and work experiences to their positions. Some may train specifically for the field, while others may have started in art or journalism and eventually wound up behind cameras at television stations. Television Camera Operators with an excellent reel of work have greater odds of securing better jobs with higher salaries. As required by many television production companies, camera operators who belong to trade unions such as the National Association of Broadcast Employees and Technicians—Communications Workers of America (NABET-CWA) or the

International Alliance of Theatrical Stage Employees, Moving Picture Technicians, Artists and Allied Crafts of the United States, Its Territories and Canada (IATSE) will also be able to secure better jobs and wages.

Advancement Prospects

In an industry with union contracts covering annual salary growth and related job changes, Television Camera Operators typically advance by being promoted within the network. They can advance to become senior camera operators or camera supervisors. As individuals retire from or leave senior positions, opportunities will also arise for Television Camera Operators to assume greater responsibilities and more complex projects. They can teach at vocational schools, create instructional videos, write articles and books, and participate in panel discussions hosted by trade associations.

Education and Training

Most television stations require a two- or four-year degree in communications, photography, or film and television production. Film school can provide an educational background well suited to this position and expose students to all areas of television and film production.

Experience, Skills, and Personality Traits

Television Camera Operators must have an excellent eye for detail and good eye-hand coordination. They must be knowledgeable and versatile in photographic equipment, as well as lighting, composition, and movement. In addition to being technically and technologically proficient, they must be skilled editors and understand how to move the flow of images, even when nothing is happening for certain periods of time, so that the picture makes sense to viewers. Television Camera Operators work closely with camera crews and take directions from directors, producers, or more senior camera operators, so the ability to work with a team and solid communication and listening skills are critical. Having a sense of humor doesn't hurt, either. Television Camera Operators usually work during weekday business hours but also work at various times during the night, as well as over weekends and holidays. Flexible individuals who are reliable, responsible, and perform well under pressure thrive in this field.

Unions and Associations

Television Camera Operators for larger television stations are usually required to be members of local or national unions in order to be employed. Camera operators may belong to the NABET-CWA or the IATSE for contract negotiation help, grievance assistance, educational resources, industry news, and job referrals.

Tips for Entry

1. If you have not already done so, get professional film training. Visit the Web sites of film and art schools near you and learn more about certification programs or continuing education classes. Set up a meeting with a department head, if possible, to learn more about the classes, job placement programs, prerequisites, and if networks recognize the school and hire graduates.

2. Read everything you can find about film and television production. Read film and video magazines and biographies about cameramen, directors, producers, etc. Learn about the masters and the innovators.

3. Find job listings by perusing the employment sections of broadcast network Web sites.

4. Be persistent, diligent, and patient. There is not one right way to go about entering this field, so try a variety of routes. One will eventually pan out. If you cannot find a freelance job, get a lower-paying or even unpaid internship if you must. Pay your dues and use the time to train and hone your skills while on the job. Networks often promote from within, so do well and you can eventually work your way up.

VIDEOGRAPHER

CAREER PROFILE

Duties: Provides professional videographic services in sound and color to families for weddings and parties and to schools and colleges for graduations, sports events, and performances; provides videographic services to city or county government agencies for recording depositions and special events and to corporate clients for conferences, presentations, trade shows, and more; creates videos for department stores for new employee training and for local police or fire departments for new equipment training programs

Alternate Title(s): Wedding Videographer

Salary Range: $50,000 to $75,000

Employment Prospects: Good

Advancement Prospects: Good

Best Geographical Location(s): Large cities and urban areas

Prerequisites:

Education or Training—Two- or four-year degree in photography, with videography training required; coursework in filmmaking beneficial

Experience—Several years of experience as a wedding photographer or assistant to a Videographer

Special Skills and Personality Traits—Excellent hand-eye coordination and steady hands; able to follow action with video camera and tell the story of the event from beginning to end; strong communication and interpersonal skills; patient; flexible; able to work all hours of day and night; physical stamina; team player; reliable and responsible

CAREER LADDER

```
┌─────────────────────────────────┐
│   Videography Franchise Owner   │
└─────────────────────────────────┘

┌─────────────────────────────────┐
│           Videographer          │
└─────────────────────────────────┘

┌─────────────────────────────────┐
│   Wedding Photographer /         │
│   Videographer's Assistant       │
└─────────────────────────────────┘
```

Position Description

Professional Videographers work for a variety of clients to help create videotapes for special events, legal documentations, employment training, and classroom education. Many Videographers specialize in weddings, and couples usually book them as part of the wedding photography team soon after they secure the reception hall and finalize the details.

They also work for local advertising agencies, department stores, theatrical and church groups, as well as legal firms, police departments, and government agencies. Hospitals and medical schools commission Videographers to create educational films for use in classrooms. Videographers are also retained by private detectives, architects, home contractors, and industrial construction companies.

Videographers prepare for jobs by scouting locations before the day of the shoot. They will physically visit the location and take notes about lighting, structures, objects, where activities will be taking place, and other factors so that they can determine a visual sequence of events. This helps them map out their time once they start shooting. They choose the appropriate equipment and cameras to match the event and may work with assistants who will hold lights or microphones and run errands, if needed. They also have preliminary meetings with clients to discuss the agenda for the evening, what will be happening when, who will be involved, and the most important people and aspects of each activity that the client wants captured on video. Large events will require them either to move from room to room to capture everything or to work with a videography team. They will take close-ups and shots from a distance. They may interview people who are attending the events, asking them to discuss their opinions and feelings about the events, or record their brief messages.

Videographers also have the challenge of assembling the footage after the event has ended. While the guests and participants may go home, the Videographer heads to the studio and spends the next few days or weeks reviewing the video, adding titles and special effects, and synching voices, music, and background sounds to the action on the screen. Videographers with training in film and video editing will be fully equipped to handle this aspect of the job and have full control of their product.

Salaries

Many Videographers are self-employed or work on a contract basis. Annual salaries can range from $50,000 to $75,000, depending upon their experience, clientele, and types of events they are videotaping. Freelance Videographers will have to allot money for such expenses as video cameras and equipment, studio rent and utilities, office equipment and supplies, as well as direct marketing and advertising campaigns to promote their business.

Employment Prospects

Videographers can expect to find good opportunities for work. Elaborate wedding celebrations are happening everywhere, every year. Families with medium-to-large budgets for these services will continue to need Videographers to help them commemorate their special occasions. Universities, law firms, major department stores and franchises, city and federal agencies, and many others will also continue to need the services of Videographers to help them accomplish their goals and promote their services. Professional Videographers who are technically skilled, have developed reputations for producing quality videos, and who have effective advertising and direct marketing campaigns will have the best chances of maintaining clientele and securing new business.

Advancement Prospects

Videographers who own their own businesses can advance by opening other videography studios in new locations. They can also purchase other franchises and consolidate with their businesses, thereby expanding clientele and photographic services. They may hire more videographers and add other services to their studios. If they work full time at a videography company, they can take on more responsibilities by becoming heads of videography departments. More senior jobs will entail more prioritization, delegation, management, and leadership skills. If they specialize in videotaping one area, they can always explore new terrain. They can also create educational programs on videography (including their own instructional videos), teach and lecture at technical or art schools and professional associations, and write and publish on the subject.

Education and Training

A four-year degree in photography, filmmaking, or other liberal arts specification may be required for some positions. Coursework in camera operation and videography is recommended. Training in videography and film editing is a tremendous asset in the field. On-the-job training as an assistant photographer or Videographer is essential.

Experience, Skills, and Personality Traits

Videographers usually have prior experience as photographers or other related employees or freelancers for wedding photography studios. They enjoy working with people, traveling to various locations for their work, and capturing stories with their video cameras. Videographers have excellent knowledge of how to operate a video camera. They know how to mesh in with crowds without intruding or disrupting the flow of activities. While they may be attending weddings and parties where people are dancing and having a good time, Videographers always keep their professional demeanor and remain focused on the work at hand. The events may be long, and they are expected to capture all of the action, so physical fitness, energy, and stamina are extremely beneficial to the position.

Unions and Associations

There are professional Videographer associations in various states throughout the country that offer Videographers benefits that can enhance their careers. For a listing of associations and their Web sites, visit the services section of Real Videographers (http://www.realvideographers.com). Professional Videographers can also join photography-related associations, such as the National Press Photographers Association and Professional Photographers of America.

Tips for Entry

1. Create a list of wedding photography and videography studios in your area. You can find them by check-

ing your phone book or conducting an online search. Call or visit the studios and ask if they have any openings in the videography department. If not, find out about other ways to get your foot in the door.

2. If you have not trained in this arena yet, check with local schools to see if they offer courses in videography. Learn as much as you can on your own, too, by reading filmmaking and videography magazines and books. It is also a good idea to read what other Videographers are doing and learn about their backgrounds. You can find information by using an online search engine and simply plugging in the keyword *videographer.*

3. Rent or lease equipment from a photographic supplier and experiment with it.

4. Your local Chamber of Commerce may also have information about videographic services and careers and postproduction services.

COMMERCIAL PHOTOGRAPHY, ADVERTISING, AND PUBLICITY

ADVERTISING PHOTOGRAPHER

CAREER PROFILE

Duties: Takes photographs of merchandise, as directed by advertising agency art directors or clients, for print advertisements in magazines, newspapers, billboards, etc.; creates work estimates and schedules; works closely with and oversees assistants and creative team; attends client meetings; manages budgets; may handle accounts receivable and payable

Alternate Title(s): Commercial Photographer

Salary Range: $50,000 to $150,000+

Employment Prospects: Fair

Advancement Prospects: Good

Best Geographical Location(s): New York, Boston, Washington, D.C., Atlanta, Chicago, Minneapolis, Denver, San Francisco, and Los Angeles

Prerequisites:

Education or Training—Bachelor's degree, with specialization in photography helpful; certification from two-year photography school may suffice

Experience—Several years of experience working as a photographer

Special Skills and Personality Traits—Strong visual and conceptual eye; creative; flexible; detail- and deadline-oriented; able to take art direction and contribute artistic insights as needed; able to work independently as well as with a team

CAREER LADDER

```
┌─────────────────────────────┐
│   Advertising Photographer  │
└─────────────────────────────┘

┌─────────────────────────────┐
│     Catalog Photographer    │
└─────────────────────────────┘

┌─────────────────────────────┐
│    Assistant Photographer   │
└─────────────────────────────┘
```

Position Description

The Advertising Photographer works closely with a team of specialists to create photographs for publication in newspapers, magazines, billboards, and television. Before work can begin, Advertising Photographers meet with clients to secure the specifics about the project so that they can estimate the time and costs involved. They determine the product and the target audience; review sketches and layouts; learn the style and approach of the photography, key staff involved in the project, when the work should be completed; and more. They create the estimate either based on a flat fee for the entire project or a day rate and include billing for their hours, any staff required, film and processing, travel, shipping and messengers, and other expenses.

If photographing clothing, Advertising Photographers, or a casting director or stylist whom they have hired, choose the models, schedule them for fittings, and then book their time for the shoot. The Advertising Photographer also hires artists to handle makeup and hair. If photographing products, Advertising Photographers create the sets based on instructions from the art directors from the advertising agency or the client. Advertising Photographers work closely with assistant photographers, who are tasked with loading and unloading film into cameras, keeping notes, taking light readings using a meter, and handling the different types of lights and other technical and administrative aspects of the shoot. On the first day of the shoot, Advertising Photographers, the client, and/or agency art director will be present to confirm that the setup and test photos match the layout sketches agreed upon at the planning meeting.

When outdoor settings are required, Advertising Photographers arrange for cars or vans with drivers for the studio team, the models, makeup artists, and agency and client representatives. Advertising Photographers make sure appropriate permits, insurance coverage, and other permissions have been secured for use of the locations, such as public sites, where shoots may be scheduled.

The Advertising Photographer coordinates and oversees a trained team to carry out the requirements of the shoot, both on-site and off. He or she is responsible for this team, the models, light and equipment rentals, and any other special apparatus to be delivered to the studio or location. When off-site, Advertising Photographers manage the project's paperwork, including receipts, petty cash, return of rental garments, purchases or rentals of props (i.e., floral arrangements, furniture, etc.), and more. Advertising Photographers confirm the signing of photo-use releases by models and are responsible for the tracking of all billable expenses, sometimes laying out monies for expenses to be reimbursed at later dates.

Advertising Photographers need to have a variety of materials on hand for use as the need arises. Some of these materials include: seamless paper backgrounds, sawhorses, solid surfaces (i.e., Plexiglas, Formica, tile, wood, glass, etc.), lights, light stands, and lighting control devices (i.e., flags, gobos, reflector boards, scrims, diffusion material, etc.). A well-equipped studio will also have on hand a variety of common art supplies, drafting materials, and household tools and materials for building sets.

Salaries

Independent Advertising Photographers who own their own studios can earn salaries ranging from $50,000 to $150,000 or more, depending on the product and the client's budget. Advertising Photographers who have established themselves in the field and are recognized names will secure higher rates and achieve annual salaries in excess of $150,000.

Employment Prospects

According to the *Occupational Outlook Handbook,* employment of photographers in all areas is expected to increase by about 10 to 20 percent, or as fast as the average, through 2012. Digital photography will be in particularly high demand, as online magazines, journals, and newspapers continue to grow. The field, however, is extremely competitive. Advertising Photographers may have greater employment opportunities if they secure representation or commit a certain amount of time from their schedules to networking and marketing their services. Reinvestment in the business and staying current with technology is also crucial, as the growth of digital photography continues.

Advancement Prospects

Advertising Photographers are at the top of the career ladder, having achieved their positions after working for years, initially as assistants, then as photographers honing their skills. While there is no one particular job that they can advance to, Advertising Photographers are always seeking new accounts and more prestigious clients. They can expand their business by having a full-service studio, replete with staff photographers, assistants, set builders, and other specialists. They can also branch out by teaching in universities, lecturing and participating in panel discussions, and writing.

Education and Training

A four-year degree is recommended, with a specialization in photography and coursework in advertising or commercial art. Advertising Photographers may also participate in two-year programs at schools such as the School of Photographic Arts and Sciences at Rochester Institute of Technology or, on the west coast, the Brooks Institute of Photography in Santa Barbara, California, among others. It is also important for Advertising Photographers to stay current with industry trends and developing technologies by participating in workshops, trades shows, and conferences, and by reading magazines, books, and Web sites.

Experience, Skills, and Personality Traits

Advertising Photographers must have a good eye for color and concept and understand how to translate their client's visions into photographs that capture consumers' attention. Awareness of popular culture and what is going on in the world is important. Because Advertising Photographers oversee a variety of people, they must have excellent communication skills, be diplomatic team leaders, and be able to juggle tasks while keeping everyone on target, within budget, and tuned into deadlines. Advertising Photographers who succeed in this business are exceptional at coordinating projects and people. In addition to being creative and experimental, Advertising Photographers are technically adept; they know how to use various cameras, materials, and techniques to achieve the desired visual effects.

Unions and Associations

For access to employment opportunities and peer support; networking, educational events, and conferences; mailing list; computer software, and equipment discounts; group health insurance; and more, Advertising Photographers can join such organizations as Advertising Photographers of America, Professional Photographers of America, Inc., and the American Society of Media Photographers.

Tips for Entry

1. Get an internship in a catalog studio or directly with an Advertising Photographer. Use an online search as

well as the local phone books to find the studios or people you are interested in working with. Contact the human resources departments or individuals to find out about internship options.

2. Look at such publications or Web sites as Black Book (http://www.blackbook.com) or Work Book (http://www.workbook.com) to see the work you admire or find photographers you would be interested in contacting.

3. Look through photography magazines in your local library or bookstore for announcements of seminars and trade fairs with consumer days. Contact the trade-show offices to find out about Advertising Photographers in your area. Contact the Advertising Photographers to set up informational meetings.

ASSISTANT PHOTOGRAPHER

CAREER PROFILE

Duties: Provides daylong assistance to a photographer, as well as to consultants (i.e., makeup, wardrobe, etc.), at the behest of the photographer; creates checklists of items needed for shoots; may run errands, including delivering packages, picking up supplies, and arranging for food and beverages for shoots; may clean the studio before and after shoots; may help build, paint, and break down sets

Alternate Title(s): Photographer's Assistant

Salary Range: $20,000 to $65,000+

Employment Prospects: Fair

Advancement Prospects: Good

Best Geographical Location(s): Major urban areas, such as Atlanta, Chicago, Los Angeles, Miami, San Francisco, Seattle, and Washington, D.C.

Prerequisites:

Education or Training—Four-year degree in photography; two-year degree from technical school acceptable; digital camera and photography design software training

Experience—Several years of experience as an intern or studio assistant in a commercial studio, portrait studio, or with a wedding photographer

Special Skills and Personality Traits—Knowledgeable about film, lighting, lenses, cameras, set-building materials, etc.; strong communication skills; good listener; able to follow directions; professional; diplomatic; physically strong; able to help build and move sets, as needed; reliable and responsible; detail- and deadline-oriented; organized

CAREER LADDER

```
┌─────────────────────────────────┐
│     Commercial Photographer     │
└─────────────────────────────────┘

┌─────────────────────────────────┐
│     Assistant Photographer      │
└─────────────────────────────────┘

┌─────────────────────────────────┐
│   Studio Assistant / Apprentice │
└─────────────────────────────────┘
```

Position Description

The Assistant Photographer is the right hand to the photographer, prepared to have the correct camera and lamps at the camera stand when called upon. He or she has learned the difference between the mini-spot and the general floodlight, the big Klieg and the small spotlight, and knows how the boom lamp creates shadow-free light across the worktable. It is the Assistant Photographer's responsibility to arrive early at the studio each day to prepare the cameras, lenses, lights, and light stands; load film; make sure the floor and

tabletops are clean and the space is completely appropriate for the day's work; and more. The Assistant Photographer may also help create sets by moving props such as chair, couches, tables, and dressers, and he or she may even paint sets. When shoots wrap, assistants are responsible for breaking down the sets and moving, packing, and shipping items, if necessary.

Assistant Photographers clean up and tidy dressing rooms before models arrive. They put out hand towels and tissues, hang clothing, and possibly even replenish beverages or snacks if there is a refrigerator on hand. If the photographer is photographing tabletops of watches, jewelry, or silverware, the Assistant Photographer will clean the glass tops and set up appropriate lights. The night before a location shoot, the Assistant Photographer thoroughly reviews the checklist, making sure all film, cameras, equipment, materials, and tools needed for the shoot have been packed carefully. If working with a larger studio and a larger budget, Assistant Photographers may also be responsible for delegating work to more junior staff, such as apprentices or interns, and coordinating with other assistants.

If the work is being done with digital cameras, Assistant Photographers set up computer equipment. Throughout the shoot, they keep track of the shots by writing down shot numbers, brief descriptions of the shots, and whether they are digital or film. Assistant Photographers prep the film for the labs and either arrange for messengers or take the film directly to labs themselves.

Salaries

Assistant Photographers can earn salaries ranging from as low as $20,000 or less to $65,000 or more, depending upon their years of experience, the types of photographers they work with, and the clients' budgets. Freelance Assistant Photographers usually charge flat day rates, which can range anywhere from $75 to $500 or more, according to several experienced professionals in the field. Assistant Photographers who are just starting out usually need to supplement their modest incomes by securing other types of part-time or full-time work.

Employment Prospects

Employment Prospects for Assistant Photographers are fair because the competition is fierce. These jobs are highly desirable and many more flock to them than there are jobs to fill. According to the *Occupational Outlook Handbook,* employment of photographers overall is expected to grow by about 10 to 20 percent through 2012. As long as photographers continue to secure work, Assistant Photographers will be likely to secure work with them.

The Department of Labor states that half of all photographers own portrait studios in small towns. They often hire new studio employees, such as Assistant Photographers, when they expand their businesses or when employees retire. These family-run studios are frequently the sole full-service wedding and portrait photographers in their communities and may provide good opportunities for work. The fastest way to start a career in a small studio is by seeking work in the late spring or early summer, a popular time of year for weddings.

Advancement Prospects

Depending on the economic or population growth of communities in various states, the advancement opportunity of the Assistant Photographer in a small studio will range from poor to good. If the studio has an active wedding-photography business, the potential for advancement is better. If the studio serves a community largely of retired or senior citizens, there are fewer opportunities once a trainee has reached a skilled performance level. Assistant Photographers who freelance in major cities can advance to become professional photographers within five or more years.

Education and Training

A four-year degree, with a specialization in photography, and coursework in computer design software (i.e., Adobe Photoshop and Illustrator) is recommended. Several years of training with a studio or wedding photographer is an excellent way to learn firsthand how daily business is conducted. Assistant Photographers must keep abreast of technological advances by reading industry magazines and books, visiting Web sites, networking with other professionals in the field, and taking classes.

Experience, Skills, and Personality Traits

Assistant Photographers must have excellent communication skills. They will be working directly with photographers and the photographers' creative teams, as well as with clients. They must be versatile at working with a variety of people. Assistants are also technologically adept in working with cameras, lights, and computer equipment. Assistant Photographers know when to follow directions and when it is appropriate to offer suggestions to photographers. They are diplomatic, professional, organized, extremely responsible, and flexible. Whether they are lighting a set or sweeping the floor of the studio, they treat each task seriously. They are always aware that they are being observed and news travels fast in the industry. In the end, an Assistant Photographer's character and the quality of his or her work will determine success in the field.

Unions and Associations

Assistant Photographers can join such associations as Advertising Photographers of America, American Society of Media Photographers, and Professional Photographers of America for educational and networking opportunities, discounts from various service providers, access to employment listings and competitions, and more.

Tips for Entry

1. Volunteer for a day at a photo studio as a messenger or to help clean or run errands. This is an excellent way to see how the studio is set up and how the sittings are arranged.
2. Visit a major resort city in which professional photography studios abound. Do your research first through

the Internet. Find the studio Web sites, look at their work, and make a list of notes and questions. Visit these studios and speak with the owners and staff about how best to enter the field. Learn what their experiences have been like.

3. Network as much as possible. This is a smaller world than you might think, and sometimes the best jobs come about through word of mouth. The more people you meet in the business, the better your chances of getting leads about upcoming shoots or job openings.

COMMERCIAL PHOTOGRAPHER

CAREER PROFILE

Duties: Creates photographs for advertisements in newspapers, magazines, billboards, posters, books, brochures, catalogs, company reports, and other media; photographs buildings and environments for reports and records; retouches photographs using digital software; may work with live models or products, depending upon specialty; sets up lights and backdrops; creates estimates, budgets, and production schedules, and secures client approvals; handles or oversees promotion and marketing of photography studio; may work with graphic and Web designers on branding; invoices clients, handles accounts receivable and payable, and oversees studio management and maintenance

Alternate Title(s): Advertising Photographer, Magazine Photographer, Portrait Photographer, Studio Photographer

Salary Range: $20,000 to $100,000+

Employment Prospects: Fair

Advancement Prospects: Fair

Best Geographical Location(s): Major metropolitan areas, such as Atlanta, Boston, Chicago, Los Angeles, Miami, New York, and San Francisco

Prerequisites:

Education or Training—Two- or four-year degree in photography; training in design software, such as Adobe Photoshop and Illustrator

Experience—Two to three years of experience as a photographer's assistant; several years of experience working in a commercial photography studio

Special Skills and Personality Traits—Strong knowledge of light and composition; agile at working with variety of cameras; computer savvy; excellent communication and listening skills; creative, with strong business-management abilities; able to work with variety of clients; entrepreneurial and self-motivated; complete knowledge of cameras, lights, films, and photography accessories; solid grasp of industry standards and practices and contract terms

CAREER LADDER

```
┌─────────────────────────────────┐
│     Commercial Photographer     │
└─────────────────────────────────┘

┌─────────────────────────────────┐
│     Photographer's Assistant    │
└─────────────────────────────────┘

┌─────────────────────────────────┐
│  Studio Intern / Studio Assistant │
└─────────────────────────────────┘
```

Position Description

Commercial Photographers create photographs to help clients advertise products and promote messages. They are technically and technologically skilled and adept at working for a variety of media and with a variety of clients, all for commercial purposes. Art directors, agency owners, product managers, and owners of stores hire Commercial Photographers to deliver photographs that capture their target audiences' attention. Architects, builders, and building owners will also hire Commercial Photographers to photograph landscapes and buildings for company reports, records, and brochures. Commercial Photographers may also photograph events and even students' art projects for portfolio pieces.

Commercial Photographers either work in their own studios or on location. They either create the backgrounds and backdrops themselves or work closely with the client's art directors or creative directors to help create the settings. Photographers make sure they have clear directions from clients before beginning the shoot. In their initial meetings, they ask the client who the advertisement is aimed toward and how the photographs will be used (i.e., billboard, poster, magazine advertisement, etc.). They include these terms in their contracts and secure clients' signatures before beginning work. They discuss the theme and style of the photographs and learn whether the client prefers soft lighting or strong color contrasts. Once all of the specifics have been reviewed, the photographer sets up the shot, choosing the lights, film, cameras, composition, and camera angles based on the client's directions. It is standard practice for Commercial Photographers to take "test" shots, usually in Polaroid, before working with actual film. The test shots provide opportunities to see what works and doesn't work in the setup, before spending money on actual film. Photographers scan the Polaroid shots and then e-mail them to clients for review and approval.

Commercial Photographers shoot in both film and digital. Digital photography enables them to synch the cameras directly to computers and easily review and retouch images using design software such as Adobe Photoshop and Illustrator. They can also scan film and retouch images, with some extra steps involved. If shooting in film, photographers usually have photography labs develop the film and review it to make sure nothing was altered in the development phase. They then will send the film to clients for approval.

Freelance Commercial Photographers are responsible for hiring staff for projects. Photographer's assistants help them with all aspects of shoots, from painting backdrops and moving props, to setting up lights, cameras, tripods, packing lists, running errands, and more. Photographers also work closely with makeup artists, stylists, and other creative crew. They negotiate employment terms with their staff and establish schedules before jobs begin. Independent photographers also negotiate contract terms and fees directly with clients. They create estimates and budgets, which they submit first to clients for approval before invoicing for completed work. Depending on their studio structure and size, they may manage all aspects of their business, from handling the bookkeeping and the bills, to making sure the copy machine has toner, the water cooler has water, and the studio space is clean and dust-free. Commercial Photographers will also be involved, to some degree, in the promotion and marketing of their businesses. They may hire writers, graphic designers, and Web designers to help them create and maintain their brand images, such as their company logos, stationery, business cards, promotional brochures and flyers, e-flashes and Web sites, and more.

Salaries

Salaries for Commercial Photographers can range anywhere from $20,000 to $100,000 or more. As in many professions, Photographers who are new to the business tend to earn lower salaries as opposed to veterans who have established clientele and enjoy repeat business. The *Occupational Outlook Handbook* cites a lower salary range for photographers overall in 2002, from $14,640 to $49,920, but does not take into account the earnings' potential for Commercial Photographers specifically. For instance, top advertising agencies generally have larger budgets and can pay their Commercial Photographers better fees. Freelance Commercial Photographers usually charge flat day rates, and the industry standard is to charge higher fees for rush jobs and work required over weekends and holidays. Photographers charge higher fees if the project is an all-rights contract, or a buy-out, and they also adjust their fees based on usage. Multiple uses require higher fees to the photographer.

Employment Prospects

The market is flooded with prospective Commercial Photographers. Competition is fierce and only those who have tremendous talent, drive, business savvy, and exceptional communication skills will survive and thrive in this business for the long term. Commercial Photographers usually secure work through a variety of avenues. They advertise in trade publications and on Web sites. They conduct promotional mailings on a regular basis. They network and secure projects through word of mouth. There is no singular right way to get work in this field, and the more avenues pursued, the better.

Advancement Prospects

Commercial Photographers are at the top of their field. Most freelance and own photography studios. They can advance by expanding their businesses, growing their client base, adding staff, and enhancing services. They can share their expertise by teaching classes in technical and art schools, as well as lecturing and writing.

Education and Training

While it is not required, a two- or four-year degree in photography is a solid base for many Commercial Photographers. Alternately, some may learn their trade by assisting Commercial Photographers or interning in commercial studios. Regardless of where they acquire their skills, Commercial Photographers must be well versed in digital photography as well as in digital design software. They can either take courses while in school or register for continuing education programs at local universities and trade schools.

Experience, Skills, and Personality Traits

Several years of experience as a photographer's assistant in a well-known and respected commercial studio is an excellent way to get a foot in the door in the commercial photography field. Successful Commercial Photographers are technically and technologically savvy. They understand cameras and computers and know how to synch the two to create images that meet clients' needs. They are creative thinkers with strong business-management skills and are adept at working with diverse people to meet deadlines. They must have excellent listening skills to clearly hear and understand what clients specifically want. Commercial Photographers must be independent workers as well as team players. They need to have the creativity and intelligence to translate clients' visions into reality, but they must also know how to collaborate with clients and creative staff to accomplish goals.

Unions and Associations

Commercial Photographers can join such associations as Advertising Photographers of America, the American Society of Media Photographers, and Professional Photographers of America for professional resources and networking opportunities.

Tips for Entry

1. Join a professional association, attend trade shows and conferences, and network. Attend the events and workshops your prospective clients attend. The commercial photography field is highly competitive, and the best way to find work is through word-of-mouth. You need to be circulating with your business cards and portfolio at the ready.
2. Read industry magazines such as *Photo District News, American Photo,* and *Digital Photo Pro.* Take workshops and read books. Keeping up with what is going on in your industry is critical.
3. Make sure you understand contract terms, industry terminology, and negotiating tactics before you start work for any client. Many professional associations offer workshops to help freelancers hone these skills. You can also glean a great deal of information through the Internet.

FOOD PHOTOGRAPHER

CAREER PROFILE

Duties: Creates appealing photographs of food for consumer and trade magazines and publications, cookbooks, and promotional literature for restaurants, culinary arts schools, cooking supply companies, gourmet stores, and supermarkets; works closely with food and set stylists to create images that will entice readers to buy the objects as well as to create the dishes on their own

Alternate Title(s): Culinary Photographer, Still Life Photographer

Salary Range: $14,640 to $49,920+

Employment Prospects: Good

Advancement Prospects: Fair

Best Geographical Location(s): Major metropolitan areas as well as cultural centers, such as Atlanta, Boston, Chicago, Los Angeles, Miami, New York, Seattle, and Washington, D.C.

Prerequisites:

Education or Training—Bachelor's degree in photography, with coursework in culinary arts, or culinary arts degree, with photography background, is recommended; training in photographic design software required

Experience—Several years of experience as commercial photographer or assistant food photographer, with advertising or publishing clients, is recommended; prior experience as assistant food stylist is beneficial

Special Skills and Personality Traits—Creative; good visual eye and hand-eye coordination; cooking and food preparation skills; strong interest in all types of food; patient; excellent interpersonal skills; team player as well as independent worker; reliable; deadline-oriented

CAREER LADDER

```
┌─────────────────────────────────┐
│       Food Photographer         │
└─────────────────────────────────┘

┌─────────────────────────────────┐
│  Assistant Food Photographer /   │
│    Commercial Photographer       │
└─────────────────────────────────┘

┌─────────────────────────────────┐
│     Assistant Food Stylist       │
└─────────────────────────────────┘
```

Position Description

Food Photographers create enticing photographic images of various types of food and prepared dishes for advertisers, publishers, restaurants, food markets, and others. They may photograph perfect-looking hamburgers and French fries for McDonald's, corn-on-the-cob slathered in butter for Waldbaum's, or creamy, chocolate-laden ice cream sundaes for Friendly's. Food Photographers consult with food stylists, prop artists, and set designers to achieve the crisp shots and the desired results. They map out shooting schedules based on the types of food they will be photographing. Some foods can endure heat from the lights throughout the day, whereas other foods must either be photographed quickly or treated to make them stay the course. With experience and training, Food Photographers know which tricks and techniques to use to "doctor" their subjects. For example, plump, consistent pancakes are usually photographed frozen. The bright yellow of margarine, as opposed to the duller hue of butter, stands out beautifully on potatoes or slices of bread. Perfect soft-serve ice cream usually isn't ice cream; it is often Dream Whip. Tortillas stay fresh, thanks to a coating of Armor-All, and hamburger buns stay straight with melted wax.

At the onset of a project, Food Photographers meet with clients to discuss the food, look, and mood they want. They then set up a shoot date, select and secure appropriate props, and hire food stylists, assistant photographers, prop movers, and whoever else is needed for the project. Food stylists are especially crucial for preparing, styling, and placing the food on the table. Food Photographers, with help from assistants, prepare the technical aspects of the shot, choosing and setting up the cameras, the camera angles, the film, lighting, and props. They take test shots to determine which lighting and angles work best and adjust until they are satisfied with the image. The food must hold up throughout, which is why Food Photographers will often substitute an object, a *food stand-in,* until all the preparations are finalized. Clients attend the shoots and review the images. Once they approve the test shots, the Food Photographer brings out the actual food, known as the *hero dish,* for the shoot.

Food Photographers often maintain their own inventory of stemware, barware, silverware, flatware, table linens, and more. They know where to locate what they need to complement and enhance the food and achieve the overall look and mood the clients are seeking in the images. Food Photographers are also constant "shoppers," always perusing magazines and stores to keep up with lifestyle design trends. They know that a certain glass or style of plate or knife can literally make or break a shot, and when they see that perfect item, they know when to nab it.

Independent Food Photographers manage and oversee their businesses. They work with graphic and Web designers to help them develop their companies' brand images (i.e., logos, stationery, brochures, Web sites). They handle and oversee direct marketing and advertising campaigns to promote their services. They network for new clients and maintain relationships with current clients. They hire and oversee staff, create contracts, negotiate fees, make sure bills are paid and invoices sent out, and plenty more.

Salaries

There are no salary ranges documented specifically for Food Photographers. However, the U.S. Bureau of Labor Statistics cites that in 2002, salaried photographers overall had annual earnings ranging from $14,640 to over $49,920. Freelance Food Photographers have the potential to earn higher salaries but must factor in costs for overhead, such as rent, equipment purchases and maintenance, office supplies, taxes, health insurance, and so on. Food Photographers who have established themselves in the business and who have good connections will secure the most work and the highest wages.

Employment Prospects

Employment of photographers in all disciplines will increase about as fast as the average for all occupations through 2012, according to the U.S. Department of Labor. Food Photographers may fare even better than other photographers over the next few years because the food and entertainment industries are expected to continue to grow. While advertising budgets may decrease, restaurants, stores, publishers, and others will still need professional photographers to help them entice diners and promote their services and products through their Web sites, menus, literature, and publications. As long as people continue to eat and remain interested in food, Food Photographers will be needed to get images of the food out there. Competition in the field will remain fierce, though, so technical and creative skills coupled with the right work background and connections will be an advantage in the job hunt. Food Photographers who keep up with technology and learn the latest digital-photographic techniques will also have an edge over the competition. More than half of the approximately 131,000 photographers working in this country are self-employed. Others work on a full-time or contractual basis for various clients. Many Food Photographers enhance their salaries and secure commissions by placing their photographs with stock photo agencies.

Advancement Prospects

Food Photographers can advance by growing their businesses and partnering with other photographers who specialize in certain commercial photography areas. If they work primarily in editorial, they can explore developing clientele in other areas, such as food manufacturing or the entertainment industry. They can write and publish books and articles and teach at arts and technical schools.

Education and Training

A bachelor's degree in photography, with coursework in advertising, culinary arts, and consumer science, is recommended for this type of work. Alternatively, a degree in culinary arts, with coursework and training in photography, is also an excellent background for a Food Photographer. Food Photographers must understand what they are photographing to best capture the images for clients. Training in preparing foods and learning about various vegetables, fruits, and grains, and other types of foods and how they interact with chemical properties and lighting is critical. Math and chemistry classes are also relevant for creating effects and treating the foods in order to get desired results. You should also be sure to take computer science classes and explore software that can store and manipulate images, such as Adobe Photoshop and Illustrator.

Schools such as the Culinary Institute of America offer a wide variety of courses for all types of students, from the layperson to prospective chefs. You can find more schools by visiting http://www.cookingschools.com. Art and technical schools throughout the country offer degrees in food photography. Look for accredited art programs on the National Association of Schools of Art and Design Web site: http://nasad.arts-accredit.org.

Experience, Skills, and Personality Traits

Photographing food requires vast amounts of patience and flexibility. It may take hours to cast the right light and sheen on a particular object, and shoots may even take days or weeks, particularly if creating images of food and prepared dishes for cookbooks. Versatile, creative Food Photographers do best in this industry. They will be able to create unadulterated images for those clients who want something simple, such as a Granny Smith apple on a plain white backdrop. They will also be able to successfully create and photograph a formal dinner with various courses. Food Photographers' eyes are trained for details. They are able to scrutinize subjects as no layperson can and adjust cameras, lenses, filters, and lighting to correct the images before capturing them on film. Naturally, of utmost importance in the food photography field is a passion about food. Food Photographers spend hours getting a bowl of carrots to look just right. This type of work would drive anyone else mad. Successful Food Photographers see what others may overlook—the unique shapes, textures, and shadows—and they appreciate the art that is in their subjects.

Unions and Associations

Food Photographers can become members of the American Society of Media Photographers and Professional Photographers of America for educational resources, networking opportunities, and discounts on various services and products.

Tips for Entry

1. Get your foot in the door by starting out as a food-styling assistant. You will have firsthand exposure to the intricacies of the business and make valuable connections.
2. If you have not done so already, take some cooking classes to learn how to prepare certain types of food. Register with a recognized and well-respected school. Name recognition is important in this industry and having this on your résumé will attract and impress prospective clients.
3. Join a cooking club and experiment with taking photos of the dishes you and others create along the way. You can even peruse your own refrigerator and experiment with taking photos of what is on your shelves. Create lighting effects and set up props. Then share your photos to see how others react and take notes on their feedback.

PHOTO STYLIST

CAREER PROFILE

Duties: Works closely with photographers, fashion and makeup stylists, and other creative crew members to create looks and moods of images for clients by choosing props and backgrounds, styles of clothing and accessories, furniture, lights, interior and exterior design objects, and other set elements; may specialize in certain areas, such as bridal, fashion, prop buying, or location scouting, or cover many areas at once; may coordinate schedules for shoots, work with models, and manage staff; attends photo shoots

Alternate Title(s): Style Consultant

Salary Range: $350 to $800+ per day

Employment Prospects: Fair

Advancement Prospects: Fair

Best Geographical Location(s): Major cities, such as Boston, Chicago, Miami, Los Angeles, New York, and San Francisco

Prerequisites:

Education or Training—Bachelor's degree, with specialization in photography, is recommended but not required; coursework in advertising, graphic design, and fashion design is helpful

Experience—One to three years of experience as an assistant Photo Stylist required; prop-buying or window-dressing experience is beneficial

Special Skills and Personality Traits—Creative; knowledgeable about fashion and lifestyle trends; organized; excellent communicator; flexible; accessible and able to work at all hours of day and night; energetic; problem solver who can think on his or her feet; able to follow directions and work well with others; reliable and responsible

CAREER LADDER

```
┌─────────────────────────────┐
│       Photo Stylist         │
└─────────────────────────────┘

┌─────────────────────────────┐
│  Assistant Photo Stylist    │
└─────────────────────────────┘

┌─────────────────────────────┐
│      Window Dresser         │
└─────────────────────────────┘
```

Position Description

Photo Stylists help photographers create the overall look and feel of photographic images for advertisements, magazines, books, Web sites, and other types of publications. Photo Stylists also work closely with art directors, assistants, makeup artists, designers, and clients throughout the shoot. Photo Stylist responsibilities vary according to the types of projects and photographers with which they are working. For instance, Photo Stylists who specialize in fashion will be responsible for helping to audition and select models, as well as choosing clothing and accessories that will look best on them, fit the theme of the photos, and effectively sell the products to the target audience.

Photo Stylists may specialize in any number of areas. They may be well versed in prop shopping and purchasing or set decorating and location scouting. Photo Stylists who specialize in food use various artistic techniques, such as glazing or painting, to enhance food and make it more appealing. Props often come into play in lifestyle images, so stylists who specialize in home furnishings will deal with chairs, tables, lamps, etc. Then there are *on-figure* and *off-figure stylists,* with on-figure stylists arranging clothes on models and off-figure stylists creating and setting up clothes against backgrounds. *Soft-goods stylists* focus on clothing, fabrics, and linens, and *tabletop stylists* will make even the most mundane item, such as a pair of pliers, look appealing by adding a dab of Vaseline or glue. *Hair and makeup stylists* work with cosmetics, and *casting stylists* locate modeling talent. Many stylists are cross-disciplined and able to work with a wide variety of clients.

Photo Stylists are magicians, in a way. They are often the go-to people for solving problems at the last minute. They may use anything from salt to duct tape to keep an object together or create a certain effect. Photo Stylists may also be tasked with designing and building props, coordinating crew schedules, securing locations and release forms, and more. They have the solutions, and when they do not, they know where to go to find what is needed. Photo Stylists create and maintain lists of props and set elements before the shoots begin, tracking delivery times and checking items upon arrival. Throughout the shoots, they make sure objects are being treated respectfully and with care. They oversee returning items once the shoot has ended and maintain receipts and financial records to assure everything is within budget.

Freelance Photo Stylists without agency representation must also continually seek work through self-promotion efforts. They must tailor their online and print portfolios to specific clients, make sure their Web sites are current, network at professional events, negotiate fees, send out invoices, oversee their own accounts receivables and payables, and, on top of all this, devote time to keeping up with trends through reading magazines and other print and online publications.

Salaries

Photo Stylists can earn rates ranging from $350 to $800 per day, depending upon their years of experience in the business and the types of projects and clients. Many Photo Stylists are freelance and must factor into their earnings costs for health insurance and general business overhead, such as rent and utilities. Experienced and respected freelance Photo Stylists can earn far beyond $800 per day, with complete coverage of expenses such as travel and accommodations.

Employment Prospects

Employment prospects for Photo Stylists are only fair because many people consider the work to be glamorous, and glamour jobs always attract more people than there are jobs available. The field is highly competitive, and it is the creative Photo Stylists with solid self-promotion skills who will secure the most work. The advertising, publishing, and entertainment industries are expected to remain steady, according to the Department of Labor, assuring at least continual employment for some Photo Stylists who have inroads. Most Photo Stylists are self-employed and work on a per-assignment basis. Another route Photo Stylists can take to secure work and avoid spending time on the job hunt is through agency representation. Reps usually receive about 20 percent commission for work they succeed in securing for their clients.

Advancement Prospects

Freelance Photo Stylists who work with mid-level publications can advance by stepping up to a bigger playing field. They can notch up their business and increase their earnings by taking on more work with major, well-recognized publications and photographers. Reputation is everything in this business; it can make or break a person's career. Photo Stylists must always keep their eyes open for opportunities to work on high-end projects with stars in the field. With years of experience, Photo Stylists can also advance to become art directors, creative directors, fashion editors, and senior photo stylists.

Education and Training

A bachelor's degree in photography is a solid educational background for this type of work. While a degree is not mandatory, many Photo Stylists have, at minimum, attended art schools and taken courses in advertising, marketing, photography, and design. Coursework is also recommended in the areas Photo Stylists may be interested in specializing in, such as cosmetology classes to learn more about fashion styling or cooking classes for food styling. Two years of experience as an intern, apprentice, or assistant photo stylist in an advertising agency, magazine publishing company, or design house is also an excellent way to learn the ins and outs of the business.

Experience, Skills, and Personality Traits

Several years of experience as an assistant photo stylist are usually recommended. Successful Photo Stylists are extremely creative yet simultaneously grounded and realistic. They are decisive but flexible, able to adjust to changing needs and schedules. They have good taste, are agile problem solvers, and have clear communication skills. They listen closely to what clients want and understand how best to work with photographers and other crew to achieve the desired images. The job requires many hats and the best Photo Stylists can wear each one well. They are patient, professional, diplomatic, and able to meet deadlines while often working under stressful conditions. Easygoing stylists who are approachable and supportive often have the largest clientele. They keep up with trends, know where to get everything and anything that is needed, and how to negotiate for the best prices. They have excellent interpersonal skills, which facilitates working with everyone from corporate executives and art directors, to models, makeup artists, and photographers. They are also familiar with photographic techniques, such as lighting and composition, understand advertising, and are familiar with product lines and designers.

Unions and Associations

Photo Stylists who are accepted as members of the Association of Stylists and Coordinators receive access to employment opportunities and referrals, as well as other professional benefits.

Tips for Entry

1. Learn about advertising and product display by securing a job in the advertising department of a retail store. Watch window display artists at work and, when appropriate, talk to them to learn more about what is involved in a typical day.

2. Join a professional association and network with the people who have the potential to hire you and refer you to jobs. Attend design shows and magazine launch parties. Go to gallery openings and fashion shows. Consider the time spent meeting and chatting with people as an investment in your future. Approach it seriously and professionally. Always have business cards with you, and always follow-up, even if it may not immediately generate results. It will be worth your while in the long run.

3. Speak with Photo Stylists to learn more about the work. Search the Internet to find stylists near you if you want to set up in-person interviews. Learn as much as you can by perusing their Web sites before contacting them.

PUBLICITY PHOTOGRAPHER

CAREER PROFILE

Duties: Provides photographs of individuals, places, and events to publicists and public relations firms to accompany press releases and magazine or newspaper articles; may work in communications or public relations departments of associations and nonprofit organizations; maintains photography libraries; negotiates fees, work estimates, and contracts; may oversee assistants

Alternate Title(s): Public Affairs Photographer, Public Relations Photographer

Salary Range: $35,000 to $60,000

Employment Prospects: Good

Advancement Prospects: Poor

Best Geographical Location(s): Boston, Chicago, Hollywood, Houston, Las Vegas, Los Angeles, Miami, New York, San Francisco, and Washington, D.C.

Prerequisites

Education or Training—Four-year degree in photography; training in digital photography and photographic design software

Experience—Several years of experience as a newspaper or magazine photographer

Special Skills and Personality Traits—Excellent interpersonal skills; knowledgeable about lighting and composition; good visual eye; friendly and accessible; able to make people feel comfortable and natural in front of the camera; detail- and deadline-oriented; ethical and professional; flexible and available to work days and evenings when needed

CAREER LADDER

```
┌─────────────────────────────────┐
│  Director of Photo Department   │
└─────────────────────────────────┘

┌─────────────────────────────────┐
│     Publicity Photographer      │
└─────────────────────────────────┘

┌─────────────────────────────────┐
│     Freelance Photographer      │
└─────────────────────────────────┘
```

Position Description

Publicity Photographers are responsible for creating photographs of a wide range of events, people, and products for use in press releases, newspaper and magazine articles, advertisements, promotional materials, Web sites, e-newsletters, annual reports, and more. Press agents, publicists, and public relations firms hire Publicity Photographers to create imagery that will help them convey specific messages to targeted audiences about the companies or individuals they represent.

Publicity Photographers may work for publicists for magazines such as *People* and *Us Weekly* and photograph celebrities to accompany articles or cover awards ceremonies and premieres. They work for the public affairs and communications department of city agencies, such as the Metropolitan Transportation Authority in New York City. They photograph subway tracks, train platforms, interiors and exteriors of trains, stairs, turnstiles, subway signs, conductors, and passengers. Their images appear in posters throughout the trains and platforms, promoting subway rules and regulations and advertising upcoming events. Their work also appears in promotional brochures and flyers and is released to magazines, newspapers, broadcast networks, and newswires.

Some Publicity Photographers are also responsible for videography and visual production, such as script development, graphic design, and editing and studio production. Publicity Photographers who work for such associations as the Red Cross take shots of volunteers in action, either in the safety of administrative offices, at fund-raising events, or on location at disaster sites. They photograph tents being set up, food being served, medical equipment, medical care and counseling, and more. The military also hires Publicity Photographers to photograph training camps, offices, equipment, living quarters, as well as military operations and exercises at home and at war.

Staff Publicity Photographers are often responsible for developing and maintaining photo libraries and fulfilling internal photo requests. They develop and process both black-and-white and color film and use Adobe Photoshop and other design software to correct color and light, crop out objects, and resize images. Depending upon the company, they may be required to operate still, motion picture, and electronic news-gathering cameras (cameras that record live events and transmit them to a studio) and to write captions for motion-picture film and photographs. They collaborate with reporters and public relations journalists in creating and producing visual stories and publicity films. They also record and file original negatives and transparencies with the staff involved in the production of the stories.

Salaries
Publicity Photographers can earn salaries ranging from $35,000 to $60,000. Annual earnings will vary for freelancers, depending upon the number and types of clients that they have. Publicity Photographers usually enjoy perks such as access to events and places from which the general public is typically barred. Travel, hotel, and other work-related expenses are also normally reimbursed. Some companies provide their staff photographers with expense accounts, use of the company car, and frequent flier mileage. Full-time staff Publicity Photographers may enjoy benefits such as profit sharing, stock options, paid vacation and sick leave, bonuses, and group health insurance.

Employment Prospects
Many people clamor to the publicity field because it is considered a glamour industry. Competition for Publicity Photographer jobs is fierce, but there will be opportunities for work, particularly in smaller publicity firms. The U.S. Department of Labor predicts employment in the public relations industry will grow by 19 percent through 2012, compared to 16 percent for all industries combined. Public relations, like advertising, is driven by the economy. As the economy expands, companies will introduce more services and products to meet consumer demands and more Publicity Photographers will be needed to help get word out to the public. Publicity Photographers will also find work as their predecessors advance to other positions or retire.

Advancement Prospects
With years of experience and good connections, Publicity Photographers can advance to become the heads of photography departments within publicity agencies and publications. They can start their own publicity agencies, and they can transfer their skills into media broadcasting. They can also move up by writing articles for trade publications or teaching in liberal arts and technical schools.

Education and Training
Publicity Photographers normally have four-year degrees from liberal arts schools or two-year degrees from photographic or technical institutes. Coursework in communications, advertising, and direct marketing can be helpful. Publicity Photographers are trained in digital photography and well versed in color and image-enhancement software programs, such as Adobe Photoshop and Illustrator.

Experience, Skills, and Personality Traits
Public relations companies and associations prefer Publicity Photographers with several years of experience as daily newspaper or magazine photographers. Publicity Photographers need to be technically accurate photographers who can work fast to meet deadlines. Their job requires travel both locally and internationally, so they must be organized and able to adapt to change. They must be able to work at all times of the day and night and in all types of weather. An ability to interact with a wide variety of people is essential in the job, and photographers who can speak other languages are particularly desirable by companies with international branches. Publicity Photographers need to stay abreast of new developments in the companies they work for, as well as be knowledgeable about the key movers and shakers, and the companies' missions and past and current projects. They must also keep up with photographic and technological advances, so they can work most effectively.

Unions and Associations
The National Press Photographers Association, Public Relations Society of America, American Society of Media Photographers, Advertising Photographers of America, and Professional Photographers of America are just some of the associations Publicity Photographers can belong to for educational workshops and conferences, networking opportunities, portfolio critiques, employment referrals, and discounts on group health insurance and other necessities.

Tips for Entry
1. Search for public relations firms and publicity agencies on the Internet. Contact them and set up informa-

tional meetings so that you can learn how they work with photographers and if they have any openings.

2. Network. The public relations industry thrives on networking. Join professional associations and attend meetings and conferences. Always have business cards, promotional postcards, or even electronic portfolios on CD with you to share at events.

3. Many nonprofits look for volunteer public affairs photographers. While it is always better for the wallet to have a salary, if you are new to the field, volunteering can be a great introduction to the field and an opportunity to create images for your portfolio.

STOCK IMAGE PHOTOGRAPHER

CAREER PROFILE

Duties: Creates photographic images (i.e., film and digital images, montages, collages) for various clients and self-initiated projects over the years; builds a substantial, diverse library of images and categorizes them by subject; participates in stock image shows and exhibitions; creates and negotiates contracts for buyers; manages and oversees a Web site gallery

Alternate Title(s): Commercial Photographer, Fine-Art Photographer, Nature Photographer, Photojournalist

Salary Range: $40,000 to $75,000+

Employment Prospects: Good

Advancement Prospects: Good

Best Geographical Location(s): Anywhere

Prerequisites:

Education or Training—Two- or four-year degree in photography; training in digital photographic and photographic design software (i.e., Adobe Photoshop)

Experience—Three or more years of professional photography experience in a commercial studio

Special Skills and Personality Traits—Knowledgeable about photography and photographic techniques; creative and innovative; savvy about stock image business practices; excellent negotiation skills; ability to understand stock image contracts; self-motivated; organized; ethical

CAREER LADDER

```
┌─────────────────────────────────┐
│    Stock Image Photographer     │
└─────────────────────────────────┘

┌─────────────────────────────────┐
│    Professional Photographer    │
└─────────────────────────────────┘

┌─────────────────────────────────┐
│    Photographer's Assistant     │
└─────────────────────────────────┘
```

Position Description

Stock Image Photographers turn the numerous images they have created over the years into stock photography libraries for sale to advertisers, publishers, and others. Stock photography means they rent the images to clients for one-time usage or other types of usage as dictated in their usage agreements and therefore have a secondary market for work they have already completed. When clients have an immediate need for photographs or are operating under tight budget constraints, they often use stock photography. Rather than commissioning photographers to create current work, which takes more time and can entail a variety of expenses, clients can peruse online photographic galleries, choose the images that best match their needs, pay the appropriate fees, and have access to those images within minutes. Stock photography is used in advertisements, books, magazines, posters, calendars, Web sites, clothing, accessories, decorative items, textile and industrial products, and more.

Stock Image Photographers choose and categorize images by subject. If they specialize in food photography, the categories can be as simple as *hamburgers, pizza, deli sandwiches, fruit, holiday dinners,* and so on. Just about any image a photographer creates can become a stock image. Depending upon their projects, clients will look for images in any number of subjects, such as scenes in offices, people in parks, backyard barbecues, landscapes, flowers, or children at playgrounds. They may want a martini on a glass table, a man lounging at the beach while using a laptop computer, or an older couple laughing as they pick fruit at a supermarket. Generic, everyday life, nonbrand images have the best potential for reuse in the stock photography market.

Stock Image Photographers may also create stock images on speculation, meaning they will take photographs of their own creation and initiative to add to their galleries and pitch to prospective clients. For instance, if a photographer wants to have images that focus on people using cellphones in a variety of venues, he or she may call a modeling agency and ask about creating images of the newest models, both for the agency and for client pitches. The photographer will photograph models using cellphones as they walk down a street, sit in a bus, shop in a store, or in other settings. The agency then uses the photos to promote their models while the photographer adds them to his or her inventory.

Naturally, Stock Image Photographers can create stock images at any time. They may be working on a commercial shoot, for example, at the Chrysler Building on a particularly beautiful day. While there, they can snap a series of shots of the building with a blue-sky, puffy white-cloud background. These pictures can make for excellent images for clients needing New York scenes or examples of architectural accomplishments.

Stock Image Photographers usually commission graphic designers to help them create stock image catalogs, brochures, and other promotional literature. They also retain Web designers to create Web site galleries and stores in which to promote and sell their stock photographs. They may hire and oversee administrative staff, such as sales associates and customer service representatives to field customer inquiries and handle transactions, as well as office managers, bookkeepers, and accountants.

Salaries

Stock Image Photographers can earn annual salaries ranging from $40,000 to $75,000 or more. Their earnings will depend upon the size and scope of their stock libraries, the quality and desirability of their images, the types of buyers, and types of usage being purchased. It costs less to buy one-time usage rights for an image than it does to use that image in a number of ways and in a variety of media. Multiple-use means more money for the photographer. Experienced and reputed photographers can sell their collections for large amounts of money to such stock image giants as Corbis and Getty.

Employment Prospects

The proliferation of online stock photography agencies has provided photographers with more opportunities to promote and sell their stock photography images. Creating their own Web site galleries and stores has also gotten easier and enabled more photographers to have a secondary market for their work. Employment prospects will depend upon a number of variables: the size of the Stock Image Photographer's library, the quality and marketability of the photographs, whether the photographer is a well-known name in his or her photographic specialty, and how the photographer chooses to promote and sell the images. Stock Image Photographers may sell their images through their own Web sites or through stock photography agencies. Those who sell on their own choose to do so because they prefer to have complete control of the business and retain more money; they set the terms and negotiate directly with clients. They choose how best to promote their stock catalogs. Stock photography agencies, on the other hand, can save photographers time by handling all of the administrative and account management tasks. They oversee the Web site gallery and may deal directly with clients and handle transactions on the behalf of photographers.

Advancement Prospects

Stock Image Photographers can advance by expanding their libraries. They can partner with other photographers who specialize in fields other than their own, for the opportunity to diversify their libraries and attract new clients. They can write articles and lecture about the business. They can also advance the field by teaching and writing about fair industry practices.

Education and Training

A two- or four-year degree in photography, with coursework in small business management and sales and negotiation tactics, is a solid foundation for this position. Training in digital photography and design software such as Adobe Photoshop is recommended. Stock Image Photographers keep abreast of industry practices and copyright issues by taking workshops offered by trade associations and technical and art institutions.

Experience, Skills, and Personality Traits

Stock Image Photographers have backgrounds in a wide variety of photographic disciplines from which they build their stock image businesses. Some may be nature photographers; others fine arts photographers or interior design photographers. They are extremely organized and are able to commit time to creating, categorizing, and cataloging image libraries. They have excellent written and communication skills. If they have full-time staff, they are adept at prioritizing and delegating work and managing and overseeing others. Stock Image Photographers are smart, ethical entrepreneurs who have a thorough knowledge of how the stock image business works and conduct their business in accordance with fair trade practices. Stock Image Photographers are self-determined, motivated individuals who are interested in extending the use of their images to make the most of its market potential.

Union and Associations

Stock Image Photographers belong to the associations that pertain to their photographic specializations. For instance, photojournalists may belong to the National Press Photographers Association for networking opportunities and educational resources. Stock Image Photographers of all disciplines may belong to the Photo Marketing Association International, Advertising Photographers of America, American Society of Media Photographers, and Professional Photographers of America for workshops and conferences, employment referrals, portfolio critiques, and discounts on medical and equipment insurance. They may also join the Association of International Photography Art Dealers for educational publications, networking opportunities, and the ability to participate in annual photography shows.

Tips for Entry

1. Make sure you understand how the stock photography business works before you dive into it. You need to protect your rights and price your work in accordance with industry standards. Read the stock artwork section of the Graphic Artists Guild's *Handbook of Pricing and Ethical Guidelines* and publications from trade associations such as the American Society of Media Photographers.

2. Join the Association of International Photography Art Dealers and learn the full details about how you can exhibit and sell your photography in their annual photography show. The show features vintage and contemporary photographic images, offered for sale by international galleries and private dealers.

3. Stock agencies such as Creative Eye, Stockphoto Network, and Media Image Resource Alliance offer a wealth of information for photographers and buyers about the stock image business. Review their catalogs or visit their Web sites regularly to keep up with industry practices and issues and to network with others in the field for advice and referrals.

EVENT AND TRAVEL PHOTOGRAPHY

BANQUET PHOTOGRAPHER

CAREER PROFILE

Duties: Photographs banquets for associations, universities, large corporations, and other organizations that host dinners and evening functions at hotels, conventions centers, and banquet sites; oversees film development and processing; sells photography packages and framed pictures to clients

Alternate Title(s): Convention Photographer, Wedding Photographer

Salary Range: $40,000 to $80,000

Employment Prospects: Good

Advancement Prospects: Fair

Best Geographical Location(s): Boston, Chicago, Las Vegas, Los Angeles, New York, and San Francisco

Prerequisites:
  Education or Training—Two- or four-year degree in photography; trained in digital photography and photographic design software programs
  Experience—Two to three years of commercial photography work; prior wedding or event photography experience beneficial
  Special Skills and Personality Traits—Detail- and deadline-oriented; excellent interpersonal and communication skills; polite and comfortable in social settings

CAREER LADDER

```
┌─────────────────────────────┐
│    Banquet Photographer     │
└─────────────────────────────┘

┌─────────────────────────────┐
│    Wedding Photographer     │
└─────────────────────────────┘

┌─────────────────────────────┐
│   Photographer's Assistant  │
└─────────────────────────────┘
```

Position Description:

Banquet Photographers photograph banquets hosted by hotels, convention centers, universities, corporations, associations, sports leagues, and many others. They cover dinner dances, holiday parties, awards ceremonies, luncheons featuring panel discussions, alumni reunions, and graduation balls. The word *banquet* doesn't always apply to their subject matter, however, as they may also be commissioned to photograph summer camp events and school proms.

Banquet Photographers take pictures of groups at tables and speakers and honorees at podiums. They photograph guests as they arrive, groups mingling during the pre-dinner cocktail receptions, and couples dancing during post-dinner entertainment. Banquet Photographers also take interior shots of the facilities, as well as exteriors of the buildings in which the banquets are held.

Banquet Photographers travel to locations for their work and have their camera equipment and gear packed and prepared in advance for shoots. For large banquets and events, they usually work with a team of photographers and assistants, all of whom are either on staff in their studios or have been commissioned as freelancers for the event. Banquet Photographers meet with clients before events to discuss the various photographic packages available, the photographic style and subject matter the client would like to see, as well as to review cost estimates and negotiate contract terms.

Normally, Banquet Photographers have digital setups on site at the banquets, so people can see previews of their photographs and request retakes if the images do not meet their expectations. Banquet Photographer also work in film, creating wide-screen images of large groups and entire rooms. Some Banquet Photographers also offer on-site printing, so that people can take the prints home immediately. Photographers can add company logos to the prints and offer various print options to clients, such as color schemes and photo borders.

Banquet Photographers also work closely with convention center and hotel managers and crew. These facilities are usually run by unions and have set job descriptions for their employees. Banquet Photographers may not be authorized to move certain objects or set up certain electrical wires if these tasks fall within an employee's domain. Photographers will contact employees throughout the location shoot to bring cartons and cases, provide and install electric wires, set up or move ladders, adjust and control overhead lights (not photographic lights, though), and more.

Freelance Banquet Photographers are also responsible for running and maintaining their businesses. They handle the promoting and marketing of their services and work with graphic designers on advertising campaigns and Web designers on the creation and maintenance of their company Web sites. They either have a bookkeeper and accountant handle the books, tax payments, and accounts receivable and payable, or they do it themselves, and they make sure their office equipment works and office supplies are stocked.

Salaries

Banquet Photographers are usually freelancers who charge flat fees or day rates for their services. They may charge anywhere from $500 to $1,500 or more per event or per day. Fees depend upon number of shots and locations involved in the project, location of the banquet or event, and the photographer's years of experience in the field. Successful Banquet Photographers who are well known and in high demand will secure higher salaries. The few Banquet Photographers who are full-time employees at commercial studios will usually enjoy such benefits as discounted group health insurance and paid vacation and sick leave. Depending upon their agreements with clients, Banquet Photographers may augment their earnings by selling images to stock photography houses.

Employment Prospects

Chances of finding work in the banquet photography field are good. The growth of group travel to resorts and to year-round convention and trade-show cities has increased the demand for on-site photography services in hotels and convention halls everywhere. The increasingly affluent middle class and the substantial growth of the senior citizen market has led to new and improved retirement and resort communities. New hotels, convention centers, and the development and expansion of seashore communities have contributed to the continual demand for Banquet Photographers.

Advancement Prospects

Freelance Banquet Photographers advance by adding more staff photographers to their studios, expanding into other areas of photography they may not already be servicing (i.e., sports, weddings, etc.), and opening more studios in new locations. Staff Banquet Photographers can advance to become senior photographers or owners of commercial studios.

Education and Training

A two- or four-year degree in photography, with training in digital photography and design software such as Adobe Photoshop and Illustrator, is usually a solid foundation for Banquet Photographers. Sales is an important part of the position, and Banquet Photographers will do well to take workshops in promotion, marketing, advertising, and small business ownership.

Experience, Skills, and Personality Traits

Most Banquet Photographers have at least several years of prior experience in commercial photography. A background in portrait and wedding photography is especially helpful to the position. Banquet Photographers are outgoing, confident, and adept at working with a wide variety of people, from clients of all ages to banquet and convention center employees. They are professional and firm, able to manage and instruct groups and individuals about when and where to pose to ensure the best images. They take photographs both indoors and outside and are skilled in lighting and composition. Banquet Photographers need to have strong communication and organization skills and be comfortable promoting their services and selling photographic packages. They must be energetic and have great stamina because they may work long days or nights and will have to travel to locations.

Unions and Associations

Associations such as Wedding and Portrait Photographers International and Professional Photographers of America provide Banquet Photographers with educational resources, employment listings, and networking opportunities.

Tips for Entry

1. Find Banquet Photographers in your area by doing an Internet search on Google or another search engine. Review their Web sites and online galleries. Read their biographies and familiarize yourself with their client lists. Contact those studios you are most interested in working for and ask about employment opportunities. If nothing else, see if you can set up informational meetings to learn more about the field and their work.

2. Contact hotels, catering halls, and convention centers to learn the names of photographers who cover ban-

quets and events. Contact these photographers to see if they need assistance with upcoming projects. If you can afford it, volunteer to help at a shoot. It will give you the chance to see if this type of work is for you and learn all the steps that are involved.

3. Visit the Web sites of corporations, associations, sports leagues, and others to see their event calendars for the coming months. Contact these groups to see if they have photography needs and schedule a meeting to discuss your services with them. Prepare for the meeting by tailoring your portfolio to include images that best represent the style and content the prospective client will prefer.

CRUISE PHOTOGRAPHER

CAREER PROFILE

Duties: Provides photography throughout a cruise, from the moment passengers board to the activities of the final night; handles sales and print orders during the voyage; keeps records of all photographs; may work with an assistant

Alternate Title(s): None

Salary Range: $1,000 to $2,000+ per voyage, plus bonus

Employment Prospects: Good

Advancement Prospects: Good

Best Geographical Location(s): Major cities with active ports

Prerequisites:

Education or Training—Two- or four-year degree in photography; training in digital cameras, design software (i.e., Adobe Photoshop, Illustrator), and photo processing

Experience—At least three years of experience as portrait studio photographer or wedding photographer

Special Skills and Personality Traits—Ability to interact well with people one-on-one and in large groups; good eye for details; sensitive to appropriate times to photograph; able to work long days and nights; high energy; productive; deadline- and detail-oriented; strong knowledge of photo development process

CAREER LADDER

```
┌─────────────────────────────┐
│  Senior Cruise Photographer  │
└─────────────────────────────┘

┌─────────────────────────────┐
│     Cruise Photographer      │
└─────────────────────────────┘

┌─────────────────────────────┐
│   Portrait Photographer /    │
│    Wedding Photographer      │
└─────────────────────────────┘
```

Position Description

Cruise Photographers are roving goodwill ambassadors who photograph passengers throughout the trip, at both the cruise lines' and the passengers' requests. Cruises may be long weekends, one- to two-week tours, or longer periods of time aboard luxury vessel lines such as Celebrity, Carnival, Royal Caribbean, Holland America, and many others departing from ports on the east and west coasts.

The Cruise Photographer is usually a member of a photography team covering indoor and outdoor youth activities, typically located outdoors at swimming pools or indoors for storytelling or game periods. The Cruise Photographer also covers adult, leisure-time events on decks and indoors, including group portraits at dining tables and at the captain's table, where special guests are invited.

Cruise ships offer photographers a finishing room and file headquarters, which feature provisions for tamper-free wall mountings of photo bulletin boards. Each day, Cruise Photographers post an array of photos taken either that day or the day before, for customers to review and select. When passengers order prints Cruise Photographers can deliver them long before the trip ends. Digital cameras speed the process and enable immediate printing and billing through electronic processing. Processing of digital printing is followed by a bill issued through the cruise operator.

The Cruise Photographer accepts special calls for group photos or for publicity photos and press coverage of special shipboard moments. Once on board the ship, the Cruise Photographer is on the job seven days a week, available and ready to photograph all activities day or night, as requested.

Typically, there is not much rest until the ship returns to its home port.

Salaries

The Cruise Photographer is often paid per voyage, and rates can range from $1,000 to $2,000 or more per month, depending on experience. The fee is negotiated in advance and usually includes a bonus or commissions for high-volume sales of the photographs. Cruise Photographers who work fast, are adept at capturing special moments, and who are friendly and have smart sales tactics will succeed in earning higher wages.

Employment Prospects

The growth of the cruise-line business and the addition of even longer voyages have changed normal shipboard employment conditions and, consequently, improved job prospects for Cruise Photographers. A new employer in the cruise field is Trans-Ocean Photos, which employs 200 photographers, many of whom are situated onboard the ships while others are located at theme parks such as Disneyland. Often husband-and-wife teams sign on for the voyage as photographer/pianist combinations. Sometimes both are photographers. Applications are best made when cruise ships are in port for crew changes, provisioning, and repairs, which is usually during weekends. More applications are now being accepted through the Internet than via mail. When ships are docked, prospective photographers should see the purser to find out about openings for later voyages.

Advancement Prospects

Staff sizes vary widely on cruise ships. The longer the cruise and the greater the number of passengers, the larger the staff needed to meet all of the needs. Cruise ships with larger staffs normally have larger photography departments and higher turnover, thus providing photographers with more opportunities to advance. Cruise Photographers with two or more years of solid, frequent cruise photography experience can advance to become senior cruise photographers or heads of the photography department. They can also write about their experiences and share tips in industry, as well as newsstand, publications.

Education and Training

A two-year degree from a technical school or a four-year degree with a specialization in photography is usually adequate for employment with most cruise lines as a Cruise Photographer. Of utmost importance is agility with digital cameras and design software, which can be learned either in the classroom or on the job as portrait or wedding photographers. Cruise Photographers must also be trained in photo-processing techniques.

Experience, Skills, and Personality Traits

Cruise Photographers are professionals who know how to retain a certain degree of decorum while they are at work. While others are vacationing aboard the ship, photographers are always mindful that they are employees, not guests, and have certain responsibilities to fulfill. They know how to be detached observers, always at the ready to photograph special, unique moments. To do this kind of work, they must enjoy working with all types of people and all age groups and have huge supplies of patience and flexibility. They need great technical and technological skills and must be adept with digital cameras, design software, and print processes. The finish room is a giant responsibility, requiring great attention to detail, organization, and deadlines. Cruise Photographers and the photography team may be processing prints and coordinating orders for anywhere from 800 to 1,500 customers, all of whom need to be served within seven to 10 days, depending on the length of the cruise. Because the job is often seven days a week, Cruise Photographers need stamina and high energy to meet all of the demands.

Unions and Associations

Cruise Photographers can join such associations as the Professional Photographers of America and Wedding and Portrait Photographers International for access to industry news, technology updates and technical advice, discounts on various services (including mailing lists for promotional purposes), educational workshops, conferences, and more. There may be other, cruise line–specific associations that might offer networking benefits to Cruise Photographers. Use Internet search engines such as Google to research these associations.

Tips for Entry

1. Read the Web sites of various cruise lines. Visit the employment sections and see if they have any job openings for Cruise Photographers.
2. To secure work in this field, be sure to create a portfolio that reflects your best portrait and event or wedding photography. Also make sure that your résumé or curriculum vitae is professional, presentable, and accurate.
3. Pursue all avenues when you are job hunting. Attend travel expos and trade shows. Bring business cards so you can take full advantage when you network.
4. Check listings in national and trade publications. You can also find jobs listed with such employment placement agencies as Cruise Job Line (http://www.cruisejobline.com) and Cruise Placement Hiring Agency (http://www.cruiseplacement.com).

RESORT PHOTOGRAPHER

CAREER PROFILE

Duties: Provides photographic services throughout the day and evening for prestigious hotels; creates portraits of guests and photographs conferences, special events, and interiors; provides photographic documentation of resort development

Alternate Title(s): Travel Photographer

Salary Range: $30,000 to $100,000

Employment Prospects: Good

Advancement Prospects: Poor

Best Geographical Location(s): Beach and mountain communities with established hotels featuring entertainment and sports facilities

Prerequisites:

Education or Training—Two- or four-year degree in photography

Experience—Two to three years of experience as a portrait or wedding photographer

Special Skills and Personality Traits—In-depth knowledge of photographic design software; skilled in color correction and enhancement; excellent people skills; energetic, flexible worker; able to work independently and on a team; familiarity with graphic design and videography; bilingual or multilingual skills beneficial

CAREER LADDER

```
┌─────────────────────────────┐
│     Resort Photographer     │
└─────────────────────────────┘

┌─────────────────────────────┐
│  Portrait Photographer /    │
│   Wedding Photographer      │
└─────────────────────────────┘

┌─────────────────────────────┐
│   Photographer's Assistant  │
└─────────────────────────────┘
```

Position Description

The Resort Photographer works with a creative team to provide daily photographic services at a single hotel. The team captures candid shots of daytime activities of guests at the beach or pool, at tennis, golf, and other sports offered at the resort, as well as at special evening events, such as dinners and theatrical performances. The coverage will include close-ups of activities, such as card playing, bingo, and other table games, as well as high angles of groups taking yoga and dance lessons or attending workshops or performances. The Resort Photographer will also cover the children's play areas and children's team sports and activities.

Resort Photographers take indoor and outdoor shots. They photograph gyms or exercise rooms, card and game rooms, billiards, hair salons, gift shops, bars, dance clubs, and the-aters. Some resorts may have restrictions about photography in bars, card rooms, or casinos. Dining areas are often only to be photographed if requested or suggested by guests at a single table. Resort Photographers may also photograph new developments and renovations at resorts. They take pictures of interior and exterior shots of buildings, sports facilities, pools, beaches, and so on for promotional purposes.

When a resort has a special dress-up evening or formal event, the Resort Photographer creates portraits of singles, children, couples, or groups by posing people in screened-off and pre-lit sections of lobbies before and after dining hours. They post signs in the immediate area informing people that photographs are subject to the guest's acceptance of the results, with print prices charged to the guest's room upon acceptance. Guests select and order prints at a cashier area and pick the prints up when checking out. Resort Photographers are often precluded from accepting payments or gratuities from guests.

Salaries

Resort Photographers work on a contract basis, typically from month to month or from season to season, and are rarely full-time employees of hotel corporations. Industry standard is to pay Resort Photographers by the month, and those wages can range anywhere from $2,500 to $5,000 or more per month. Rates will vary depending on the size and prestige of the resort and the Resort Photographer's expertise. Resort Photographers are frequently provided with commissions for their work, as well as room and board, saving them money on rent and food while they are on the job. They are often also given limited access to sports facilities and other resort amenities. Often Resort Photographers hire their own assistants and, in some cases, work alongside their family members.

Employment Prospects

According to the Department of Labor's *Occupational Outlook Handbook,* employment in hotels and other accommodations is expected to increase by 17 percent through 2012, compared with 16 percent growth projected for all industries combined. Resort Photographers have good chances of finding work throughout the year at resorts around the world. The largest, most prestigious resorts will, naturally, offer the most opportunities. Resort Photographers who have commercial photography experience, are able to adjust their schedules to travel, and can pick up and relocate within short notice will have the greatest advantage in securing contracts. Monthly and seasonal employment also assures a higher rate of staff turnover within resorts as compared to other industries so that there are often openings.

Advancement Prospects

Because Resort Photographers are contractual workers, opportunities for advancement within hotel corporations are poor. In some instances, resorts with large creative departments may have hierarchical structures, consisting of junior-, middle-, and senior-level photographers, where photographers can move up the ladder. Most Resort Photographers, however, advance by expanding their technical expertise; they can hone their videography, graphic design, or Photoshop skills. They can write books and articles about their work, both from the human-interest level as well as from the business and technical side. They can also teach workshops and speak at conferences hosted by trade associations.

Education and Training

Most resorts do not require photographers to have specific educational backgrounds. Well-rounded and successful

Resort Photographers, however, draw from the strong basis of a four-year degree in photography or art. Resort Photographers must have an excellent working knowledge of digital photography and be trained in photographic design software, such as Adobe Photoshop. Customer service or retail experience can be useful since Resort Photographers deal directly with the public on a daily basis.

Experience, Skills, and Personality Traits

The Resort Photographer is generally an experienced, prior owner of a small portrait or commercial studio. He or she is adept at working with digital equipment and at lighting, composition, and creating portraits of people. Resort Photographers need to not only be technically and technologically skilled but also have the ability to instantly create a rapport with people they have never before met. They must be accessible, approachable, and friendly. People are there to have fun; photographers must have the same attitude to capture that spirit. They must also be capable of working independently as well as with a team. Resorts offer services and events around the clock, and Resort Photographers are on call for everything on the calendar. Stamina, energy, organization, attention to detail and deadlines, reliability, and responsibility are key characteristics of successful Resort Photographers. Many resorts are located overseas in exotic locations. Resort Photographers who speak several languages, such as English, French, and Spanish, may have the extra advantage when seeking employment.

Unions and Associations

Professional Photographers of America and Advertising Photographers of America provide Resort Photographers with access to employment listings, educational resources, and networking opportunities.

Tips for Entry

1. If you are not yet working in a commercial studio, seek an assistant or apprentice position at a photography studio that covers events and activities. Make sure the work you'll be doing closely matches a portion, at least, of what Resort Photographers do, such as photographing conferences, weddings, and creating portraits of individuals and groups.

2. Create a list of the resorts for which you would like to work. Make sure that the activities the resorts offer are activities you are interested in photographing. In other words, if you love the water and swimming, pursue resorts that offer pool and beach activities. If you have no interest in skiing, delete ski resorts from your list. Use an Internet search engine, such as Google (http://www.google.com), to find the Web sites for these resorts and see the amenities they offer. Contact personnel departments or visit the resorts in

person to find out about employment opportunities and application requirements.

3. Immerse yourself in the resort and travel business. Read travel books and industry magazines and check the back pages for employment listings. You can also find job advertisements on the Internet, at such sites as Escape Artist (http://jobs.escapeartist.com) and Jobs Abroad (http://www.jobsabroad.com).

SAFARI PHOTOGRAPHER

CAREER PROFILE

Duties: Photographs animals in their natural habitats, landscapes, and local cultures in such places as Africa, India, and South America for magazines, newspapers, book publishers, and Web sites; may organize and manage tours to remote areas of the world where wildlife roams freely

Alternate Title(s): Travel Photographer, Wildlife Photographer

Salary Range: $25,000 to $75,000+

Employment Prospects: Fair

Advancement Prospects: Fair

Best Geographical Location(s): Major cities, to establish business and attract clients; Africa, Alaska, Botswana, Kenya, India, South America, and other locations, for actual photography work

Prerequisites:

Education or Training—Four-year degree in photography; degree or coursework in zoology and biology beneficial

Experience—Five or more years of commercial photography work; experience as daily newspaper, sports, or wedding photographer beneficial

Special Skills and Personality Traits—Strong interest in and knowledge of wildlife; adventurous spirit; excellent eye for detail; culturally aware; some multilingual abilities helpful; patient; flexible; adaptable to change; physically fit and healthy; friendly; organized; leadership abilities; strong communication and interpersonal skills

CAREER LADDER

```
┌─────────────────────────────────┐
│    Safari Tour Owner/Operator    │
└─────────────────────────────────┘

┌─────────────────────────────────┐
│       Safari Photographer        │
└─────────────────────────────────┘

┌─────────────────────────────────┐
│     Commercial Photographer      │
└─────────────────────────────────┘
```

Position Description

Safari Photographers photograph animals, people, and places in remote locations around the world. They work for magazine and book publishers, Web sites, safari and adventure tour companies, advertising agencies, public relations firms, and tourist boards. In addition to photography work, they may also lead tours, taking groups of amateur or professional photographers to picturesque sites that they discovered through their own experiences.

Safari Photographers study animals to understand their behaviors and patterns and also determine the best times to set out from camp to photograph them. Through their own observations, as well as discussions with national parks officials and locals, they learn about the animals that inhabit the region in which they operate. They find out the specific types of animals in the area, the number of animals in the herds or prides, and the exact locations of watering holes, hunting grounds, and shelters from the day's heat. They may photograph a variety of animals or focus specifically on one animal for the duration of their trip. Either way, they set out early each day with appropriate equipment and gear to take photos of the animals in their natural environments. They will photograph zebras grazing in the plains, hippopota-muses cooling themselves in lakes, lions chasing down gazelles, eagles feeding their young. They may photograph landscapes in the evenings for dramatic, moonlit images. They may spend a day scouting various locations, making detailed notes about the specific site, time of day, lighting, and composition pluses or minuses.

While Safari Photographers may focus primarily on wildlife, many also create dramatic and beautiful photo-graphic images of the people and culture of the regions to which they travel. They may photograph tribes people, mar-ketplaces, homes, rituals and celebrations, daily life activi-ties, and more. Their cultural studies may be exhibited in museums and galleries around the world.

Safari Photographers learn everything they can about where they travel. Whether they have been commissioned by a travel magazine or the trip is self-initiated, they make sure they understand all of the following, and more, before they book their flight:

• political climate of the region
• languages spoken and cultural mores
• climate
• common illnesses, health hazards, prevention and treat-ment
• food and water availability
• licenses and permits that may be required

They study maps, learn the basics of the local languages (at least enough to get by), and create lists of photographic equipment and supplies they will need to pack. They may hire assistants, interns, and others for their photography team, depending upon the scope and size of the project. They will oversee and manage their teams, making sure each person is prepared for the work ahead.

Salaries

Annual salaries for Safari Photographers can range from $25,000 to $75,000 or more. Earnings depend on their years in the field and the types of clients for which they work. Most Safari Photographers are freelancers, which means they have the burden of covering many of their expenses, especially if they are just starting out. They will need to allot money from their earnings for the purchase and main-tenance of photographic equipment, film and development, and travel gear. Clients usually reimburse photographers for travel, food, and related expenses. Safari Photographers can supplement their incomes by teaching safari and travel pho-tography, writing articles, and selling and licensing their work to stock agencies.

Employment Prospects

The safari photography field is extremely competitive. Only a select few have established themselves as the top Safari

Photographers, and they normally only reach this level after having committed years to the industry. And while the select few rise, advances in technology have made it easier than ever for people from all walks of life to take photographs, retouch their own images, and flood the field. This is not to say that experienced, technically skilled photographers are not still needed, but it does mean that the market is that much more overloaded with applicants, many of whom are willing to lower their standards to secure work. Another benefit and detriment to the field is stock photography. Clients can now easily find and purchase exotic images from online stock photography agencies.

Safari Photographers who can secure work with maga-zine publishers and tourist boards and prove they are reli-able, deadline-driven professionals have the best chances of receiving referrals to other clients and projects. Many Safari Photographers must work in other areas of photography to supplement their incomes. Some may maintain commercial photography studios in major cities. Still others may teach in universities and technical or vocational schools.

Advancement Prospects

There is no standard career ladder for Safari Photographers. The good news is that they have options from which to choose, and advancement will depend on their strengths and interests. After years of hard work, freelance Safari Photogra-phers who have entrepreneurial spirits and excellent connec-tions can open their own safari and adventure-tour operations. They may lecture at conferences hosted by professional asso-ciations and teach at universities. They may write books and magazine articles about their adventures. Safari Photogra-phers may also exhibit their photographs at galleries and museums and license their work to stock agencies.

Education and Training

A four-year degree is recommended for Safari Photographer work. Degrees can be in zoology or biology, with course-work in photography, or vice versa. On-the-job training as a Safari Photographer's assistant is highly recommended. Safari Photographers must also be trained in digital photog-raphy and photographic design software programs, such as Adobe Photoshop and Illustrator.

Experience, Skills, and Personality Traits

Safari Photographers usually have backgrounds in commer-cial photography. The skills needed to photograph live news or sports events for newspapers or magazines, or weddings for portrait studios, are very similar to those used in safari photography. A Safari Photographer must have an excellent eye for detail, be tuned into his or her environment at all times, and know the perfect moment to take a picture. The job requires the ability to study animals and understand their behaviors. This knowledge is especially helpful in determining when it is safe to be near animals to take photos and when to keep at a distance. Safari Photographers must be curious about the world and have adventurous spirits. The work requires extensive travel and often uncomfortable and dangerous environments, so it is not a field for the faint of heart. Physical fitness, sound health, stamina, and energy are crucial in the position. Safari Photographers must also be technologically proficient. They must be adept at digital photography and fluent in photographic design software programs.

These skills are especially crucial when photographers are on location in remote areas. For instance, if a photographer is on a three-week tour in the Kalahari Desert and under deadline to get work to his editor in New York City, he or she can upload the images from the digital camera directly to a computer, correct light, color, or size using Adobe Photoshop, then transmit via e-mail or Wi-Fi for near-immediate receipt. Knowing how to do all of this is the key to building a professional reputation in the safari photography business.

Unions and Associations

There are no known associations dedicated solely to Safari Photographers. They may belong to such associations as the American Society of Media Photographers and Professional Photographers of America for educational workshops, industry news, contests, networking opportunities, and employment referrals. Safari Photographers can also find useful information and resources through the Travel Photographers Network (http://www.travelphotographers.net).

Tips for Entry

1. Immerse yourself in travel photography. Read travel magazines such as *Outdoor Life, National Geo-* *graphic, Condé Nast Traveler, Global Traveler, Travel & Leisure, Travel Africa Magazine,* and many others. See what other Safari Photographers are doing by visiting their Web sites. You can find many by using a search engine, such as Google (http://www.google.com), and plugging in the key words: *Safari Photographer.* Safari Bill (http://www.safaribill.com) is an excellent Web site with useful information. Another Web site with great resources is Wild Safari (http://www.wildlifesafari.info).

2. Take a summer job with a safari tour operation group. Secure work as a photographer's assistant, if possible. If there are no photography positions open, work as a camp assistant or in any other capacity so you can see firsthand how tours run and the tasks and skills involved in being a Safari Photographer.

3. Secure an internship or entry-level job in the creative or editorial department of a travel magazine. Having your foot in the door of a travel publication can be an excellent way to learn how editors, creative directors, and publishers think and what it is they look for in article and photography submissions.

4. If you can afford to, take a self-funded trip to test the waters. Go on safari and treat the trip as you would a professional job. Research the location, get the right gear, and create a packing list. When you get back, pitch your pictures to magazine publishers and others and see what happens. In the end, you will know if this is the kind of work you want to pursue. And if nothing else, you will most likely have some good stories to share!

TRAVEL PHOTOGRAPHER

CAREER PROFILE

Duties: Travels around the world photographing people, places, and events for advertising, marketing, and editorial clients; works closely with creative directors, models, stylists, assistants, and other creative staff; negotiates contracts; creates estimates, production schedules, and invoices; scouts locations; handles accounts receivable and payable; handles self-promotion and marketing

Alternate Title(s): Photojournalist

Salary Range: $40,000 to $100,000

Employment Prospects: Good

Advancement Prospects: Limited

Best Geographical Location(s): Boston, Fort Lauderdale, Houston, Miami, New York, and Seattle

Prerequisites:

Education or Training—Bachelor's degree in photography

Experience—Three or more years of experience as a commercial photographer; several years of experience as a photographer's assistant or studio assistant for studios with travel-related clients

Special Skills and Personality Traits—Digital photography and design software expertise; adept at independent work and teamwork; flexible attitude; able to travel on short notice; diplomatic; sensitive to and respectful of diverse cultures and communities; curious about other cultures and places; excellent research and organizational skills

CAREER LADDER

```
┌─────────────────────────────────┐
│       Travel Photographer       │
└─────────────────────────────────┘

┌─────────────────────────────────┐
│     Commercial Photographer     │
└─────────────────────────────────┘

┌─────────────────────────────────┐
│        Studio Assistant /       │
│     Photographer's Assistant    │
└─────────────────────────────────┘
```

Position Description

Travel Photographers work on assignment for magazine editors or pitch ideas to editors either before or following their trips. They travel to cities, rural areas, and remote locations near or far and photograph landscapes, architecture, people, animals, foliage, as well as events. Their work is published in magazines, books, travel brochures and posters, and on Web sites. If photographing for advertising clients, they work closely with models, wardrobe stylists, makeup artists, creative directors, assistants, and others. They may be responsible for hiring and overseeing creative staff, depending upon the client and the project.

Travel Photographers prepare extensively for their trips. They read as much as they can about the countries they plan to visit. They learn about the people, the customs, and the basic language they will need to get through the day. They scout locations through literature and online research or firsthand before the first day of the shoot. If working with a crew, they create a shoot schedule. They identify the objects they plan to photograph and then they determine the angles that will work best and where specifically to capture those angles. It may mean standing at a street corner near a café 10 blocks away or setting up on a building rooftop just down the street. They need to know these locations in advance so they can strategize when and how to get there and so that they can secure any required permissions from the city's officials. Travel Photographers review current maps to orient themselves to the terrain. They also familiarize themselves in advance with the modes of transportation available and nearby conveniences (i.e., public facilities, restaurants, film supply stores). Also of great importance is knowing whom to contact for specific things, as well as when and how to get licenses and permits to photograph at certain locations.

Travel Photographers create thorough and accurate lists of photography equipment needed on location and make sure each and every item is packed. If they hire assistants to handle these tasks, they are still responsible for overseeing that everything is accurate and complete. They keep careful track of all of their expenses and save all of their receipts. When they return from their trips, they create expense reports, which they submit to clients along with copies of all receipts for reimbursement. Typically, they secure approval for expenses in meeting with clients prior to travel.

Salaries

Travel Photographers can earn salaries ranging from $40,000 to $100,000 or more, depending on clientele and types of projects. Travel Photographers usually charge a per-diem rate ranging from $500 to $1,000 or more, plus all travel expenses. Contract terms usually list one-time use only. Travel Photographers, like all photographers, charge more when the agreement requires that the images be used more frequently and in other media. They enhance their salaries by also selling images to stock photography houses and licensing agencies. Freelance Travel Photographers may travel first and pitch their images afterward to publication editors. To take this approach, they must be able to front the costs for their trips and cover all related expenses.

Employment Prospects

Travel Photographers face fierce competition because many consider the field to be glamorous and ideal. Consequently, there are far more prospective Travel Photographers than there are jobs to fill. Travel Photographers secure work by keeping up with what is going on in the world. They follow the news closely by reading newspapers and magazines, watching the news and documentaries on television, listening to the radio, and networking through memberships to professional associations. Smart photographers know to pitch magazine and book publishers well in advance about events, festivals, or special celebrations that will be happening in particular countries and cities next year or even the following year.

Advancement Prospects

Most photographers aim to make travel photography the pinnacle of their careers. For many, this is the ultimate way

to combine adventure with work, having already committed years to honing their skills in commercial photography. If they do not already own their own studios, they can always advance to become studio owners. Many Travel Photographers branch out by doing things to enhance their careers that require skills other than photography, such as writing articles and books about their travels, to accompany their photographs. They also teach and participate in speaking engagements and panel discussions.

Education and Training

A four-year degree in photography, with coursework in photographic design software, is a beneficial background for Travel Photographers. Depending on where they travel, a working knowledge of the local language can also come in extremely handy. Classes in history can be helpful in choosing and understanding shoot locations.

Experience, Skills, and Personality Traits

Travel Photographers need to have their photographic skills down solid to succeed in this field. They are often in unfamiliar turf, where everyday conveniences may not exist. It stands to reason that organization, follow-through, attention to details and deadlines, and self-initiative are absolutely critical. Travel Photographers must be excellent researchers and diligent and self-driven enough to do their homework before arriving at locations. They must understand local cultures and etiquette and have some familiarity with other languages, at least enough to communicate the essentials. They must know whom to contact and how best to contact them to arrange for the things they will need throughout the shoot, such as water and food, any last-minute photographic items, or even modes of transportation to remote spots. Above all, Travel Photographers must be deeply curious about other places and people and know how to convey what they learn in their images in ways that inform and rivet viewers as never before.

Unions and Associations

To date, there are no known associations dedicated specifically to Travel Photographers. Many photographers participate in online forums and access valuable information and resources through Travel Photographers Network (http://www.travelphotographers.net). Depending upon their specialties and clientele, they also join Advertising Photographers of America and Professional Photographers of America for educational conferences, employment listings, and discounts on various professional services.

Tips for Entry

1. Visit a local travel office and collect a handful of brochures on Egypt, India, Greece, Spain, Morocco,

and other places that interest you. As you look through the brochures, study the types of photos that have been chosen to promote various places and entice people to book their trips.

2. View your city as if you were a Travel Photographer. Map out what you plan to shoot, the angles and where you will need to be located to capture those angles, times of day to shoot, and then head out "on location." Or plan an actual trip. Put together a portfolio of your best images from the trip and target your pitch to magazines that you think will be interested in the location.

3. Check the newsstand or your local public library for consumer travel magazines. Study the photographs, the locations chosen, the lighting, and the angles. Learn as much as you can about the images and the styles each magazine has chosen to print.

WEDDING PHOTOGRAPHER

CAREER PROFILE

Duties: Photographs all aspects of weddings, everything from pre- to post-ceremonies, at homes, in churches and at receptions, and outside in various settings; creates portraits of couples and their families; may create videotapes of weddings; usually works with assistants; meets with couples to discuss photography services and negotiate terms of agreement

Alternate Title(s): Bridal Photographer

Salary: $25,000 to $100,000

Employment Prospects: Good

Advancement Prospects: Fair

Best Geographical Location(s): Major cities and suburbs

Prerequisites:

Education or Training—Four-year degree in photography; training in digital photography and photographic design software

Experience—Several years of experience as an assistant photographer; one to two years of experience as a lighting assistant, portrait studio intern, or apprentice

Special Skills and Personality Traits—Excellent at lighting and composition; able to recognize and capture special moments; reliable and deadline-oriented; organized; flexible and patient; exceptional people skills; able to work with individuals and groups of all backgrounds and ages

CAREER LADDER

```
┌─────────────────────────────────┐
│   Wedding/Portrait Studio Owner  │
└─────────────────────────────────┘

┌─────────────────────────────────┐
│      Wedding Photographer        │
└─────────────────────────────────┘

┌─────────────────────────────────┐
│       Portrait or Wedding        │
│     Photographer Assistant       │
└─────────────────────────────────┘
```

Position Description

Wedding Photographers work closely with assistants and in coordination with wedding service providers to create still photographs or videotapes of these special occasions. They and their team are responsible for lighting, sound, and still photography. Before the day of the wedding, they hold planning meetings with the future bride and groom and their families to discuss all aspects of the wedding and what is expected photographically. In this meeting, they discuss the bride's dress, the number of people in the wedding party, where the wedding will take place, who the important people among family and friends are to photograph, and more. They secure the address where the bride and her family will

be preparing for the wedding, locations of churches, synagogues, or other venues, and the address of the catering hall or wherever the reception is taking place. They discuss the specifics regarding the vehicles in which the bridal party will travel, as well as vehicles for the trip to the portrait studio after the ceremony and before the reception.

Wedding Photographers also discuss with the religious leaders the rules regarding photography. In many religious houses, flash photography is either prohibited or limited during ceremonies. Wedding Photographers arrive early to learn the specifics and discuss possible alternatives (i.e., restaging of the ring exchange after the ceremony has ended). They discuss the shots they would like to take and secure permission to take those shots from various locations within the religious establishment.

Wedding photography studios often have mandatory shot lists, meaning shots that Wedding Photographers must get and shots that must be within that studio's style. Wedding Photographers create and follow schedules for the pre-wedding photographs. They may start at the bride's home, photographing the bride preparing at a dressing table or her mother adjusting her veil. They may pose wedding parties in private or public gardens, in backyards or at nearby parks. Many create a story line of the day for the photo album, starting with a photograph of the flowers and wedding invitation, ending with the rice throwing and then the bride and groom waving goodbye from their departing limousine, and everything in between.

Salaries

Annual salaries for Wedding Photographers can range from $25,000 to $100,000 or more. Spring and summer are peak times for weddings, and Wedding Photographers will typically see a rise in business during these seasons. Studios usually pay Wedding Photographers per job and by the day, with more experienced photographers earning higher wages. They may hire photographers for weekend-only positions or on a seasonal basis. *The Professional Photographer* magazine publishes, in most issues, advertisements for Wedding Photographers for weekend work as backup photographers in New Jersey, Pennsylvania, Delaware, Missouri, and the West Coast. These jobs usually pay $1,000 for the weekend.

Because these are considered once-in-a-lifetime celebrations, families are often willing to spend small fortunes to ensure that all of their needs are met. Wedding photography is one area in which they have no qualms about splurging, making this a timelessly profitable industry. Families usually purchase photography packages from wedding photography studios. Couples receive the proofs, which they review and from which they choose pictures. Packages usually include the wedding album, an 11″ × 14″ portrait of the couple, and several 8″ × 10″ framed pictures. Studios enhance their income by offering extras outside of the package deals, such as extra photo albums and prints for parents and other family members and friends. They will also charge premium rates if people choose to commission specific photographers to cover the weddings.

Employment Prospects

The affluence of middle-class couples, the increasingly familiar second marriages of more mature couples, and the opportunity for a special party for couples already established in their communities has measurably widened the opportunities for wedding photography. Further, the first-time married couples have increasingly invested in full-color and sound videotapes, all supplementing the traditional framed bridal portraits. The traditional wedding has become more a Hollywood setting and less a small group at the altar. People are waiting a little longer to get married these days and saving their money for extravagant gala ceremonies. Those wanting a traditional wedding now have a budget that never would have been possible for their parents. Wedding Photography studios and teams are now larger and more involved in weddings than ever before. Jobs in the wedding industry are therefore growing to keep up with this demand.

Advancement Prospects

If working in studios with large staff structures, Wedding Photographers can move up to become the heads of photography and video units, as their employers grow. As studio owners retire, Wedding Photographers can also move up to become the new owners. If they already own their own studios, they can advance by expanding their staff, adding backup teams, and opening more studios in other locations.

Education and Training

A four-year degree in photography, with training in lighting, composition, and digital photography, is a sufficient educational background for Wedding Photographers. Ongoing training to keep up with current technological advances is critical in this industry. Wedding Photographers maintain their skills by joining professional associations and attending trade conferences and educational workshops.

Experience, Skills, and Personality Traits

Wedding Photographers usually have three or more years of prior experience in commercial or portrait photography studios, working first as studio assistants or interns, moving up to handling lights, then to photographer's assistant. Wedding Photographers are particularly adept at creating flattering images and capturing special moments in hectic and often unconventional environments. They are poised professionals who know how to remain calm and instill calm when everything around them is otherwise.

They know how to arrange outstanding photographs by managing crowds, directing family members and brides and groups, large groups and individuals, all while being unobtrusive, especially during solemn moments. Wedding Photographers must have poise, confidence, and self-control to be the silent but important witnesses at these staged events. They are respectful of religious halls and in polite but firm command when pushing crowds must be separated and intruding floral arrangements must be moved.

Unions and Associations

Wedding Photographers join such associations as Wedding and Portrait Photographers International and Professional Photographers of America for employment referrals, photography competitions, news about the industry, annual conventions and trade shows, and educational publications.

Tips for Entry

1. Search online directories, the Yellow Pages, and newspaper and magazine advertisements for wedding and bridal portrait studios. See if they have any assistant opportunities or offer to drive or provide porter services, so you will have the chance to see firsthand a wedding photography team at work.

2. Check with photo department chiefs at local newspapers for introduction to staff members who are weekend wedding photographers.

3. Check bulletin boards at local supermarkets and beauty parlors for ads by independent Wedding Photographers. Offer to assist at one or more weddings.

FINE ARTS AND EDUCATION

DIGITAL PHOTOGRAPHY CONSULTANT

CAREER PROFILE

Duties: Trains and advises camera store personnel, photography teachers, professional photographers, and the general public; teaches courses in classrooms and at trade shows; may field questions through Web sites and the Internet; helps photographers set up digital photography equipment; consults with technology developers on new products

Alternate Title(s): Digital Photography Trainer

Salary Range: $15,000 to $40,000+

Employment Prospects: Good

Advancement Prospects: Good

Best Geographic Location(s): New York, Boston, Philadelphia, Washington, D.C., Atlanta, Chicago, St. Louis, Dallas, Denver, San Francisco, and Seattle

Prerequisites:

Education or Training—Two- or four-year degree in photography; thorough training in digital cameras and design software, such as Adobe Photoshop and Illustrator

Experience—Several years of experience as a professional photographer, using digital cameras, recommended; camera store and customer service background helpful; one to two years of teaching or consulting experience beneficial

Special Skills and Personality Traits—Well versed in digital photography; knowledgeable about camera brands, technology, and computer software and hardware; organized; personable; excellent communication, public speaking, and presentation skills; patient; good listener; flexible; able to work with wide variety of people; deadline-oriented

CAREER LADDER

```
┌─────────────────────────────────────┐
│  Digital Photography Consultant      │
└─────────────────────────────────────┘

┌─────────────────────────────────────┐
│  Photographer                        │
└─────────────────────────────────────┘

┌─────────────────────────────────────┐
│  Assistant Photographer              │
└─────────────────────────────────────┘
```

Position Description

First-time purchasers of digital cameras often experience confusion about the cameras' performance and capabilities. Digital Photography Consultants have thorough knowledge about camera brands and models and a solid grasp of each camera's benefits and drawbacks. They share this knowledge by advising camera store employees and customers; teaching classes at photography stores, computer stores, and digital photography conferences and trade shows; as well as writing articles for trade publications. They may also be hired by professional studios to troubleshoot digital camera issues. While most Digital Photography Consultants are also professional photographers, many are active photography and computer hobbyists who have a wealth of knowledge and passion about the field. Digital Photography Consultants also advise businesses about the cameras, computer equipment, and hardware and software they will need to achieve their goals.

Digital Photography Consultants prepare for their classes and presentations in advance. If they are working for specific stores with specific products, they discuss the products and features the employer wants emphasized. They may prepare their presentations with PowerPoint or with other design software, such as Adobe Photoshop and Illustrator, and field questions during the session. They may also answer questions through the help sections of digital camera–brand Web sites. Photographers often hire Digital Photography Consultants to help them set up, maintain, and troubleshoot their digital photography equipment. Technology developers also call upon consultants to serve as *testers* of new products and software, helping them work through the kinks and enhancing the features before releasing for mass distribution.

Salaries

Salaries for Digital Photography Consultants can range anywhere from $15,000 to $40,000 per year, depending on their level of experience, client base, and geographical location. Consultants who have at least five or more years of professional photography experience and are based in major urban areas can secure higher wages. Those who work for major digital camera stores or professional associations will also earn higher incomes. Many Digital Photography Consultants are freelancers who work in other capacities as well. They may also be professional photographers, computer consultants, Web designers and Web consultants, or camera store owners. Some stores may offer consultants base salaries and commissions or bonuses for camera sales. If teaching or lecturing, Digital Photography Consultants might earn between $100 to $300 or more per class, depending on the store, product, conference, or trade show.

Employment Prospects

According to Lyra Research, Inc. (as published in InfoTrends Library, http://www.itlibrary.com), digital still-camera shipments exceeded 63 million units worldwide in 2004, a 35 percent increase over 2003, and shipments are expected to surpass 100 million units in 2008. As first-time digital camera buyers continue to flood the marketplace, Digital Photography Consultants will continue to be needed. Consultants can find work as teachers at camera stores, in art and technical schools, in continuing education programs offered by colleges and universities, and through professional associations, annual photography trade shows, and conferences.

Advancement Prospects

There is no clear, specific career ladder for Digital Photography Consultants. Many who enter the digital photography field have diverse backgrounds and can therefore advance in equally diverse ways. If they work in structured environments, Digital Photography Consultants may advance to senior or management levels, where they oversee staff, han-

dle budgets, develop other educational programs, and take on increasingly higher-level responsibilities. Others may expand their scope by becoming columnists in trade and newsstand publications, writing articles and books, and lecturing and teaching at various venues.

Education and Training

A bachelor's degree in photography is recommended. Either structured training or self-taught knowledge of digital cameras, design software, and computer software and hardware is essential. Digital Photography Consultants who have on-the-job training as photographers may have a better appreciation of photographers' concerns and issues with equipment and product specifications.

Experience, Skills, and Personality Traits

Digital Photography Consultants can have a wide range of prior professional experience. Some have worked at least for several years or more as commercial photographers. Others have an avid interest in photography but may have gained their digital photography knowledge by immersing themselves in the technology, taking classes, and reading books and magazines. Some may even have a background in computers and be technologically agile. Whether speaking one-on-one to customers or teaching large groups at conferences, schools, or trade shows, Digital Photography Consultants must have excellent communication skills and be strong public speakers. In addition to being organized in their presentations, they must also be able to translate technical jargon into language that customers and students will grasp. Individuals who do well in this field are flexible and entrepreneurial. They enjoy working offbeat hours when needed. They realize the importance of keeping up with technology and stay abreast by regularly reading trade publications and books, taking classes, and networking at professional events. Digital Photography Consultants who are in high demand are extremely knowledgeable without being arrogant. They are professionals who enjoy educating people, troubleshooting problems, and helping people choose digital photography equipment that is appropriate to their needs and goals.

Unions and Associations

There are no unions or associations devoted solely to Digital Photography Consultants. Consultants can explore full or associate membership in such organizations as Photo Marketing Association International, Professional Photographers of America, and Advertising Photographers of America for networking opportunities, educational resources, and other benefits.

Tips for Entry

1. Professional photographers and avid, fully knowledgeable and qualified hobbyists are often hired by

photography shops to teach evening and weekend classes. Check with stores in your area to find out about employment opportunities.

2. Computer maintenance centers also seek Digital Photography Consultants to help people troubleshoot digital camera issues when synched to the computer. Check job listings by visiting maintenance center Web sites directly and searching employment sites such as Yahoo! HotJobs (http://hotjobs.yahoo.com) and Monster (http://www.monster.com), as well as the employment section of the New York Times on the Web (http://www.nytimes.com). You may also find jobs listed in the back sections of trade publications.

3. Regional offices of major electronic product companies also hire Digital Photography Consultants to train their own salespeople or to advise and teach at trade shows. Find these companies by doing an Internet search. Contact the human resources departments to inquire about employment opportunities.

FINE ARTS PHOTOGRAPHER

CAREER PROFILE

Duties: Creates photographic images for exhibition in museums and galleries; creates images for home and office interiors commissioned by individuals and corporations; mounts or frames images for display; works closely with gallery owners and managers on shows; may work with models, celebrities, and average citizens; may photograph products, objects, buildings and homes, street settings, and landscapes; secures licenses, permissions, and releases when appropriate

Alternate Title(s): Environment Photographer, Landscape Photographer, Photojournalist, Portrait Photographer

Salary Range: $10,000 to $250,000

Employment Prospects: Good

Advancement Prospects: Good

Best Geographic Location(s): Boston, Chicago, Dallas, Los Angeles, New York, San Francisco, Santa Fe, and Seattle

Prerequisites:

Education or Training—Four-year degree in art and photography; coursework in photographic design software and printing processes and techniques; courses in painting, sculpture, and art history helpful

Experience—Several years of experience as a photographer's assistant or studio assistant; apprenticeship in gallery beneficial

Special Skills and Personality Traits—Passionate about experimenting with photography and printing processes; extremely creative and innovative; excellent visual eye; strong knowledge of color and lighting; individualistic; self-motivated; familiar with art history and photography history, including cameras, accessories, photographic techniques, film-development processes

CAREER LADDER

```
┌─────────────────────────────────┐
│     Fine Arts Gallery Owner      │
└─────────────────────────────────┘

┌─────────────────────────────────┐
│      Fine Arts Photographer      │
└─────────────────────────────────┘

┌─────────────────────────────────┐
│   Photographer's Assistant /     │
│        Studio Assistant          │
└─────────────────────────────────┘
```

Position Description

Fine Arts Photographers create photographic images, based on their own individual visions, for display and sale in galleries, auction houses, and museums. They may also be commissioned by wealthy individuals and corporations to create works for interior decor in homes, offices, prestigious resorts, and other facilities. They experiment with a wide variety of photographic processes in their work, such as photo gravure (images produced from an engraving plate), daguerreotype (the first successful photo process, based on using copper plates instead of film), calotype (the first photo process to use paper negatives), ambrotype (a process using glass negatives), ferrotype (a process using iron-plate negatives), cyanotype (blueprint making), and hybrids of their own invention. Their mission is to highlight the ordinary or extraordinary or transform one to the other. Pioneers of fine arts photography include Edward Weston, Ansel Adams, and Man Ray. In the 1930s, Weston transformed beach sand, tree limbs, and gleaming vegetables into classic studies. Ansel Adams used his technical skills and exceptional timing to capture beautiful landscapes and skyscapes. In 1981, his extremely popular photograph *Moonrise, Hernandez* sold at an auction for $71,500. Emmanuel Radnitsky, aka Man Ray, was heralded for photographing Dada and surrealist images, part of a school of art that featured deliberately irrational and often dreamlike subjects. One of his small photos recently auctioned for $250,000. Californian Mark Klett only two decades ago aimed his view camera at the still-visible trails of the Lewis and Clark expedition. O. Winston Link captured the dwindling moments of America's great railroad engines puffing into stations at night in countless villages and towns.

Fine Arts Photographers not only create interesting, lovely, or bizarre images but also comment on what is going on in the world and enlighten society by photographing subjects that disturb, provoke thought, and incite debate and controversy. One example is the work of Robert Mapplethorpe, who initially created art with photographic images before moving fully into photography. He photographed pornographic stars, friends, and lovers, shedding light on sexuality and the beauty, strength, and fragility of the body at a time when AIDS and HIV were part of a new lexicon. He also created floral studies using old cameras and photographic techniques.

Salaries

The Fine Arts Photographer is self-employed, with an earnings capacity beyond that of most studio photographers. Earnings can range from as low as $10,000 to more than $250,000, depending upon the number of pieces commissioned and sold during the year. Many Fine Arts Photographers hire representatives to secure gallery and museum showings and negotiate contracts and fees. Photographers find commission-paid agents by asking for recommendations from photography gallery and museum curators and by speaking with other photographers and perusing such trade books as *American Showcase* and *Workbook*. Fine Arts Photographers also publish their work in books, magazines, posters, postcards, advertisements, calendars, greeting cards, and other formats. They can augment their salaries through advantageous licensing agreements.

Employment Prospects

Fine Arts Photographers often edge their way into the field while working simultaneously as photojournalists, museum, travel or studio photographers, or in any other number of photographic disciplines. Because Fine Arts Photographers are freelancers and self-directed, they can enter this discipline in any number of ways and secure sales and commissions if their styles and themes engage an audience. Employment prospects are good but are completely dependent upon the photographer's creativity, technical skills, and initiative.

Advancement Prospects

Fine Arts Photographers can advance to become fine arts gallery owners, if this part of the business interests them. They can write books to accompany their artwork. They can also become speakers as part of lecture series offered by schools, museums, and arts associations, or they can teach.

Education and Training

Fine Arts Photographers should have at least a four-year degree in art or photography for a well-rounded educational background. The field requires in-depth knowledge of contemporary art and a strong appreciation of the fine arts photography stories of the past 50 years. Coursework should include art history, either as taught in colleges and art schools, or in local museums. Training in and appreciation for various photography equipment and processes, both old and new, enable Fine Arts Photographers to more fully experiment and explore when creating their imagery. Training in Adobe Photoshop and Illustrator is also recommended.

Experience, Skills, and Personality Traits

Fine Arts Photographers usually bring several years of experience in a photographic or arts discipline to their work. They are immersed in and passionate about photography history and are well aware of the works and techniques of the fine arts photography masters who preceded them. They study these masters and can become influenced by them, but successful photographers are still able to retain and express their individuality in their imagery. Fine Arts Photographers work independently and must be self-motivated. They must be curious and adventurous in their work, always tuned into past and current economic, social, political, and religious issues. They must be able to translate their passions and interests into styles and themes that spark interest. The fine arts photography field is extraordinarily competitive and only the wise and the innovative survive and thrive.

Unions and Associations

There are no known associations or unions dedicated solely to Fine Arts Photographers. To learn more about business standards and practices in exhibiting fine arts photography, photographers subscribe to literature and visit the Web site of the Association of International Photography Art Dealers. Fine Arts Photographers can also join such trade associations as Professional Photographers of America for contract assistance, lobbying efforts to protect copyrights, credential programs, educational workshops and literature, and access to discounted insurance for equipment, liability, and health.

Tips for Entry

1. Create a list of the photographers, past and present, whose work interests and inspires you. Learn as much as you can about their work by reading books, perusing Web sites, and visiting galleries and museums. Read their biographies to learn their backgrounds, influences, and creative processes.

2. If you are ready to pursue this field, secure a photography representative. Before you set up meetings to see if you have a fit, make sure your portfolio represents your best work and reflects styles and themes that have current market potential.

3. Network as much as possible. Attend gallery showings and talks where curators, museum and gallery directors, and representatives will be in attendance. Always have postcards with you that feature a sample of your work that reproduces well and include all of your pertinent contact information.

4. Another great way to gain exposure in the fine arts photography field is through photography competitions. There are millions of them, though, and navigating through the rules and regulations can be a slippery slope. If you choose this avenue, approach with extreme caution. Make sure you understand the fine print first before registering and sending in your work. You can learn more about ethical and unethical contest rules and regulations by reading the art contests guidelines in the Graphic Artists Guild's *Handbook of Pricing & Ethical Guidelines* (11th edition). You can also seek advice from the American Society of Media Photographers.

MUSEUM PHOTOGRAPHER

CAREER PROFILE

Duties: Photographs full exhibitions, individual displays, holdings in storage, and special events for museum publicity and archives; prints negatives; may mount and frame photographs for displays

Alternate Title(s): Commercial Photographer

Salary Range: $35,000 to $60,000

Employment Prospects: Good

Advancement Prospects: Fair

Best Geographical Location(s): Boston, New York, Philadelphia, Washington, D.C., San Francisco, and Los Angeles

Prerequisites:

Education or Training—Four-year degree in photography, art, or art history; advanced degree may be required by some museums

Experience—Three years or more as a photographer at a known and respected commercial studio; experience photographing products for catalogs; some experience in a museum environment beneficial

Special Skills and Personality Traits—Computer savvy; adept at photographic technical processes; strong interest in history; detail-oriented; able to work independently and on a team; patient; respectful of and careful with artwork

CAREER LADDER

```
┌─────────────────────────────────────────┐
│   Director of Photography Department      │
└─────────────────────────────────────────┘

┌─────────────────────────────────────────┐
│         Museum Photographer               │
└─────────────────────────────────────────┘

┌─────────────────────────────────────────┐
│        Commercial Photographer            │
└─────────────────────────────────────────┘
```

Position Description

Museums throughout the world feature paintings, photographs, sculptures, crafts, and ethnic artifacts mounted on walls or displayed in glass cases. When museums acquire new pieces for display and exhibition, they need Museum Photographers to photograph the collections. These photographs accompany press releases and appear in newspaper articles, museum brochures and Web sites, auction catalogs, and art books and postcards typically sold in museum stores. The photographs may also be used for wall-size displays and prominent posters throughout the museum, as well as throughout other venues around the country. They serve as visual records for museum archives, as well as for conservation and insurance purposes, particularly if pieces are being shipped. Museums can e-mail the images to art experts for review and verification. Museum Photographers also photograph interior spaces when museums are setting up galleries. Historical societies hire Museum Photographers to photograph artwork for their publications and Web sites.

Photographs may also be used for authentication and to detect forgeries. For example, Museum Photographers photograph paintings outside of their frames, which hide a small portion of the image around the edges, for museum records. These frame-less images are seen only by an exclusive few, thereby diminishing the chances of a forger recreating the artwork in its true, complete state.

Museum Photographers work closely with museum curators, exhibition designers, public relation directors, and education directors in creating the images that best meet the museum's needs. They discuss which objects to focus on and which aspects of the objects to highlight. For some paintings and artwork, they may use ultraviolet or infrared photography. When paintings are restored, the original (and old) paint will photograph differently under different kinds of lights. There are scientific aspects to this work, and Museum Photographers understand art materials and the chemical makeup of the pieces with which they work. This knowledge helps them determine the proper photographic equipment and techniques to use.

Salaries

Museum Photographers can earn salaries ranging from $35,000 to $60,000, depending upon the museum's budget and the photographer's years of experience. Staff Museum Photographers may not earn higher salaries than freelancers, but they will enjoy benefits that freelancers must allocate funds for, such as paid vacations, bonuses, group health insurance, and immediate and often free access to museum events and offerings.

Employment Prospects

The American Association of Museums reports that there are approximately 15,500 to 16,000 museums in the United States, a number based on separate surveys by the National Conference of State Museum Associations and the Institute of Museum and Library Science. Large or small, all museums depend on photographers to create the images they need to help promote the artwork and entice the general public to visit the collections. Large museums such as the American Museum of Natural History in New York City and the Smithsonian Institution have full-time photographers to continually create photographic inventories as well as photograph new and revised exhibitions. These institutions also employ photographers for all archaeological and travel activities conducted abroad. Museum Photographers work on staff or on a contract basis; they work in studios located within museums or in their own studios.

Museum Photographers can also find work with organizations that provide museum-related services, such as the Science and Society Picture Library (SSPL) in England. SSPL represents the collections of various museums and historical societies, such as the Science Museum, the National Railway Museum and the National Museum of Photography, Film & Television. They create online records containing digital images and transparencies from the museums' collections and loan them for various fees to clients for reproduction. Museum Photographers are on hand to photograph images from the collection, as well as for on-location filming projects.

Advancement Prospects

Staff Museum Photographers who work for larger museums can advance to become department heads. Museum Photog-

raphers with advanced degrees in art history, conservation, or library science may be able to work their way up to become directors of photographic collections. This requires research and data-management skills and experience in cataloging and archiving electronic images. It also calls for much less actual time behind the camera. To advance to this type of position, Museum Photographers need to have firsthand knowledge of the practices and standards involved in managing museums' collections and should acquire several years of experience as an assistant to a collections director.

Education and Training

A four-year degree in photography is a solid foundation for Museum Photographers. Some museums require photographers to have advanced degrees and coursework in art curatorial and conservation studies. Museum Photographers should be adept at working with digital photography and trained in photographic design software.

Experience, Skills, and Personality Traits

Museum Photographers need to have at least three to five years of experience as commercial photographers under their belts to handle the serious responsibilities of the job. Catalog photography experience is particularly beneficial to this type of work, as they will be photographing a variety of objects often for advertising and promotion. Museum Photographers are photographing original creations and must be extremely knowledgeable about cameras, lighting, current and historical art materials and chemical compositions of those materials, as well as how to handle the artwork without harming it. They must be particularly adept at lighting surfaces to highlight textures and differences in colors.

Museum Photographers will collaborate with a variety of museum staff, sometimes under tight deadlines and sometimes on projects that last for months or years. They must have patience, flexibility, and speed to deliver quality work. Success in this field requires thoughtfulness, respect for the ideas of others, strong communication skills, and an appreciation of budget and time constraints.

Unions and Associations

Museum Photographers can join the American Association of Museums for educational resources, job listings, grant opportunities, and networking events. They can also join the Professional Photographers of America for photography-related benefits.

Tips for Entry

1. Create a portfolio featuring your best product photography, from jewelry to home decor. If you have prior catalog photography experience, include photographs from this body of work, also.

2. Contact the public relations and communications departments of local museums and inquire about employment opportunities. See if you can set up informational interviews.

3. Visit the museums and collect promotional literature to familiarize yourself with the collections and styles of the photographic images.

PHOTOGRAPHY CURATOR, MUSEUM

CAREER PROFILE

Duties: Directs photographic collectibles departments within museums; plans for periodic displays based on social themes and various current and historical issues; coordinates loans of appropriate images for exhibits in American and overseas museums; liaises with museum's education directors regarding school tours and educational programs related to photographic collections; may train docents in leading tours through photographic exhibitions; liaises with museum's public relations department regarding press releases, exhibition openings with press coverage, and other communications-related issues; may deal with public inquiries directly

Alternate Title(s): Photography Administrator, Photography Director

Salary Range: $30,000 to $70,100+

Employment Prospects: Fair

Advancement Prospects: Fair

Best Geographical Location(s): Large cities, such as Chicago and New York, with private and public museums that have existing photographic image holdings

Prerequisites:

Education or Training—Four-year degree in photography, art, art history; master's degree in photography history or art history; Ph.D. required by some organizations

Experience—Four or more years of experience as an associate photography curator

Special Skills and Personality Traits—Extremely knowledgeable about photography, photographic history, and current and past photographers; knowledgeable about the era or genre in which the museum specializes; aware of and interested in current events and issues; passionate about educating and enlightening the general public; creative, innovative, and imaginative

CAREER LADDER

```
┌─────────────────────────────────────┐
│   Chief Curator / Museum Director     │
└─────────────────────────────────────┘

┌─────────────────────────────────────┐
│        Photography Curator            │
└─────────────────────────────────────┘

┌─────────────────────────────────────┐
│   Associate Photography Curator       │
└─────────────────────────────────────┘
```

Position Description

Photography Curators oversee and manage photographic exhibitions and collections within museums. Photography Curators have diverse responsibilities, and the smaller the museum, the more diverse those responsibilities will be. They may research collections and come up with plans for exhibitions based on current collections. They may collab-orate with museum education directors to create educational programs tailored to tour groups, students, and senior citizens. They may also participate in lectures and help create and coordinate seminar programs.

Photography Curators are responsible for maintaining the permanent photographic collections and make recommendations and prepare proposals to appropriate museum executives for purchases and acquisitions. They are also involved in loaning photographs to museums and requesting loans from other institutions. They are responsible for authenticating, evaluating, and categorizing photographs. They work closely with exhibition designers in creating exhibitions and consult with other museum administrators as well in determining appropriate wall spaces, display cases, lighting, and designs for exhibitions. They collaborate with the public relations and communications departments in preparing information about exhibitions and collections for museum brochures and promotional literature, press releases and announcements, and the museum's Web site. They also work with educational departments in training docents to lead students and groups through exhibitions.

Administrative tasks are an intrinsic part of the Photography Curator position. Curators create department budgets and may also document collection in management databases. In smaller museums, Photography Curators may have more direct contact with the public and will field inquires by phone, e-mail, or mail from museum visitors, scholars, professors, art and photography dealers, and staff at other museums and arts institutions. They may also write articles for trade and academic publications.

Salaries
Photography Curators can earn annual salaries ranging from $30,000 to $70,100. Earnings will vary depending upon the size of the museum or institution and the curator's years of experience. The *Occupational Outlook Handbook* cites $33,720 as the median annual earnings for archivists, curators, and museum technicians in 2002 in museums, historical sites, and similar organizations. Curators who work in large, well-funded museums earn far higher wages than those who work for small institutions. The federal government also pays higher salaries, with museum curators earning an average annual salary of $70,100 in 2003.

Employment Prospects
Job prospects for Photography Curators is expected to remain very competitive, as there are many more people interested in this field than there are jobs to fill. According to the *Occupational Outlook Handbook,* employment of curators is expected to increase by 10 to 20 percent, about as fast as the average for all occupations, through 2012. Art and history museums are the largest employers in the museum business, so job opportunities will be best there. More public and private organizations are focusing on establishing archives and organizing information and records, and public interest in this information and art history, overall, is simultaneously increasing.

Advancement Prospects
Photography Curators who work for large museums and institutions can advance to become chief curators, depart-

ment heads, and, with years of extensive experience, eventually museum directors, depending upon the structure of the staff. Curators in small museums can advance by taking positions of greater responsibility at larger museums. They can enhance their skills by writing articles for trade publications, exploring new areas of photography, and giving lectures at other institutions and educational facilities. They can also advance by attracting and coordinating high-profile exhibits at their museum.

Education and Training
Most museums require Photography Curators to have a master's degree in art history or photography history, with coursework in particular eras and genres. Some museums may require doctoral degrees. Photography Curators who hold two degrees, one in museum studies (museology), one in a specialized subject area such as art history or photography, will have better chances of securing work. Curators take continuing education workshops to maintain their knowledge of the field. Museums, historical societies, and museum associations, as well as the National Archives, offer educational programs and training for curators and other museum professionals.

Experience, Skills, and Personality Traits
Museums prefer to hire Photography Curators with extensive museum experience, which can be five or more years of prior experience as associate curators. Photography Curators must be adept in handling rare photographs and be knowledgeable about photographers and their backgrounds. Diplomatic skills are critical in this job, as Photography Curators interact not just with museum staff but with the general public as well. They must have excellent written and verbal communication skills, be organized, efficient, and deadline-oriented. Proficiency with Microsoft Word, Excel, and database-management programs is a must. Some museums may also require multilingual skills. Curators need to be creative and imaginative. They must know how to choose and organize photographic content and materials and the designs and displays that will most accurately and effectively convey the themes of the exhibitions. A key component to this job is intellectual curiosity, a deep understanding of photography, and a passion for sharing this knowledge with the purpose of educating and enlightening the general public.

Unions and Associations
Photography Curators and other museum professionals join the American Association of Museums and the Society for Photographic Education for educational workshops, annual conferences, networking opportunities, and employment referrals. They also keep up with industry issues and developments by joining Professional Photographers of America.

Tips for Entry

1. Get an internship in a photography museum or art museum with photographic exhibitions. The best way to get work in this field is by already having a foot in the door. Internships provide excellent opportunities to learn the intricate details behind forming museum collections and creating exhibitions.

2. Join a professional association such as the American Association of Museums. Take workshops and attend events. Go to photography exhibitions and openings. Network whenever possible and tell people that you are looking for work. You just might meet someone who can offer you your next job.

3. Create a list of the museums you would like to work for and look at the employment sections on their Web sites. You can also find job listings at no cost on the American Association of Museums Web site (http://www.aam-us.org).

PHOTOGRAPHY INSTRUCTOR

CAREER PROFILE

Duties: Teaches students of all ages and skill levels various aspects of photography, from shooting pictures and developing film, to creating prints and evaluating finished photos; works for schools with continuing education programs, as well as in high schools, or teaches members of clubs and professional associations

Alternate Title(s): Photography Teacher

Salary Range: $15,340 to $60,000

Employment Prospects: Good

Advancement Prospects: Good

Best Geographical Location(s): Major cities, such as Atlanta, Boston, Chicago, Miami, Los Angeles, New York, and San Francisco

Prerequisites:

Education or Training—Bachelor's degree in photography recommended; photo instructions training or teaching certification may be required by some employers

Experience—Five or more years of experience as a professional photographer; some experience training or teaching others about photographic techniques and processes in classroom settings

Special Skills and Personality Traits—Excellent knowledge of photography techniques and processes, as well as the history of photography and photographic trends; passionate about sharing knowledge and educating and interacting with others; clear verbal and written communication skills; good listener; organized; reliable; patient; diplomatic; energetic

CAREER LADDER

Photography Instructor

Commercial Photographer

Photographer's Assistant

Position Description

Photography Instructors teach photography to students of various ages and skill levels, from high school students to adults in professional associations, community centers, photography centers, and so on. They research and organize lectures about photographic techniques and processes and also train students in such darkroom work as developing and printing images. Photography Instructors will tailor their classes to students. Some classes may be strictly lectures covering the technical aspect of photography as well as the art forms. Instructors will discuss shutter speeds, f-stops, knowing what differentiates a good picture from a bad picture, how to take pictures of subjects that are in motion, light and composition, framing shots, camera settings, effects, depths of field and contrast.

Instructors will also discuss photography history, sharing images and facts about professional photographers and photography innovators from the past. They may show slides and films and arrange field trips to galleries and museums. They may assign students photography work outside of the classroom, then guide peer reviews and critiques.

If the school or institution has a darkroom, Photography Instructors will demonstrate how to develop exposed film and supervise students in everything from mixing and properly handling development chemicals to printing the film. They will orient students to the darkroom before turning off the lights, explaining the different machines and enlargers and how adjusting exposure times will create different effects in the images. Once the students print their film, they will examine the prints in the classroom to see what needs to be changed.

Instructors help students understand how to examine the work with a critical eye, see where to enhance or adjust, and how to make the corrections. They will teach them how to salvage a poorly shot image, such as by *dodging* and *burning,* where they can make an image lighter or darker in certain areas by increasing or decreasing the picture's exposure time to light. Students can also use light filters to change images in the darkroom.

Photography Instructors are also responsible for writing course descriptions and bios; fielding prospective students' questions; meeting with students to discuss their work and provide guidelines and referrals, as needed; providing support, encouragement, and constructive help to students; coordinating and establishing class schedules with schools or community centers; and taking class attendance and filing paperwork as specified by their employers. In addition to teaching duties, self-employed Photography Instructors must also handle promoting their services, networking for future work, maintaining relationships with current clients, pitching classes and negotiating fees, invoicing clients, and paying their bills.

Salaries

Photography Instructors' earnings are based on the types of schools and organizations that employ them and their respective budgets. Nonprofit organizations and community centers generally have smaller budgets and may pay as little as $20 per hour or as high as $60,000 per year. According to the U.S. Department of Labor, *self-enrichment teachers,* meaning those who teach as part of continuing education programs or at art and community centers, earned median salaries of $29,320 in 2002. Overall, annual salaries that same year ranged from as low as $15,240 to $55,090 or more. Instructors in technical and trade schools earned $50,470. Salaries for full-time Photography Instructors may also be enhanced by such benefits as medical insurance, paid vacations and sick time, and educational discounts for family members.

Employment Prospects

The future looks bright for Photography Instructors, according to the U.S. Department of Labor's *Occupational Outlook Handbook.* Through 2012, employment for all self-enrichment teachers, including Photography Instructors, will grow faster than the average for all occupations, with jobs opening up due to employees relocating or retiring from their positions. People who are interested in pursuing new hobbies, as well as retirees who will have more time to take classes, will account for much of the growth in the field. Classes that require hands-on education and demonstrations, such as photography, will be extremely popular. Larger high schools, community centers, and professional associations will continue to need Photography Instructors to round out their educational programs. About 280,000 people held self-enrichment, adult literacy, and remedial education instructor jobs in 2002. About 20 percent were self-employed and many additional Photography Instructors were volunteers. As digital photographic technology evolves, the need for skilled and knowledgeable Photography Instructors will also remain strong, as students will need to learn digital photographic software and how to use the latest equipment and processes.

Advancement Prospects

Photography Instructors can advance by moving on from community centers to more prestigious professional associations and schools. They may teach more classes with larger student bodies. Instructors with years of experience and tomes of student testimonials can command more work and higher rates. They can also advance by becoming photographic consultants, expanding their own commercial photography businesses, participating in lectures hosted by professional organizations, contributing articles to trade publications, as well as writing and publishing their own books.

Education and Training

Educational requirements will vary depending upon the schools and institutes in which Photography Instructors teach. Professional associations, community centers, and private high schools may require Photography Instructors to have a certain number of years of professional photography experience. Public high schools usually require Photography Instructors to have teaching certificates and specific work backgrounds. Many instructors train by sitting in on photo classes and observing instructors or by working as assistants to instructors. A B.A. in photography is always a solid educational foundation for Photography Instructors. To find accredited schools with photography programs, visit the Web site of the National Association of Schools of Art and Design, http://nasad.arts-accredit.org.

Experience, Skills, and Personality Traits

Photography Instructors must be well versed in photography to effectively educate others. They must know how to shoot pictures, develop film, and examine and correct images, and they must also understand how different cameras work.

They need to have a solid grasp of lighting and composition, framing, lenses, filters, shutter speeds, and more. A big part of the job also entails demonstrating equipment and techniques. To engage students and keep them interested, Photography Instructors must know how to organize their thoughts and be able to choose the right words that will get the messages across. They will be teaching individuals of all ages, skill levels, and personalities. Some students will be seriously interested in photography as a career; others may be approaching the class from a hobbyist perspective. Successful Photography Instructors embrace all of the differences and tailor their lessons and feedback to each student. They are knowledgeable but at the same time approachable. They must have vast amounts of patience and flexibility and also be good time managers and extremely organized. Diplomacy is also important, particularly when reviewing and critiquing students' work.

Unions and Associations

Photography Instructors receive such benefits as job listings, educational resources, and useful newsletters and magazines through membership to the Society for Photographic Education. They may also join the Professional Photographers of America for networking opportunities, workshops, and discounts on professional services and products.

Tips for Entry

1. Find out about teacher certification requirements by contacting the National Council for Accreditation of Teacher Education (http://www.ncate.org).
2. Contact Photography Instructors and set up meetings to learn more about what's involved in doing this type of work. Ask about their work and educational backgrounds to get a better idea of what is required. Make sure to find out what they think the pros and cons are of the job.
3. See if you can audit photography classes, with the mission of observing Photography Instructors in action. Otherwise, take several classes and take notes on the way the teachers organized their lectures and the different techniques and tactics they use to keep students interested and engaged. Record key phrases and questions and any language that will help you create your own style of instruction.
4. Volunteer to teach a class at a community center or through a professional organization. It is an excellent way to test the waters and see if this is for you. If the class goes well, students will refer colleagues and friends to you for future classes. You can then start charging appropriate fees for your services.

PHOTOGRAPHY TEACHER (HIGHER EDUCATION)

CAREER PROFILE

Duties: Teaches aspects of photography (i.e., cameras, accessories, lighting, composition, darkroom techniques) at colleges, universities, and technical schools for photography; teaches aspiring professional photographers, continuing education classes, and amateur photography groups; may give private consultations and workshops; creates course outlines and syllabi; assigns projects and homework; reviews, critiques, and grades work; handles administrative tasks as required by schools (i.e., filing attendance and performance records)

Alternate Title(s): Instructor, Lecturer, Professor

Salary Ranges: $23,080 to $92,430

Employment Prospects: Good

Advancement Prospects: Poor

Best Geographical Locations: Major metropolitan areas and major university towns

Prerequisites:

Education or Training—Four-year degree in photography; master's degree may be required by some schools; in-class training with an experienced Photography Teacher beneficial

Experience—Minimum five years of experience as a professional photographer; one to three years of experience in classroom setting helpful

Special Skills and Personality Traits—Able to translate technical content to student-friendly terms; interested in sharing information and being part of the education process; skilled at engaging and motivating others; strong interpersonal and communication skills; passionate about photography; knowledgeable and tuned in to current photography practices and technology; organized; patient; personable and accessible; good sense of humor; able to relate to students young and old

Special Requirements—Certification or licensing requirements will vary by state and school

CAREER LADDER

```
┌─────────────────────────────┐
│     Photography Teacher      │
└─────────────────────────────┘

┌─────────────────────────────┐
│    Freelance Photographer    │
└─────────────────────────────┘

┌─────────────────────────────┐
│   Photographer's Assistant   │
└─────────────────────────────┘
```

Position Description

Photography Teachers educate students about single-lens reflex (SLR) cameras and digital cameras, photographic equipment, film, lighting, camera angles, backdrops and props, choosing subjects to photograph and framing shots, developing and printing processes, and retouching images with design software. They teach in the art departments of colleges and universities and in art and technical schools.

They tailor their classes to specific levels. Beginning photography students will learn the basics about how the camera and all of its accessories work, how to take pictures using black-and-white and color film, and developing and printing images. Advanced students will learn the finer details of lighting and composition, as well as darkroom and printing techniques.

Photography Teachers create course descriptions for schools to publish in educational catalogs and on their Web sites. They field prospective student inquiries by e-mail and telephone and provide students with class outlines, required reading lists, and what they should bring to class. They may teach classes either in-person or online. Photography Teachers demonstrate camera techniques, show slides, and discuss photographic themes and styles. They discuss the history of photography and the latest developments in the technology. They also demonstrate styles by introducing students to the work of famous and respected photographers in the field, taking trips to photo galleries and museums, and having guest speakers visit classes. Photography Teachers are responsible for assigning homework, monitoring each student's performance on projects, and conducting group and individual critiques of work. They also meet with students one-on-one to review and advise on their portfolios.

Photography Teachers are also responsible for filing appropriate paperwork with school administrators by certain deadlines. They must take attendance, keep track of grades, and maintain performance reviews. They must also maintain their own education on the photography field. Photography Teachers stay tuned in by reading industry publications, frequenting Web sites, attending trade shows and conferences, attending photo shows, and networking as much as possible.

Salaries

Salaries for college-level educators vary by state and by each institution's budget. Full-time photography educators do not have special status and are paid according to the same salary scales as other professional educators. The starting salary for staff teachers in many schools is in the $30,000 range. Four-year schools generally pay higher than two-year schools, and private institutions usually pay lower wages. The *Occupational Outlook Handbooks* cites $64,455 as the average salary for full-time faculty, based on a 2002–03 survey by the American Association of University Professors. Professors earned approximately $86,437; associate professors, $51,545; instructors, $37,737; and lecturers, $43,914.

Photography educators who create and market their own workshops, independent of schools, have the potential to earn higher salaries. They will have to factor in overhead costs, though, such as advertising and promotion, travel, rent, utilities, and personal health insurance. Many Photography Teachers also supplement their incomes by consulting or writing and selling articles to publishers or by working as freelance photographers.

Employment Prospects

The future looks bright for Photography Teachers, especially those who seek part-time work. According to the Department of Labor's *Occupational Outlook Handbook,* more college and university teaching jobs are expected to open up; many of the positions will be for part-time or non-tenured teachers. Employment of teachers overall is expected to increase much faster than the average, by 36 percent or more, for all occupations through 2012. Part-time Photography Teachers will work weekdays, nights, or weekends. Those who have flexible schedules will have more opportunities from which to choose.

Advancement Prospects

Staff Photography Teachers can advance to become department heads, deans, or presidents of universities. The natural next step for part-time and nontenured Photography Teachers is to join the school's staff of educators. Freelance Photography Teachers usually teach while still practicing their profession, so advancement in the school system is often not what many are seeking. Advancement may also come by moving to a position at a larger or more prestigious college.

Education and Training

A four-year degree in photography is usually the minimum requirement to teach, although some universities may only hire Photography Teachers with graduate degrees. Part-time teachers who work for art schools and continuing education programs may not be required to have degrees. Of utmost importance is years of experience in the field, the quality of their work, and their ability to share knowledge and successfully educate others. Photography Teachers should have some prior training or orientation to teaching, either by working as assistants to Photography Teachers or devoting time to observing live classes.

Experience, Skills, and Personality Traits

Photography Teachers should have at least five years of prior professional photography experience, as well as some experience in the education and consulting end of the business. They must be able to share what they know in ways that are logical, engaging, and effective. To do this, they need to be able to organize their thoughts into lectures that fit the class levels and schedules. Patience, flexibility, excellent written and verbal communication skills, and the ability to work with groups as well as with individuals are key to enjoying this type of work. Photography Teachers must be dedicated to their students and willing to help them learn and succeed.

Special Requirements

Some schools may require teachers to be licensed according to state guidelines. Photography Teachers should be clear on the requirements in their state before applying for positions.

Unions and Associations

Photography Teachers can belong to such associations as the National Photography Instructors Association, the National Education Association, the Society for Photographic Education, and the Society of Teachers in Education of Professional Photography. Full-time teachers usually join the United Federation of Teachers, or other teachers' unions, for support in securing fair contracts, wages, and treatment. Photography Teachers may also belong to professional organizations such as Professional Photographers of America for industry-related resources.

Tips for Entry

1. Make sure you have the appropriate certification or license to teach in the schools where you would like to work.

2. Contact the heads of the art departments at local universities and colleges or technical schools that offer photography programs. Explain that you are interested in teaching and ask if you can speak with the Photography Teachers about observing a class.

3. Prospective employers will need to see your portfolio and check your references before hiring you. Put together work that best reflects your interests and style and make sure your list of references is up-to-date.

MEDICAL AND SCIENTIFIC PHOTOGRAPHY

ARCHAEOLOGICAL PHOTOGRAPHER

CAREER PROFILE

Duties: Photographs archaeological objects for museums, universities, publications, etc.; works closely with archaeologists and other specialists; photographs in studios, and travels to and works on-site at excavations; may oversee assistants and interns

Alternate Title(s): None

Salary Range: $20,000 to $35,000+

Employment Prospects: Fair

Advancement Prospects: Limited

Best Geographical Location(s): Diverse sites around the world

Prerequisites:

Education or Training—Four-year degree in photography; master's degree helpful; coursework in archaeology and history beneficial; design software training (i.e., Adobe Photoshop and Illustrator)

Experience—Minimum three to five years as an assistant archaeological photographer, with studio and excavation photography experience

Special Skills and Personality Traits—Knowledgeable and passionate about archaeology and social and cultural history; extremely detail-oriented and organized; physically healthy and able to work in challenging weather conditions and landscapes; able to work independently and with a team; strong knowledge of lighting; patient and flexible; curious; adventurous spirit

CAREER LADDER

```
┌─────────────────────────────────────┐
│   Archaeological Photographer        │
└─────────────────────────────────────┘

┌─────────────────────────────────────┐
│   Assistant Photographer             │
└─────────────────────────────────────┘

┌─────────────────────────────────────┐
│   Studio Assistant / Intern          │
└─────────────────────────────────────┘
```

Position Description

Archaeological Photographers at excavation sites around the world, from Greece to Sri Lanka and beyond, have a single responsibility to the archaeologist: preserve every step of the expedition. Archaeological Photographers are responsible for documenting items found at digs for archeological records. Some may record the actual excavation itself, from breaking ground to covering the site in the end. Each photograph is an important record of the dig, which is why Archaeological Photographers take a scientific, methodical approach to their work. Artifacts may be intact or in hundreds of pieces. The Archeological Photographer may shoot shards of pottery and statues, pieces of clothing and bones, or entire sarcophagi. Those who photograph for books and magazines may take a more artistic approach to their work and pay closer attention to composition, color, and lighting.

Archaeological Photographers may photograph artifacts in studios or directly on site at excavations. If working at excavations, they might be in any number of geographical locations: in the desert or jungle; on mountains; in sand pits, bogs, swamps, and caves; aboveground or below the sea. They are well prepared for these challenges with appropriate photography equipment and tools, as well as technical gear and clothing. Archaeological Photographers need to be particularly mindful of their equipment because they are working in conditions that are inherently harmful to cameras, lenses, film, and lights. While dust, sand, grit, water, and other elements are always concerns for any photographer, they are huge problems for Archaeological Photographers working in the field. Archaeological Photographers must be aware of and prepare for the conditions in which they operate. Taking proper precautions is critical. For instance, a photographer working on an underwater site will need to familiarize himself or herself with underwater equipment. Lenses cannot be changed at depth, so planning is especially important. On the opposite side of the spectrum, working in a dusty or desert environment forces photographers to consider the risks of sand and grit on moving parts and optical surfaces. It is useful and economical to know that underwater camera equipment is also well suited to desert conditions, as the seals designed to keep out water work just as well at keeping out dust. Dual-purpose equipment can be a great money-saver. When working in extremely cold conditions, fluids that normally keep a camera lubricated can actually turn into sludge. Photographers working under arctic conditions need to have their equipment serviced and prepared with special lubricants designed for this type of weather. Another useful tip is to wear external battery packs inside a coat to keep equipment functioning under frigid conditions.

Salaries

Archaeological Photographers usually work on a freelance basis and earn wages on a project-by-project basis. Annual salaries can range from $20,000 to $35,000 or more, depending on the number of excavations and projects the Archaeological Photographer is able to secure. There are very few long-term employees because expeditions may span only a few months or extend over several years. Archaeological Photographers typically charge flat rates for projects, with all expenses included.

Employment Prospects

According to the *Occupational Outlook Handbook,* employment of archaeologists is expected to grow by about 10 to 20 percent through 2012. As archaeologists are employed, so will Archaeological Photographers secure work. More expeditions are occurring due to increased private funding to museums, colleges and universities, and philanthropic groups. Competition will be fierce, though. Photographers with advanced degrees and experience working with archaeologists will have a much-needed edge.

Advancement Prospects

There is no specific job to which Archaeological Photographers can advance. They can expand by working on digs that are different from what they normally have done in the past or by securing steady employment. They can write for various publications, participate in panel discussions, and teach at colleges and on the graduate-school level.

Education and Training

A four-year degree in photography, with coursework in archaeology and history, is recommended. Some educational institutions may require Archaeological Photographers to have advanced degrees. Skill with computer design software (Adobe Photoshop) is required.

Experience, Skills, and Personality Traits

Several years of prior experience as an assistant to an Archaeological Photographer is recommended. To succeed in this field, Archaeological Photographers must have great patience and be passionate about archaeology. Photographing artifacts and expedition sites, traveling to excavations, and witnessing the discovery of new worlds can be overwhelmingly exciting. At the same time, the reality is that many photographs will be needed of countless, often unidentifiable pieces and particles of those finds. The Archaeological Photographer who is deeply interested in learning about other cultures and how people lived eons ago will enjoy this work immensely and thrive in the field.

Archaeological Photographers who work at excavation sites must be hale and hearty. Weather, terrain, and other factors will strive to distract from the work at hand. Photographers who are in good physical shape, extremely focused, and have flexible attitudes will overcome the challenges to achieve the goals of the project. They must also be adept at working independently and as part of a team and be capable of taking and following instructions from archaeologists and dig leaders. They must also be educated about and respectful of local customs.

Unions and Associations

There are no associations specifically committed to Archaeological Photographers. Membership in such organizations as the Association of Archaeological Illustrators and Surveyors and the Archaeological Institute of America, however, offers access to educational publications, news about current and upcoming expeditions, networking opportunities, and other beneficial resources.

Tips for Entry

1. Volunteering or interning is the best way to get exposure to this world and also gain invaluable on-the-job training. Volunteer as an assistant in a museum or at an archaeological program in a university.
2. Immerse yourself in the field by reading as much literature as possible. Read archaeology magazines and frequent Web sites to learn about upcoming excavations and help that may be needed. Visit the library

and take out books about digs, archaeologists, and other specialists in the field.

3. Use Internet search engines to find information about Archaeological Photographers. Read their biographies and visit their Web sites. If you get the sense they might be approachable, e-mail a note asking if they can spare a few moments to answer questions about their work. Tell them you are considering entering the field and that their feedback will be extremely beneficial.

MEDICAL PHOTOGRAPHER

CAREER PROFILE

Duties: Photographs medical conditions for patients' records and treatment; photographs medical procedures for scientific papers, records, textbooks, pamphlets, and teaching models, as well as for use in educational films, slides for future classes at medical centers, and evidence in civil and criminal legal procedures; keeps detailed records of photographs and slides; handles accounts receivable and payable

Alternate Title(s): Biomedical Photographer

Salary Ranges: $25,000 to $50,000+

Employment Prospects: Fair

Advancement Prospects: Poor

Best Geographical Location(s): Major urban areas and all cities with teaching hospitals

Prerequisites:

Education or Training—Two- or four-year degree in photography; coursework in health-related subjects (i.e., biology, medicine, etc.) beneficial; design software training (Adobe Photoshop)

Experience—Several years of experience as a professional portrait or commercial photographer; some experience assisting or working in some capacity with a Medical Photographer beneficial

Special Skills and Personality Traits—Strong interest in health, medicine, and science; detail-oriented; able to work with diverse people, from patients to medical personnel; comfortable with medical terminology; excellent communication skills; diplomatic and sensitive; adept at computer software programs; PowerPoint knowledge helpful

CAREER LADDER

Medical Photographer

Professional Photographer

Photographer's Assistant

Position Description

Medical Photographers aid medical research and education by taking photographs of medical conditions, as well as by taking photographs to help in the prevention of certain conditions. For instance, some Medical Photographers may work closely with dermatologists to help detect the early signs of skin cancer. They will photograph a patient's entire body each year, which enables dermatologists to compare photographs from year to year and identify any changes in skin markings. Medical Photographers may photograph eye conditions to assist ophthalmologists in formulating their diagnoses.

Medical Photographers either work on site at doctors' offices or in their own studios, providing patients with comfortable, clean, private dressing rooms. Medical Photographers may also regularly visit rehabilitation hospitals to photograph and track body changes due to scoliosis, spinal injury, obesity, and other conditions. They may photograph surgical procedures for later use in teaching hospitals. They photograph patients before operations for close-up shots of the injuries, photograph them on the operating table from start to finish, and then take further close-ups following the operation. Patients use these photographs as proof when filing insurance claims. Medical Photographers may also photograph autopsies.

Larger hospitals generally have dedicated staff photographers who specialize in the areas being photographed. Smaller hospitals usually hire freelance Medical Photographers who are multidisciplined and able to juggle many projects. Some Medical Photographers also use video cameras in their work. Depending on the size and structure of the hospital, Medical Photographers may be tasked with producing charts and graphs, digitizing X-rays, and creating slides for presentations. Their photographs are often used in brochures, advertisements, textbooks, and other literature. Some Medical Photographers are also skilled in graphic design or Web design. They may work with medical centers to create Web sites to help patients learn about certain conditions and diseases.

Medical Photographers manage their schedules. Doctors and hospitals often refer patients to them and leave it to the photographers to book the photo sessions and confirm the locations and all of the specifics (i.e., conditions to photograph, types of images being created). Freelance Medical Photographers must also bill clients, handle the photo studio's accounts receivable and payable, and maintain office equipment and supplies.

Salaries

Medical Photographers can earn salaries ranging from $25,000 to $50,000 or more, depending upon clientele, geographical location, and number of years in the field. A Medical Photographer's fee may be derived from grants teaching hospitals receive for their services. Patients pay fees directly to photographers either on a per-photography-session or per-package basis. The photography package usually includes the photography session plus the types of photographs commissioned, which may be 35-millimeter slides or 8″ × 10″ or 9″ × 12″ digital prints. Medical Photographers may also enhance their salaries by creating images for use as evidence in legal procedures.

Employment Prospects

The medical photography field is small and highly competitive, thus employment prospects are expected to be only fair for Medical Photographers. According to the *Occupational Outlook Handbook,* employment of photographers overall is predicted to increase about as fast as the average for all occupations, or by about 10 to 20 percent, through the year 2012. Patients and doctors who seek medical histories through photographs will continue to hire Medical Photog-

raphers but generally will hire those they are most familiar with and have developed a relationship with over time, particularly if the conditions being photographed are of a sensitive nature. Medical Photographers have greater chances of finding work with rehabilitation centers, which normally need photography services for post-corrective surgery, prior to and after operations, and for diagnosis or further medical follow-through. Medical Photographers can also find work with teaching hospitals, universities, and medical book and magazine publishers.

Advancement Prospects

Medical Photographers are usually freelancers. Most work independently with no or very little staff assistance and are already at the top of their profession. While there is no specific job to which Medical Photographers can advance, they can grow their businesses and expand their skills by lecturing and writing, teaching at technical schools and universities, and exploring other areas of medical photography.

Education and Training

A four-year degree in photography is typically a solid foundation for Medical Photographers. While most do not need to have a background in the particular medicine or science they are photographing, having a grasp of the language, terminology, symptoms, and treatments is helpful. Photographers who train for one to two years with Medical Photographers receive great exposure to this field. They need to be well versed in digital photography and trained in software design programs such as Adobe Photoshop and Illustrator, as well as such Microsoft Office programs as PowerPoint.

Experience, Skills, and Personality Traits

Successful Medical Photographers have artistic skills coupled with a strong interest in health and medicine. Because they work with a wide variety of people, from doctors to patients, they need to have exceptional communication skills. They must have the knowledge to speak with doctors about the conditions and diseases they will be photographing and the diplomacy, tact, and sensitivity to help patients feel comfortable and safe while they are being photographed. Some conditions are difficult enough for patients to handle, so Medical Photographers must present themselves professionally yet humanely while they work. They may work from the studio, at hospitals, in doctors' offices, and at patients' homes. It is important that they be able to travel as needed and maintain a flexible attitude.

Unions and Associations

For educational and networking opportunities, technical expertise, and advice geared specifically to medical communications specialists, Medical Photographers can join the BioCommunications Association and the Health and Science Communications Association. Medical Photographers can also join the Association of Medical Illustrators, either as full or associate members, depending upon their art disciplines. For professional photography resources and discounts on services, they may also join Professional Photographers of America.

Tips for Entry

1. If there is a teaching hospital in your community, call and ask to speak with the Medical Photographer. Ask for an appointment to discuss the possibility of assisting or observing.

2. Speak with your family doctor about upcoming medical trade shows. Attend these shows and be sure to bring business cards with you. Network and speak with exhibitors and attendees about their medical photography needs. Find out the names of the Medical Photographers they work with and contact them to learn more about the type of work they do.

3. Research the medical photography field to learn which conditions are photographed. Check the public library for reference books and conduct Internet searches on medical photography and Medical Photographers.

4. Search for medical publishers to see which photographers they hire and the types of photographs they publish.

OCEANOGRAPHIC PHOTOGRAPHER

CAREER PROFILE

Duties: Provides photographs of the environment above and below the ocean; photographs beaches, harbors, inlets, and relevant natural and human-made elements for scientists, researchers, the U.S. Coast Guard, the U.S. military, builders of bridges, dams, and other human-made structures, historians and agencies in Congress and state legislative departments; may write and pitch articles and photographs to magazine and book publishers

Alternate Title(s): Marine Photographer

Salary Range: $20,000 to $50,000+

Employment Prospects: Fair

Advancement Prospects: Fair

Best Geographical Location(s): Seacoast university cities, Washington, D.C., and major harbor cities

Prerequisites:

Education or Training—Master's and doctoral degree; on-the-job training with oceanographers and Oceanographic Photographers

Experience—Research work at institutions, environmental centers; prior writing or teaching experience beneficial

Special Skills and Personality Traits—Strong interest in marine life and oceans, science, research, and math; comfortable in the water; skilled diver; knowledgeable about cameras, film, lighting, and accessories that work best under water; physically fit, with excellent stamina; excellent interpersonal and communication skills; able to work independently and on a team; organized; logical; detail-oriented

Special Requirements—Specialized scuba diving license required by various states and countries

CAREER LADDER

```
┌─────────────────────────────────┐
│        Marine Scientist         │
└─────────────────────────────────┘

┌─────────────────────────────────┐
│   Oceanographic Photographer    │
└─────────────────────────────────┘

┌─────────────────────────────────┐
│      Researcher or Teacher      │
└─────────────────────────────────┘
```

Position Description

Oceanographic Photographers photograph images both below and above water for research about marine life, water conditions, and environmental changes and impacts. They may document coral reefs and fish habitats, water temperatures and currents, tides and circulation. They photographically monitor land erosion of beaches and inlet shorelines periodically at high and low tides at the request of the town-ships, the U.S. Coast Guard, and for local environmental groups. Oceanographic Photographers often speak about their work and their findings at science and research conferences and sometimes even at city and town council meetings focused on local environmental issues.

Most Oceanographic Photographers specialize in an area of oceanography and are trained in underwater photography. Their area of expertise may be in marine biology or marine geology, in which they study seabeds and coastal interactions or analyze marine bacteria, algae, and animals and their interactions. They may specialize in computer modeling, in which they will create simulations of various processes in the ocean to help predict sea level and climate changes. They work in offices, laboratories, and travel to various parts of the world to conduct fieldwork in small boats or large research vessels. They take notes on what they observe, date-stamp photographs, and use computers to analyze the data. Oceanographic Photographers also spend a great deal of time keeping up with research and news in the field by reading scientific journals and publications. They may work with interns, delegating assignments to them and guiding them in their work.

Some Oceanographic Photographers write articles to explain the research and the stories behind their photographs or team with writers to help them tell the stories. They pitch their ideas to magazines, such as *National Geographic, Outdoor Life, BioScience,* and others. Once the stories are accepted, they negotiate the terms of agreement. Some magazines will cover travel and other expenses. If not, photographers or writers can approach resorts in the areas where they plan to travel, explain that they have been commissioned to write an article, and that they plan to include pictures and information about the resorts in the article. In exchange for this promotion, many resorts offer complementary rooms and meals. Oceanographic Photographers may also work closely with educational textbook publishers in covering various aspects of the field for high school and college students.

Salaries

Salaries for Oceanographic Photographers can range from $20,000 to $50,000 or more, depending upon their years of experience, the agencies for which they work, and the number of paying projects they are able to secure. Oceanographic Photographers may work for government or nongovernmental organizations and museums as freelancers, consultants, or staff employees. Many freelance photographers also write and publish articles in magazines and books. Photographers who have established themselves in the business and who are known for high-quality images of unique subjects in remote parts of the world usually secure the most work and the highest rates. Oceanographic Photographers may also write research proposals and secure grants to cover expenses for projects.

Employment Prospects

Oceanographic photography is incredibly competitive and only a few top-notch photographers are able to successfully commit 100 percent of their time to the field. Many Oceanographic Photographers are freelance, and those who are well connected secure the commissions. Networking and going on lecture circuits, even if it means you must lecture for free, are key to building a name in the business. There are no statistics currently available for employment predictions for Oceanographic Photographers. A close parallel, however, can be drawn to the employment rates of oceanographers and other related scientists. According to the *Occupational Outlook Handbook,* the overall employment of environmental scientists and geoscientists is expected to grow by about 10 to 20 percent, about as fast as the average for all occupations through 2012. Public policy will spur the job growth, inducing organizations and companies to comply with environmental laws and regulations. Environmental scientists and Oceanographic Photographers will be needed by these companies to research and analyze the environment, particularly the waters and shorelines, to help determine specific changes they may need to make to meet the standards.

Advancement Prospects

There is no standard career ladder in the oceanographic photography field. Some Oceanographic Photographers may advance by heading research teams and organizing more complex projects. Others may get ahead by pursuing further studies in particular areas of oceanography and securing postdoctoral degrees. They can also advance by teaching, lecturing, and writing.

Education and Training

Oceanographic Photographers usually have advanced degrees in oceanography, biology, chemistry, or other related subjects, with training in underwater photography. Many have master's and doctoral degrees.

Experience, Skills, and Personality Traits

Oceanographic Photographers must be passionate about science, research, marine life, oceans, and the environment. They need to understand the science behind their photographs. They must be curious and creative, detail-oriented, and have strong communication skills. Much of their work entails writing and reporting about their research, experiments, studies, and findings, so strong writing skills are important. They also must be tenacious and persistent in pitching ideas to magazine and book publishers. Naturally, they must be healthy, in good physical shape, and be comfortable in and around the water. Multilingual skills and appreciation and respect for other cultures are also important qualities.

Special Requirements

Oceanographic Photographers need to have a specialty license for underwater photography. They must first receive certification in advanced scuba diving to receive the specialty license. Visit the Professional Association of Diving

Instructors Web site (http://www.padi.com) for details about how to get certified.

Unions and Associations

There is no union or association specifically dedicated to Oceanographic Photographers. Those photographers who are licensed and teach diving can join the Professional Association of Diving Instructors. Oceanographic Photographers may also join Professional Photographers of America and American Society of Media Photographers for career-enhancing membership benefits. Nikon Professional Services is another organization that offers professional photographers who use Nikon equipment updates on technology, news about other professionals in the field, various classes, and more. The American Littoral Society also offers members useful information about local environmental issues and events.

Tips for Entry

1. Conduct an Internet search for summer workshops including underwater photography training. If you have not done so already, get certified in scuba diving.
2. Visit the Web site of the Archaeological Institute of America (http://www.archaeological.org) and see if they have upcoming tours of underwater sites. E-mail or call them to find out about openings for volunteer underwater photographers.
3. Join the Professional Association of Diving Instructors. Take advantage of networking opportunities, further training, and employment referrals.
4. If you have already been diving and taking photographs, enter as many underwater photography contests as possible to start getting your name out there and building connections.

OPHTHALMIC PHOTOGRAPHER

CAREER PROFILE

Duties: Works at ophthalmology practices and performs ophthalmic photography; helps ophthalmologists diagnose and treat eye diseases by performing fluorescein angiography, fundus photography, and optical coherence tomography; reviews patients' charts; attends meetings and seminars; trains on site in surgical procedures and imaging technology; may be required to transport records and supplies to sites

Alternate Title(s): Biomedical Photographer, Ophthalmic Photographer/Technician, Ophthalmic Photographer/Angiographer, Retinal Angiographer

Salary Range: $23,000 to $50,000+

Employment Prospects: Good

Advancement Prospects: Good

Best Geographical Location(s): Major cities and suburban areas

Prerequisites:

Education or Training—High school diploma may suffice for some positions; most practices will require two- or four-year degrees, with training in ophthalmic photography and angiography

Experience—Two or more years of experience in specialized ophthalmology in hospitals, laboratories, or health-care organizations

Special Skills and Personality Traits—Working knowledge of fundus photography; knowledgeable about 35-millimeter film processing; understands how to read patients' charts; excellent communication and interpersonal skills; calm, presentable, and professional demeanor

Special Requirements—Certification as a clinical ophthalmic assistant, clinical ophthalmic technician, or clinical ophthalmic medical technologist is mandatory in many practices; cardiopulmonary resuscitation (CPR) certification is also often required

CAREER LADDER

```
┌─────────────────────────────────┐
│  Ophthalmic Photographic         │
│  Supervisor /                    │
│  Certified Ophthalmic            │
│  Medical Technologist            │
└─────────────────────────────────┘

┌─────────────────────────────────┐
│  Ophthalmic Photographer         │
└─────────────────────────────────┘

┌─────────────────────────────────┐
│  Ophthalmic Photographic         │
│  Assistant                       │
└─────────────────────────────────┘
```

Position Description

Ophthalmic Photographers photograph eyes to help ophthalmologists determine eye disorders, diseases, and treatments and to help them discern congenital problems and document surgeries. Photographers use specialized cameras (i.e., the fundus camera, which documents the retina) and microscopes to take two- and three-dimensional photographs of various aspects and angles of the eye, under the supervision of opthalmologists. The patient sits facing the photographer, looking through the microscope and camera lens, and follows the photographer's instructions before the shot is taken. An angiogram, which is an examination of blood vessels, is achieved by injecting patients with a contrast medium, a fluorescent dye, which eventually flows into the retina or iris vessels. This is also known as fluorescein or indocyanine-green angiography. Ophthalmic Photographers alter light by using various filters.

In addition to fundus photography and angiography, Ophthalmic Photographers perform a variety of ophthalmic photographic functions, such as slit-lamp photography, external eye photography, videography, and optical coherence tomography imaging. They not only photograph eyes to create baseline medical records and document disorders but may also contribute work to new research projects in collaboration with other medical departments and organizations.

Ophthalmic Photographers process and develop black-and-white and color photographic materials, using manual or automated methods. They may prepare photographs for meetings, conferences, and ophthalmic photographic exhibitions. They may also be responsible for maintaining patients' records in hard-copy files as well as in computer databases. They review and choose ophthalmic photographic equipment and supplies for purchase, as well as maintain and repair the equipment. They coordinate patient scheduling of diagnostic exams and may give patients vision tests. Ophthalmic Photographers may also be responsible for instructing resident physicians in fundus photography procedures, training other Ophthalmic Photographers in fundus and external eye photography, as well as in fluorescein angiography, and may supervise medical photographers in their work.

Salaries

Salaries for Ophthalmic Photographers are commensurate with experience and can range from $23,000 to $50,000 or more. Most Ophthalmic Photographers are full-time employees of hospitals, health-care organizations, or laboratories. Upper-level Ophthalmic Photographers, such as certified ophthalmic medical technologists, with six or more years of experience, will command higher wages. In addition to steady salaries and annual raises, Ophthalmic Photographers may enjoy such benefits as medical, dental, and life insurance; 401Ks; profit sharing; paid vacations and sick leave; disability; and continuing education and certification assistance or reimbursement.

Employment Prospects

Ophthalmic Photographers usually work in private practices, clinics, laboratories, and hospitals, as well as in academia. According to the Mississippi Hospital Association (http://www.mshealthcareers.com), Ophthalmic Photographers have good chances of finding work at least through 2012. As baby boomers age and the elderly population continues to grow, so, too, will the need for diagnostic eye exams and photographic materials.

Advancement Prospects

With years of experience, Ophthalmic Photographers can advance to become supervisors in ophthalmic photographic departments. They can freelance as consultants to private practices, hospitals, and health-care clinics. They can become faculty members at technical schools and universities and share their knowledge by writing articles for medical journals and Web sites. Those who have lower-level certification can find greater employment opportunities by seeking higher-level certification as medical technicians or technologists.

Education and Training

For gainful employment, Ophthalmic Photographers usually need at least a two-year degree, with an emphasis on science, and two years of vocational training in ophthalmic diagnostic photography and angiography. Certification is the next step after completing vocational training. Ophthalmic Photographers keep up with research, photographic techniques, and technology by regularly attending continuing education workshops and conferences and reading ophthalmic journals and books.

Special Requirements

Ophthalmic Photographers must be certified as clinical ophthalmic assistants (COAs), technicians (COTs), or medical technologists (COMTs) to perform photographic services for patients. They can receive certification through such organizations as the Joint Commission on Allied Health Personnel in Ophthalmology (JCAHPO; http://www.jcahpo.org). To receive certification, photographers must complete and pass exams for lower-level certification and pass hands-on tests for higher-level certification. At JCAHPO, the COA exam is at the entry level, the COT is the intermediate level, and the COMT is advanced. Some ophthalmic departments may also require cardiopulmonary resuscitation (CPR) certification, in case a patient has trouble breathing or experiences a cardiac emergency. The American Red Cross offers classes and certification in infant, child, and adult CPR.

Experience, Skills, and Personality Traits

Ophthalmology practices normally require photographers to have between three and six years of prior diagnostic eye-photography experience, preferably in medical schools, health-care organizations, or laboratories. Ophthalmic Photographers must be knowledgeable about film processing and, at minimum, understand the basics of fundus photography. They must be adept at taking close-up photographs, duplicating slides, and working in hectic environments. Long days and overtime are often required, so dedication and flexibility are key characteristics in the position. Ophthalmic Photographers must also be independent and self-motivated, as well as capable of interacting with patients and staff. To enjoy this field, photographers need to be passionate about science, research, and helping people maintain and improve their eyesight.

Unions and Associations

Ophthalmic Photographers join the Ophthalmic Photographers' Society, Inc. for membership newsletters, industry journals and educational publications, employment listings and referrals, and discounts on certification programs (http://www.opsweb.org). They may also join Professional Photographers of America for educational resources, annual conferences, and networking opportunities.

Tips for Entry

1. Get work in an ophthalmic department as a trainee. Use an Internet search engine, such as Google, to find hospitals, private practices, and health-care organizations near you. Locate the employment sections for job listings or contact the human resources departments directly to find out about openings and how to apply.

2. Join the Ophthalmic Photographers' Society and subscribe to the society's *Journal of Ophthalmic Photography* and *The OPS Newsletter.*

3. Hone your skills by taking continuing education courses that focus on digital imaging, fundus photography, and fluorescein angiography.

4. Prospective Ophthalmic Photographers can also find job opportunities through myriad employment placement Web sites, such as HealthJobsUSA (http://www.healthjobsusa.com), HealthCareerWeb (http://www.healthcareerweb.com), Monster (http://www.monster.com), Hotjobs (http://hotjobs.yahoo.com), as well as through the U.S. Department of Health and Human Services (http://www.os.dhhs.gov).

SCIENTIFIC PHOTOGRAPHER

CAREER PROFILE

Duties: Photographs various subjects to illustrate or record scientific or medical data or phenomena for scientists and medical researchers; may prepare microscope slides; creates photographic procedures and plans for work

Alternate Title(s): Medical Photographer

Salary Range: $50,000 to $75,000

Employment Prospects: Good

Advancement Prospects: Fair

Best Geographical Location(s): Silicon Valley, California; Boston; Phoenix; and Seattle

Prerequisites:

Education or Training—Four-year degree, with specialization in a scientific discipline (chemistry, biology, physics, etc.) beneficial; master's degree or doctoral degree may be required

Experience—Several years of experience in photography, preferably in a lab or science department of university, research facility, or governmental agency

Special Skills and Personality Traits—Strong interest in science and research; extremely knowledgeable about photographic equipment and photographic science techniques; good team player; clear communicator; strong listening skills; detail-oriented and organized; patient; diplomatic; objective photographer; able to follow directions

CAREER LADDER

```
┌─────────────────────────────────────┐
│   Head of Scientific Photography     │
│            Department                │
└─────────────────────────────────────┘

┌─────────────────────────────────────┐
│      Scientific Photographer         │
└─────────────────────────────────────┘

┌─────────────────────────────────────┐
│   Assistant Scientific Photographer  │
└─────────────────────────────────────┘
```

Position Description

Scientific Photographers create accurate, objective photographic images of experiments and scientific procedures for scientists to use in their analyses, measurements, and research data. These photographic images may be incorporated into scientific, medical, or forensic reports or be published in articles and research papers as visual support of scientific discoveries and issues of debate. Their work may also appear in such magazines as *Discover, Science,* and *Scientific American.*

Research organizations, universities, and government departments hire Scientific Photographers to work closely with their scientists on a wide range of projects. They may photograph high-speed events up close or use remote cam-

eras to photograph missile paths or the progress of explosions. Scientific Photographers use specific photographic techniques and technologies to capture these images. Tools and techniques common to the trade include ultraviolet and infrared photography, thermal imaging, and time-lapse photography. Scientific Photographers also use micrography in their work, by attaching a camera to a microscope and taking a picture of the object on the microscope slide. They often assist in the preparation of specimens to be photographed by preparing slides. Many Scientific Photographers also use 16- or 35-millimeter video camcorders or movie cameras to record images and experiments.

Scientific Photographers are responsible for reviewing and selecting appropriate photographic equipment for purchase. After they learn what the assignment is, they plan the photographic methods and techniques that will be needed to complete the job. They position cameras, select the exposures, set up all of the equipment, which can range from microscopes and telescopes to X-rays and infrared lighting. They may photograph fragile documents and material for archival records. They may also develop film and create prints, slides, and transparencies. Normally, Scientific Photographers specialize in the field they are covering, such as chemistry, medicine, physiology, astronomy, or others.

Scientific Photographers are also experimenters and inventors in their own right. An excellent example of this is the story behind the earliest-known scientific photographs of a galloping horse in 1872. These photographs helped settle a dispute and inspired scientists, inventors, and researchers for years to come. According to historical reports, then California governor Leland Stanford bet $25,000 that all four feet of a galloping horse are sometimes completely off the ground, but he needed visual proof to win. Stanford commissioned Photographer Eadweard Muybridge, who was doing government survey work at the time, to photograph a galloping horse. Muybridge experimented first with still photography, which proved useless. Through trial and error, he eventually succeeded by using multiple cameras, with trip threads attached to the shutters, to take a series of photographs. The series was of Occident, a white horse, running against a black, painted background, showing the horse in different positions in each photograph. When flipped through, the series was also an early crude action movie that inspired further experiments and developments in that field. And yes, all four hooves of the galloping horse left the ground, and Stanford won his bet.

Salaries

Annual salaries for Scientific Photographers can range from $50,000 to $75,000. Their earnings will depend upon their educational backgrounds, number of years in the field, and the type of organizations for which they work. Scientific Photographers who specialize in research and experimentation in photographic science (i.e., researching and inventing new photographic equipment and techniques) can apply for grants and financial assistance to help meet business and overhead costs in their work.

Employment Prospects

Scientific Photographers have good chances at finding employment opportunities because the skills required are so specialized. Due to the rigorous educational and photographic technique requirements, there are not as many photographers flocking to the scientific photography field as there are to the more glamorous fields, such as entertainment or sports photography. Scientific Photographers with advanced degrees in the scientific areas of the companies

that are hiring, as well as the proper photographic training, will have the advantage in the hunt for employment.

Advancement Prospects

Scientific Photographers can advance to become heads of photography departments within industrial laboratories and research facilities. They may also move into other areas of science, which they may not have yet covered, after first securing advanced degrees in these areas. They may write and contribute to the magazines that focus on the areas they photograph. They may also write books, give workshops and lectures at universities and scientific association conferences, and participate in expeditions around the world. Scientific Photographers may also advance by pioneering new techniques or contributing to scientific breakthroughs.

Education and Training

A four-year degree in chemistry, biology, physics, or any other scientific area the photographer chooses to work in is recommended in the position. Many companies require Scientific Photographers to have a master's or doctoral degree. Scientific Photographers must be trained in digital photography and photographic design software, as well as the various photographic techniques they will use in their work, such as thermal imaging or micrography. They must also have some training and education in the scientific procedures they are photographing.

Experience, Skills, and Personality Traits

Several years of experience as a photographer in a lab or science department of a governmental organization is helpful. Scientific Photographers must be passionate about science and research and have a strong knowledge of the specific scientific disciplines in which they work. They must be technologically adept because their work requires absolute accuracy. They work closely with scientists and researchers, so they must have excellent interpersonal and communication skills and be able to follow directions to meet deadlines. They must know which equipment, cameras, and techniques to use. This type of work requires a great deal of objectivity and the ability to properly prepare for shots and patiently wait for the right moment to take them.

Unions and Associations

There are no associations dedicated solely to Scientific Photographers. They can belong to the American Association for the Advancement of Science for educational publications and films, access to research papers and scientific news, networking opportunities, and discounts on various services. They can also join Professional Photographers of America for professional resources.

Tips for Entry

1. If you are still in college, speak with your chemistry, biology, or physics professor about creating a portfolio of scientific photographs for review and incorporation into your final grade for the semester.

2. Create your own scientific images for your portfolio by following the examples of early scientists. Visit the online encyclopedia MSN Encarta (http://www.encarta.msn.com), read about Isaac Newton's three laws of motion, then create scientific photos, illustrating these laws. Follow the same path with Galileo's projects, such as his night-sky studies using primitive telescopes.

3. Join the American Association for the Advancement of Science and regularly peruse the Web site for employment referrals and networking opportunities.

NEWS MEDIA AND ENTERTAINMENT PHOTOGRAPHY

DOCUMENTARY PHOTOGRAPHER

CAREER PROFILE

Duties: Takes photographs of living conditions, human conditions, natural environments, wars, and other political, social, and cultural activities in cities and rural areas to document history and inform the public; provides photographic information for researchers, social scientists, world leaders, and others who can analyze and comment on conditions and affect change when needed; travels around the world

Alternate Title(s): News Photographer, Photojournalist, Press Photographer

Salary Range: $14,640 to $49,920+

Employment Prospects: Fair

Advancement Prospects: Fair

Best Geographical Location(s): Major cities where media hubs exist

Prerequisites:

    Education or Training—Bachelor's degree in photojournalism; training in digital photography and photographic design software

    Experience—Five or more years of experience as a news photographer; travel photography and portrait photography experience beneficial

    Special Skills and Personality Traits—Excellent visual sense; passion for current events and world history; interest in cultural, political, and social studies; politically aware; able to choose visual images that best capture the stories; professional; diplomatic; curious; intuitive; excellent written and verbal communications skills; multilingual capabilities helpful; adaptable to change; creative, fast thinker and problem solver

CAREER LADDER

```
┌─────────────────────────────┐
│   Documentary Photographer   │
└─────────────────────────────┘

┌─────────────────────────────┐
│      News Photographer       │
└─────────────────────────────┘

┌─────────────────────────────┐
│   Photographer's Assistant   │
└─────────────────────────────┘
```

Position Description

Documentary Photographers comment on what is going on in the real world by capturing it photographically. They pursue their subject matter either through their own personal interests and convictions, or they work according to assignments received from government and social agencies; magazine, newspaper, and book publishers; or other media. Their work may appear in publications like the *New York Times, Newsweek, Time, Life,* and many others. Documentary Pho-

tographers, like photojournalists, can ignite public outcry and change by pointing their camera lenses at such topics as people's living conditions or the consequences of environmental disasters. In the early 1900s, Documentary Photographers enlightened the world to the horrendous living conditions in city slums, helping to pave the way for new legislation to protect residents in these areas.

    Documentary Photographers map out their stories well in advance of traveling to the location(s) for photography shoots. They might work closely with other researchers and writers or alone, hiring photographer's assistants and other crew as needed. This type of work can be drawn out over long periods of time because the topics are often serious and require painstaking attention to the facts to ensure accuracy in the pictures. It is often necessary to follow up later to make sure the facts still hold true and the stories remain worth telling. Documentary Photographers may also exhibit and sell their work in galleries, possibly raising funds for the issues they have documented. They may travel to war zones and photograph war victims, troops, machinery, destruction, or surrounding cities and villages. They may do a photographic study of people with disabilities who have found interesting and empowering ways to overcome those disabilities, or they may simply photograph them in their daily lives. They may also document gentrification in neighborhoods, areas of towns and cities that have fallen into disrepair, towns where populations have dropped dramatically due to industries closing, and more. The subject matter will vary widely.

Salaries

Documentary Photographers can earn annual salaries ranging from $14,640 to $49,920 or more, depending upon their experience, connections, and subject matter. According to the U.S. Department of Labor's *Occupational Outlook Handbook,* the median annual earning for full-time, staff photographers working at newspapers and periodicals was $31,460. Documentary Photographers are normally freelancers who, unless well established in their fields, supplement their incomes by providing other photographic services. If they are shooting overseas, for instance, they can provide photographs for travel, resort, or lifestyle magazines, thereby sparing the magazines from sending other photographers to the locations. Documentary Photographers may also secure grants for their work, to help cover expenses.

Employment Prospects

It is difficult to predict employment prospects specifically for Documentary Photographers. Many work independently and therefore are able to secure commissions and grants, providing they have new stories to tell that impact the world. Employment of photographers for all disciplines and media is expected to increase at a rate average with all occupations, about 10 to 20 percent, through 2012. Documentary Photographers may secure additional work as more magazines, newspapers, and journals make their publications available on the Internet and as the public's demand for more in-depth, truthful stories increases. Declines in the print newspaper industry, however, may reduce demand for photographers.

Advancement Prospects

Documentary Photographers are typically at the top of their field. True advancement for many will be the day when they can commit 100 percent of their time and energy to documentary photography. This may take years of commitment to the field, honing their skills until they are a recognized name in the industry. They can also advance by writing articles and books to accompany their photographs, as well as delving into other media such as film and television broadcasting. They can always expand their documentary photography studios by adding more photographers and others to their staff and offering more photographic services.

Education and Training

A four-year degree in photography, with emphasis on documentary photography and photojournalism, is beneficial. Coursework in world history, cultural studies, and political science can provide a solid reference ground for this position. Training in digital photography and photographic design software programs is highly recommended.

Experience, Skills, and Personality Traits

Documentary Photographers can have diverse backgrounds. Many will have prior experience as news or press photographers and photojournalists. Some will have commercial photography and portrait photography experience. What they bring to their work is a desire to document the facts and not to create illusions about what is being seen. They are often compelled to tell a story that the world needs to know about and will work relentlessly and sometimes for little or no money to accomplish this goal. Documentary Photographers are sensitive and intuitive about how to photograph people and places, and they know how to tell a story visually. They know what makes for good images and how to communicate with people in ways that encourage natural behavior and the expression of true emotions. This sounds easier than it actually is. Documentary Photographers will often photograph people dealing with difficult situations. Many may be in remote areas of the world and in cultures where photographers are either not welcome or are shunned or feared. They are patient, flexible, excellent communicators who can secure people's trust. They are technically skilled and able to work in all weather conditions day or night. They are also adept at working alone and at working with journalists and reporters. Documentary Photographers must also remain aware of their surroundings, recognize when situations become dangerous, and know how to deal with it.

Unions and Associations

Documentary Photographers may join groups such as the International Association of Documentary Photographers and AmericanPhotojournalist.com for access to Web blogs and online message boards, industry news, employment referrals, self-promoting Web portfolios, employment listings, and photography critiques. They may also join the American Press Institute, American Society of Media Photographers, or National Press Photographers Association.

Tips for Entry

1. Research and create a list of documentary photography studios in cities near you. Find their Web sites and read about the issues that they cover and where they have traveled. Contact the studios that most interest you and see if you can set up an informal meeting to discuss the field. Bring a thorough list of questions with you, business cards, and a portfolio and solicit advice and referrals. Be sure to follow up with a letter expressing your gratitude for the person's time and advice and giving your contact information so that you can continue to be in touch.

2. This is a hard field to enter, so be prepared to pay your dues. Get an entry-level job, an internship, or even volunteer for a little while, if you can afford to, in a documentary photography studio or a studio that provides documentary photography among other photographic services. Have an open mind, be flexible, and remember that this is your training ground. You are investing time in a future career, and this is your opportunity to learn as much as you can about the field. Use your internship experience wisely!

3. Join professional associations and check their Web sites for employment listings in the field. You may also find job listings as well as other educational resources and career tips on such sites as Mediabistro (http://www.mediabistro.com), JournalismJobs (http://www.journalismjobs.com), the New York Times on the Web (http://www.nytimes.com), Monster (http://www.monster.com), Yahoo! HotJobs (http://hotjobs.yahoo.com), and others.

ENTERTAINMENT PHOTOGRAPHER

CAREER PROFILE

Duties: Creates photographs for publicists and advertisers to promote theaters, nightclubs, concert halls, and other stage settings where audiences pay to be entertained; photographs entertainers for CD covers, postcards, business cards, and headshots

Alternate Title(s): Glamour Photographer, Portrait Photographer

Salary Range: $25,000 to $75,000+

Employment Prospects: Good

Advancement Prospects: Fair

Best Geographical Location(s): Chicago, Hollywood, Los Angeles, Las Vegas, Miami, New York, and San Francisco

Prerequisites:

Education or Training—Two- or four-year degree in photography; training in digital photography and design software programs essential

Experience—Three or more years of experience as portrait photographer in commercial studio

Special Skills and Personality Traits—Solid knowledge of lighting and composition; excellent communication and people skills; professional yet outgoing and friendly; reliable and self-motivated; organized; deadline-oriented

CAREER LADDER

```
┌─────────────────────────────────┐
│   Entertainment Photographer    │
└─────────────────────────────────┘

┌─────────────────────────────────┐
│     Portrait Photographer       │
└─────────────────────────────────┘

┌─────────────────────────────────┐
│    Photographer's Assistant     │
└─────────────────────────────────┘
```

Position Description

Entertainment Photographers work closely with talent agents and entertainers to create photographs for publication in newspapers, magazines, playbills, television, billboards, and other media. Their work is often on display inside and outside theaters, in train and subway cars and stations, and on the sides of buses. Show publicists, advertising agencies, and club owners also hire Entertainment Photographers to photograph performers, including dramatic actors for stage, TV, and film; comedians; cabaret performers; musicians; magicians; circus performers; and many others.

Entertainment Photographers speak either directly with entertainers or with their talent agents to schedule photography sessions. They may be responsible for hiring and scheduling wardrobe, hair, and makeup stylists, as well as photographer's assistants, for the shoots, negotiating the terms of employment and day rates, and overseeing their work. They learn in advance from clients how the photographs will be used and the types of poses and emotions they are expected to capture. Entertainment Photographers normally schedule follow-up meetings with entertainers or their representatives to review the pictures and choose the best images for print. Entertainment Photographers may work out of their own studios or attend performances and photograph entertainers live on stage. They may also attend press conferences to get publicity shots for newspapers and magazines.

Entertainment Photographers are normally freelancers. They are responsible for all aspects of running and maintaining their businesses, including creating company brand identities and promotional literature; researching and contacting prospective clients; creating advertising and marketing campaigns; scheduling appointments, negotiating agreements, and drafting work estimates, budgets, and contracts; invoicing clients; handling bills and tax payments; maintaining photographic equipment and office machinery; stocking office supplies; and networking.

Salaries
Annual salaries for Entertainment Photographers vary depending upon their years of experience, their reputations in the field, and the economy. The entertainment field is driven by the economy and when things are going well and employment is up, people spend more money on luxuries such as plays and concerts. Earnings can range from $20,000 to $75,000 or more. Entertainment Photographers who are smart marketers and know how to effectively network have the potential to secure more work and higher wages.

Employment Prospects
Entertainment Photographers who are located in major cities with numerous theaters and entertainment centers will have good opportunities to find employment. As long as the entertainment field continues to overflow with actors seeking work and auditioning for parts, Entertainment Photographers will be needed for promotional photography purposes. Employment of photographers in general is expected to increase about as fast as the average for all occupations through 2012, according to the *Occupational Outlook Handbook*. Demand for photographers who create portraits should increase as the population grows. Entertainment Photographers who have good connections in the field will have the advantage of securing job referrals and word-of-mouth advertising.

Many photographers include entertainment photography among myriad commercial photographic services available at their studios. They may also offer portrait photography of babies and children, adults and their families, as well as of corporate executives. They may photograph weddings, events, conferences, and banquets. While specializing in a particular niche may benefit some photographers financially, others find that by expanding and rounding out their services, they also increase their employment options and earnings.

Advancement Prospects
Entertainment Photographers are normally independent employees who own their own photography studios. There is no specific career ladder for them to climb. They advance by expanding their studios and adding more photographers with different specializations to their services. If they have worked solely with theater entertainers, they may branch out by photographing writers, musicians, and fitness celebrities.

Depending upon the terms of their agreements with clients, they can license their photographs and sell their work to stock houses. They may also teach in technical and art schools, write articles and columns for industry magazines and newspapers, and write and publish books.

Education and Training
There is no education requirement for Entertainment Photographers, but a two- or four-year degree in photography can provide a solid foundation for their careers. Coursework in lighting and composition, as well as some exposure to theater and the performing arts, is relevant to an Entertainment Photographer's daily work. On-the-job training in portrait photography is also extremely helpful.

Experience, Skills, and Personality Traits
Entertainment Photographers begin their careers as photographer's assistants in commercial photography studios and move on to become portrait, wedding, or event photographers. They work with a diverse group of people, including talent agents, publicists, entertainers, publication managers, and many others, and thus must have excellent interpersonal skills, professionalism, and diplomacy. They can only succeed if they are driven, responsible, reliable, and creative in the ways they market their services to prospective clients and maintain their current client base.

Successful Entertainment Photographers are skilled at making people feel comfortable and natural in front of the camera. Knowing how to bring out the best in people is a critical component in creating images that will best promote the individuals and the shows in which they perform. Entertainment Photographers must be outgoing and personable to enjoy this work. In addition to being technically versed, they are fluent in digital photography and photographic design software, such as Adobe Photoshop. They need these skills to adjust and enhance images for framing, color, and lighting. Entertainment Photographers are motivated, energetic, and responsible. They are adept at juggling shooting schedules, keeping appointments, working well with demanding personalities, and delivering prints to clients on time.

Unions and Associations
Entertainment Photographers can join several associations for networking and career advancement opportunities, such as Advertising Photographers of America, American Society of Media Photographers, and Professional Photographers of America.

Tips for Entry
1. The best way to get into this business and start building important connections is by getting a foot in the door,

sometimes by whatever means possible. Get an internship or assistant position in a commercial photography studio that specializes in entertainment photography.

2. Contact talent agencies to find out the names of Entertainment Photographers they use for their clients' headshots. You can also check playbills to see celebrity photos and photographers who have been credited for the shots. Contact the photographers to see if they need any assistance or if you can volunteer to help during a shoot.

3. Search for employment opportunities on such Web sites as EntertainmentCareers (http://www.entertainment careers.net), Monster (http://www.monster.com), and Yahoo! HotJobs (http://hotjobs.yahoo.com).

4. Read industry publications such as *Backstage Magazine* and check employment listings in the classifieds section.

FASHION PHOTOGRAPHER

CAREER PROFILE

Duties: Photographs designer clothing in studios, on location, at fashion shows and special events for magazines, newspapers, department store advertisements, catalogs, and Web sites; may create images for gallery or museum exhibitions; works closely with publication picture editors, advertising clients, writers, stylists, makeup artists, models, assistants, and others; handles casting sessions; may handle promotion and marketing of photography studio; creates estimates; handles accounts receivable and payable

Alternate Title(s): Lifestyle Photographer

Salary Range: $350 to $2,000+ per day

Employment Prospects: Fair

Advancement Prospects: Fair

Best Geographical Location(s): New York City, Chicago, Los Angeles, and San Francisco; major international cities such as London, Milan, and Paris

Prerequisites:

Education or Training—Bachelor's degree in photography; trained in digital cameras and design software programs (Adobe Photoshop and Illustrator); coursework in fashion design history and advertising beneficial

Experience—Several years of freelance experience as a commercial, portrait, or wedding/event photographer

Special Skills and Personality Traits—Awareness of and appreciation for fashion and popular culture; excellent communication skills; able to work with various people; diplomatic; patient; energetic and creative

CAREER LADDER

```
┌─────────────────────────────────────┐
│        Fashion Photographer          │
└─────────────────────────────────────┘

┌─────────────────────────────────────┐
│  Assistant to Fashion Photographer / │
│    Portrait Photographer Assistant   │
└─────────────────────────────────────┘

┌─────────────────────────────────────┐
│          Studio Assistant            │
└─────────────────────────────────────┘
```

Position Description

Fashion Photographers help designers enhance and promote their work by creating eye-catching images for advertisements and articles in magazines, such as *Harper's Bazaar, Mademoiselle,* or *Vogue,* and newspapers; for billboards; for department store catalogs, inserts, and promotional signage; for television; and for Web sites. They photograph men and women in various designer clothing labels and accessories. Fashion Photographers who work on high-end fashion photography often photograph models and celebrities at design houses, at fashion shows, and on location around the world.

Depending on the size of the studio and the staff, Fashion Photographers may be responsible for handling casting sessions and choosing models. Even if clients are choosing the models, photographers still contribute their thoughts about who they think will work best for the images. Fashion Photographers also hire and book wardrobe, set, and hair stylists, makeup artists, assistants, and other crew as needed. If working with advertising or publishing clients, art directors may either create the sets or make suggestions for the sets. Art or creative directors are typically present during shoots to oversee the work. Throughout the shoot, it is the Fashion

Photographer's responsibility to make sure that art directors and clients are happy with how things are progressing and to discuss and make adjustments should issues arise.

Freelance Fashion Photographers are responsible for managing other aspects of their business. In addition to overseeing office equipment maintenance and making sure they are adequately stocked with office supplies, they handle marketing and promoting their business. They may buy mailing lists and create promotional mailings by hiring designers or doing it themselves. They will contact agencies, publishers, fashion houses, and other prospective clients by telephone or e-mail, set up meetings, and drop off their portfolios and other promotional literature. They will either hire a bookkeeper and accountant to handle their accounts or take care of the accounts receivable and payable themselves. Fashion Photographers may or may not assume any of these tasks based on their annual salaries, size of the studio, and their strengths and interests.

The fashion world transcends time. Designers have the freedom to draw from the past and present in their creations and can imagine and interpret the future in their lines. Fashion Photographers stay tuned into all of the trends and keep abreast of designer news by reading fashion magazines (*Vogue, In Style*), trade publications (*Women's Wear Daily*), and regularly visiting fashion news Web sites.

Salaries

Fashion Photographers' salaries can vary widely, depending upon years of experience, clients' budgets, whether celebrity models are being photographed, how the photography will be used, and more. Fashion Photographers usually charge anywhere from $350 to more than $2,000 per day, plus expenses. Photographers who are celebrities themselves, meaning they are among the top photographers in the field and are known names, can command extremely high day-rates and annual salaries well in excess of $200,000.

Employment Prospects

As in all glamour businesses, the fashion industry is highly competitive and employment prospects are only fair. The notion of working with models, top designers, and advertisers and being part of a trendy world draws more applicants than there are jobs to fill. Word-of-mouth and having connections in the fashion world are the best ways to secure work. Fashion Photographers need at least several years of prior experience as professional photographers to fully grasp how the business works. They also need prior professional work so that they will have *tear sheets* (published magazine pages) to add to their portfolios. Many Fashion Photographers get their first taste of the business by working as studio assistants. Commercial photographers often have the edge in securing jobs because they are experienced in working with products which advertisers and clients are

trying to promote. The skills used in commercial photography are the same as those needed to help promote designer clothing.

Advancement Prospects

Fashion Photographers are at the top of the career ladder in this field. Staff photographers who work in small studios will have few opportunities to advance, whereas the larger studios may have more turnover and offer greater chances for growth. Fashion Photographers can advance by moving to larger studios, expanding into other types of photography (i.e., beauty, entertainment, travel), participating in panel discussions and lecture series, teaching at the university level, and writing articles or books.

Education and Training

Most Fashion Photographers have either a two- or four-year degree in photography. Coursework in art and fashion history and training in digital cameras and design software, such as Adobe Photoshop and Illustrator, are beneficial in this field. On-the-job training as a studio assistant or as an assistant with a wedding photography or event photography team can provide skills that will help later during fashion shoots.

Experience, Skills, and Personality Traits

Fashion Photographers must have several years of commercial photography experience or solid work experience assisting a Fashion Photographer. Because the job is demanding on many levels, Fashion Photographers must have great energy and stamina, as well as multitasking abilities, to keep everyone happy and to meet deadlines. Their job is often more than photographing models; it entails coordinating a great number of details and people. This requires patience, diplomacy, excellent communication skills, wit, and good humor. Fashion Photographers set themselves apart by being as visionary in their approaches to photography as designers are in their creations. To succeed in this business, photographers must be imaginative and creative, as well as technically and technologically versed.

Unions and Associations

There are no associations or unions specifically dedicated to Fashion Photographers. For networking and educational opportunities and other career-enhancing benefits, Fashion Photographers can join such associations as Advertising Photographers of America, American Society of Media Photographers, and Professional Photographers of America.

Tips for Entry

1. Volunteer, get an internship, or assist a Fashion Photographer. If you have even just one connection in the

fashion business, take advantage and contact that person. One of the best ways to get into this fiercely competitive field is through referrals.

2. Make sure your portfolio contains images that are appropriate to the magazines, stores, or advertising agencies you approach. If you have tear sheets of your published work, be sure to include those as well.

3. Read as much as you can about Fashion Photographers. Do an Internet search by keying in *fashion photographer* in Google. Go to the bookstore or library and find biographies and autobiographies about Fash-

ion Photographers. Learn who and what influenced and inspired them, how they approach and solve problems, what kind of lighting and props they use, and anything else you can find.

4. Look through American and European fashion magazines. Pay attention to the stories the fashion advertisements are telling and how the photographers helped tell these stories. Note the differences in composition, layout, and photographic style. And take notes while you are doing this, so you can reference them in the future.

MAGAZINE PHOTOGRAPHER

CAREER PROFILE

Duties: Photographs people, events, products, and more for regional, national, international and trade magazines; attends editorial and art meetings; creates budgets, estimates, and schedules; works closely with editors, writers, art and creative directors, and other magazine staff; responsible for hiring assistants; may be responsible for organizing and archiving photographs

Alternate Title(s): Editorial Photographer, Photojournalist

Salary Range: $15,000 to $50,000+

Employment Prospects: Fair

Advancement Prospects: Fair

Best Geographical Location(s): Atlanta, Boston, Chicago, Dallas, Los Angeles, Miami, New York, San Francisco, and Washington, D.C.

Prerequisites:

Education or Training—Two- or four-year degree in photography or art

Experience—Three or more years of experience as a freelance photographer for a commercial studio

Special Skills and Personality Traits—Excellent communication skills; detail- and deadline-oriented; energetic; organized; professional; flexible attitude; able to travel when needed; strong knowledge of digital photography and design software

CAREER LADDER

```
┌─────────────────────────────┐
│   Magazine Photographer     │
└─────────────────────────────┘

┌─────────────────────────────┐
│   Professional Photographer │
└─────────────────────────────┘

┌─────────────────────────────┐
│   Photographer's Assistant /│
│   Photography Studio Assistant│
└─────────────────────────────┘
```

Position Description

Magazine Photographers help magazines meet their editorial goals by taking photographs as assigned, as well as pitching photographs to accompany articles or to appear as stand-alone stories. Magazine Photographers may work on staff or on a contract or freelance basis. They may photograph people, animals, or various objects in studio sets, in homes, and at locations both locally and internationally. Depending on the slant of the magazine, Magazine Photographers may be assigned to cover events such as weddings, court trials, gala openings of restaurants and stores, concerts, political debates and elections, protests and rallies, sports events, or celebrity appearances. They are adept at working in tranquil environments as well as in areas where there may be strife. Some assignments will be dangerous, which is why most photographers secure appropriate business and personal insurance.

Magazine Photographers may be given only one or two days' notice of their assignment, or they may have long setup times in which they will meet with editors, art directors, and others to discuss the job requirements. Magazine Photographers prepare their budgets and estimates for approval and request cash advances when needed for out-of-pocket expenses. They are careful to keep receipts and records of all of their transactions to include with their invoices and any requests for reimbursement. They are responsible for hiring assistants and other crew (after first securing client approval), coordinating schedules, and overseeing staff during shoots.

Salaries

The median annual salary in 2002 for photographers was $24,040, according to the *Occupational Outlook Handbook.* Photographers who worked for newspapers and periodicals earned slightly higher wages at $31,460. Staff Magazine Photographers may earn higher incomes than freelancers because they do not have the burden of covering their own overhead and expenses (i.e., rent, photography equipment, health insurance). Freelance Magazine Photographers usually charge day rates, which can range anywhere from $500 to $1,000 or more. They will bill for expenses as well as for the type of usage. In other words, if their photograph is used as a full-page cover of a magazine, they will be paid more than if it is used only in the table of contents. The fee scale will depend upon the size, placement, and the frequency of placement in the magazine.

Reuse is another arena in which Magazine Photographers can secure higher incomes. Providing the original contract was for one-time use only and not an all-rights sale, if a photograph has been published in one magazine and is later picked up by a textbook or another magazine, that textbook or magazine publisher must pay for the reuse.

Most Photographers who work in editorial do so for the exposure. While the pay may be less than that of other industries, securing a photo credit line in a magazine with a wide circulation is all-important. Photographers should be sure to include a clause in their contract about credit-line omissions. Many double their fees when their name is not published with their work, with the justification being that they have lost countless opportunities for future jobs and money.

Employment Prospects

Competition is fierce for Magazine Photographer positions. These are highly desirable jobs, and the market is flooded with candidates. According to the *Occupational Outlook Handbook,* employment of photographers overall is expected to grow by only 10 to 20 percent through 2012. Magazine Photographers who have a distinct, unique style and have established reputations as professionals will have the advantage in finding work. Novice photographers can find work at local publications as entry to this field. There they will learn firsthand how to work on assignment, meet deadlines, and effectively collaborate with key editorial and creative staff.

Advancement Prospects

Staff Magazine Photographers can advance to become photography or creative editors, depending upon their skills and years with the magazine. Freelance Magazine Photographers are typically at the top of their field. For them, growth may be taking new and different assignments, covering topics and environments they have not delved into before. They may share their experiences by lecturing at conferences hosted by professional associations and universities, participating in panel discussions, and by also teaching college and continuing education students.

Education and Training

A two- or four-year degree in photography or art is a solid foundation for this type of work. Training in digital photography and design software, such as Adobe Photoshop, is required.

Experience, Skills, and Personality Traits

Magazine Photographers must be interested in the topics they are covering to successfully and accurately capture them. While they must have a distinct style that sets them apart from other photographers, they must also be comfortable with the commissioning magazine's slant and approach in order to meet its creative needs and fit within its parameters. Magazine Photographers will work in any number of places: in their own studios, on sets, and at diverse locations around the world. They must have the energy and stamina to travel and put in long days and odd hours. And regardless of where they work, they must be organized. Either they or their assistants must be able to keep track of shoot schedules, equipment lists, and equipment and accessories for packing. Excellent communication skills, self-motivation, and an ability to inspire trust are key skills needed to succeed in and enjoy this work. Magazine Photographers will not always be photographing under ideal circumstances and will need to call upon local residents for cooperation and assistance during shoots. Diplomacy and tact are also critical.

Unions and Associations

Magazine Photographers can join the American Society of Media Photographers (ASMP), the National Press Photographers Association, and the Professional Photographers of America for educational, employment, and networking opportunities.

Tips for Entry

1. Familiarize yourself with contracts. Understand the terms, the terminology, and the industry standard. Make sure you know all of this and have defined what your *own* work standard is before you sign anything. Professional associations such as ASMP can provide you with contract language and guidance.
2. Put together a portfolio that not only reflects your best work but is also specifically tailored to the magazines you approach.
3. Create a list of the magazines for which you would like to work. Research the names of the photo editors and e-mail or telephone to briefly introduce yourself. See if there is a convenient time to meet or find out the schedule for portfolio drop-offs and pickups.

4. If you drop your portfolio off for review, be sure to get a signed receipt that includes the date and time of your drop-off and the name of the person receiving it. This will be added insurance in case your portfolio gets lost or misplaced.

5. Freelance for local magazines or even magazines published by nonprofit organizations. While the pay may be lower than publications for the mass market, you will gain excellent firsthand experience and have tear sheets to add to your portfolio.

PAPARAZZO

CAREER PROFILE

Duties: Takes candid photographs, often of private moments, of celebrities without their awareness or without their permission; sells photographs to tabloid newspapers and gossip magazines

Alternate Title(s): Celebrity Photographer, Tabloid Photographer

Salary Range: $25,000 to $50,000+

Employment Prospects: Fair

Advancement Prospects: Poor

Best Geographical Location(s): Hollywood, Los Angeles, Miami, New York, San Francisco, and Washington, D.C.

Prerequisites:

Education or Training—Two-year degree in photography; training in digital photography and photographic design software

Experience—Two or more years of experience as a wedding, event, or portrait photographer

Special Skills and Personality Traits—Must be interested in following and photographing celebrities; tenacious, persistent, and thick-skinned; able to work at all hours of day and night to secure shots; patient; must be able to deal with stress, angry people, threatening bodyguards, and, on occasion, physical injuries, lawsuits, and possible jail time

CAREER LADDER

```
┌─────────────────────────────┐
│        Photo Editor         │
└─────────────────────────────┘

┌─────────────────────────────┐
│         Paparazzo           │
└─────────────────────────────┘

┌─────────────────────────────┐
│   Freelance Photographer    │
└─────────────────────────────┘
```

Position Description

A Paparazzo is a photographer who follows celebrities and takes surprise photographs of them while they are in their daily walks of life (i.e., shopping, eating, visiting friends, and so on) or while they are doing something uncharacteristic or looking uncharacteristic. Often their mission is to capture celebrities in embarrassing situations and sell the pictures to publications that thrive on debunking the myths of perfection surrounding stardom. The targets are leading figures in television and film, politics, royalty, the crime world, music, sports, and other high-profile careers.

The plural form of Paparazzo is paparazzi, which means "annoying insect" in Italian. To the famous movie director Frederico Fellini, who coined the phrase, it was synony-

mous with the aggressive, overly determined magazine photographers who besieged his movie studio doorways, waiting to capture new photos of the stars. When limousines arrived, the photographers would chase celebrities down the street just to get their shots.

Paparazzi spend a lot of time in their cars, driving around celebrities' homes and cruising by restaurants, bars, clubs, stores, and salons that celebrities are known to frequent. They travel by whatever means possible to get close to celebrities and wait patiently, sometimes for hours. They camp out in doorways, hide in bushes and trees, and even take rowboats to remote spots. They hunt, or *trawl,* for stars and stories. They hope for a celebrity to step out of a doorway, stroll down a sidewalk, or appear in a storefront. Better yet is if the celebrity appears with someone they are rumored to be romantically involved with. In addition to photographs that add fuel to the gossip fire, the most coveted and highly sought-after photographs are of those celebrities who are extraordinarily private and successful at evading the press.

Some Paparazzi photograph celebrities from a distance, choosing not to intrude on their personal space by using long camera lenses for telephoto close-ups. Others chase celebrities down by foot and by car, causing hazardous situations and angering or scaring celebrities. Emotions can get out of hand in these scenarios, and it is not uncommon for bodyguards or celebrities themselves to take control of the situations by violent measures. Scuffles, fistfights, broken cameras and gear, and more, go with the terrain. Many celebrities issue restraining orders against photographers. For instance, Princess Diana had won a restraining order against one English Paparazzo in the same year she died. The crash that killed her was blamed on a car chase by the Paparazzi.

Celebrity photographers have the power to spread good or bad publicity about celebrities, which is why they have mixed reputations in the photography field and the world at large and why many celebrities hate them.

Salaries

The Paparazzo is a freelance photographer whose annual salary can range from $25,000 to $50,000 or more. Earnings will depend upon the number of photos sold throughout the year, as Paparazzi are only paid when publications buy their work. Depending upon the size of the publication, its circulation, and whether the content is "hot" or not, a single photograph can sell for as low as $35 or as high as $500,000 or more. Tenacious, hard-working paparazzi who are consistently able to be at the right place at the right time will be able to secure higher wages.

Employment Prospects

The celebrity photography field is fiercely competitive. The ratio of photographers to celebrities can be hundreds to one, making it extremely challenging for neophytes entering the business. Photographers need to be living and working where celebrities are, and those photographers who are doggedly committed to their work, to the point of being consumed by it, are usually the ones who take and sell the photographs tabloids want. Employment prospects are best for the determined, aggressive, thick-skinned photographer who knows how to track down the stars and photograph them at just the right time.

Advancement Prospects

Paparazzi are usually freelancers who establish relationships over the years with editors and publishers of a variety of tabloids and celebrity gossip magazines and Web sites. There is no specific career track for them to follow. They can advance to become photo editors of celebrity magazines or start their own tabloids or gossip publications. They can

write articles or columns about their experiences, appear as guest speakers at association conferences, and teach classes.

Education and Training

A two-year degree in photography is a sufficient educational background for a Paparazzo. Photographers must be trained in digital photography and photographic enhancement software, such as Adobe Photoshop.

Experience, Skills, and Personality Traits

Two or more years of experience as a freelance portrait, event, or wedding photographer for a commercial studio is usually helpful in this position. Magazine or newspaper photography experience is also beneficial. Paparazzi need to have solid knowledge of digital and film photography. They need to be passionate about the entertainment world because they will be spending all of their time physically tracking down celebrities. They must love learning about celebrities' lives, their relationships, their successes and failures, their weaknesses and strengths. They must also be extremely knowledgeable about how and where they spend their time. The Paparazzo is usually not welcomed with open arms. He or she must be able to deflect the negatives in order to maintain a livelihood. He or she must be able to deal with being yelled at, threatened, and even sometimes assaulted. This is a tough, uncomfortable job, and it takes a certain personality to enjoy the challenges and thrive in the work. Aggressive, persistent, sharp individuals who can consistently be at the front of the crowd before the competition arrives have the best chances to succeed in this business.

Unions and Associations

There are no associations specifically for Paparazzi. The American Society of Media Photographers, National Press Photographers Association, and Professional Photographers of America can provide useful benefits to help enhance their careers.

Tips for Entry

1. Visit your local supermarket or newsstand and buy all of the tabloids on sale. Peruse them and see the types of photographs they are publishing.
2. Read celebrity magazines like *People, Us Weekly,* and *Entertainment Weekly.* Stay in the loop on celebrity news (i.e., family issues, relationships, and upcoming projects). The only way to know who is important to photograph and who is in the spotlight is by keeping up with the magazines the fans are reading.
3. Look for a video or DVD of the MTV show, "The Assignment with Iann Robinson: Paparazzi," which aired in 2003. Rock journalist Robinson investigated the trade by spending time with celebrity photographers and Paparazzi photographers and shedding light on the distinction between the two.

PHOTOJOURNALIST

CAREER PROFILE

Duties: Helps document history by photographing news items such as courtroom trials, accidents, arrests of criminals, events surrounding wars, protests and rallies, presidents and political figures, and more, for print and online newspapers, wire services, magazines, television networks, and the Internet; often travels and works on locations around the world; may also write stories to accompany photographs; works closely with editors and photography directors

Alternate Title(s): Documentary Photographer, News Photographer

Salary Range: $27,600 to $75,000+

Employment Prospects: Fair

Advancement Prospects: Fair

Best Geographical Locations: New York, London, Berlin, Paris, Rome, and other large cities that are home to major news outlets

Prerequisite:

Education or Training—Bachelor's degree in photography, with coursework in communications, journalism, and history; trained in digital photography and photographic design software

Experience—Three or more years of experience as a newspaper or magazine photographer

Special Skills and Personality Traits—Knowledgeable about digital photographic technology and software; self-determined; intellectually curious; diplomatic and professional; culturally aware; multilingual skills beneficial; strong communication skills; able to interact with a variety of people on many different levels; energetic, with great stamina to work long days and nights; physically fit

CAREER LADDER

```
┌─────────────────────────────────────┐
│  Director of Photography / Editor    │
└─────────────────────────────────────┘

┌─────────────────────────────────────┐
│          Photojournalist             │
└─────────────────────────────────────┘

┌─────────────────────────────────────┐
│ Magazine or Newspaper Photographer   │
└─────────────────────────────────────┘
```

Position Description

Photojournalists photograph breaking news, individuals, and issues for newspapers, magazines, wire services, and broadcast networks. Their work appears in print and on the Internet. Some Photojournalists cover local news within their community, where they photograph meetings and press conferences at city halls, as well as school functions, concerts, plays, street and highway accidents, weather-related events, and other issues that impact people within the community. Other Photojournalists may travel around the world and specialize in covering international events, such as political elections, protests and rallies, cultural stories, and wars, often risking their lives to help people see what is happening beyond their backyards.

Photojournalists tell stories with their pictures and often enlighten the world to important issues. They are freelancers or staff employees. They work on assignment, come up with their own ideas and pitch them to editors, or fund their own trips and pitch photographs and stories afterward. Their work also frequently inspires outrage and change. W. Eugene Smith's photographs from the 1970s documented innumerable villagers harmed by mercury poisoning in Minamata, Japan, where a factory was dumping chemicals into the water, causing birth deformities and physiological damages. Smith's photographs helped the cause of the victims, who were eventually compensated. Lewis W. Hine's photographs of children working in cotton mills and coal mines contributed to social efforts that culminated in passage of the Child Labor Act of 1916. The work of Jacob Riis, beginning in 1889, depicted the awful conditions of New York city slums of the period and led to direct action by Theodore Roosevelt, who was then the New York City police commissioner, and later efforts to improve living conditions.

Today Photojournalists work with 35-millimeter cameras, a variety of lenses, and lighting gear. They are increasingly working with digital photography and downloading their images directly into computers. They develop their own film manually or with film-processing machines and scan the negatives into computers to create digital files. Many Photojournalists work alone and are responsible for everything, including promoting their services, booking assignments and negotiating contracts, handling travel arrangements and creating equipment packing lists, securing permissions and licenses to photograph in public places, and invoicing clients and handling the bookkeeping.

Salaries

Photojournalists earn salaries ranging from $27,600 to $75,000 or more, depending upon the medium in which they work and their years of experience. Other determining factors include the size of the publication or broadcast network and geographical location. According to the 2002 Radio-Television News Directors Association and Foundation (RTNDA)/Ball State University survey, TV photographers earned starting salaries of $26,600. A city-based Photojournalist with a bachelor's degree in mass communications or journalism and five years of experience in the field can earn an average salary of $34,900, as cited in PayScale (http://www.payscale.com). Many staff Photojournalists freelance, also, and enhance their incomes by selling photographs to other media.

Employment Prospects

Competition is keen for Photojournalist positions. There are not enough positions to keep up with the masses of people interested in this field. The Department of Labor's *Occupational Outlook Handbook* does not cite statistical information for Photojournalists specifically, but does state that employment of news analysts, reporters, and correspondents is expected to grow more slowly than the average for all occupations through the year 2012. This lag in growth is expected to result from newspapers and broadcast networks merging, consolidating, and closing. As online magazines and newspapers grow, so, too, will Photojournalist and other news-related positions. Because the work can be heavily taxing, some positions will open up as Photojournalists burn out and move into other fields or simply retire. There may be greater opportunities for work with local, small newspapers and broadcast networks.

Advancement Prospects

With years of experience, Photojournalists can advance to become directors of photography or editors, depending upon their strengths and interests. They can move to larger publications and better-known networks. If they have not done so before, they can become feature article writers and columnists. Photojournalists can share their experiences by participating in industry conferences and gatherings as guest speakers, and they can teach at the university level.

Education and Training

A four-year degree in photography, journalism, or mass communications is preferred for the position. Education in press law and ethics is of utmost importance. Hands-on training in digital photography, photographic design software, and technology is recommended. Some publications and networks offer training or financial assistance and reimbursement for workshops.

Experience, Skills, and Personality Traits

To successfully handle the responsibilities and challenges of this position, Photojournalists must have at least three or more years of prior experience as newspaper or news magazine photographers. They must be passionate about their work and aware that their presence can actually influence events. While committed to taking pictures that communicate stories truthfully and fully, they know when to draw the line on risks they are willing to take. Photojournalists must know how to stay calm in all situations and be able to work efficiently, creatively, and with technical accuracy under deadline pressure. Technical and technological proficiency are critical skills in photojournalism, more so now than ever before. Photojournalists can be in a jungle, the desert, at sea, or in the mountains, equipped with digital cameras, computers, and cell phones. They must know how to coordinate every piece of equipment and be versed in software programs in order to deliver quality pictures to publishers. Travel is an intrinsic part of photojournalism, and Photojournalists need to be flexible, organized, and adaptable to change. They must be ready to go at the drop of a hat. They often travel to different countries and are immersed in a wide variety of cultures. Sensitivity to and respect for people and cultural practices are important. Multilingual abilities can also be extremely helpful in this field. Photojournalists also need to be physically fit to carry heavy camera gear and have stamina to work long days and nights, either indoors or outside, in all weather conditions.

Unions and Associations

Photojournalists can join the online group AmericanPhotojournalist (http://www.americanphotojournalist.com) for access to message boards, employment listings, photography critiques, and self-promoting portfolio options. They may also join the American Press Institute, American Society of Media Photographers, National Press Photographers Association, and the White House News Photographers' Association for employment referrals, information on business and negotiating practices, networking opportunities, updates on copyright laws, and more. Some publications may require Photojournalists to belong to unions such as the Newspaper Guild.

Tips for Entry

1. *Life* magazine is rich in photojournalism and an excellent resource for Photojournalists of all levels. You can find scores of issues at your local library. Study the work of W. Eugene Smith, Margaret Bourke-White, and many others. Learn the subjects they covered and how they chose to photograph those subjects. Treat this study as you would a class—take detailed notes for future reference.

2. Set up informational interviews with photographers who work at newspapers in your city. Buy them coffee or lunch, have a list of questions prepared, and ask them their top-three recommendations for ways to get into this field. And if possible, have several different photographers look at your portfolio and critique it for content and presentation.

3. Intern at a magazine, newspaper, or television station. Many Photojournalists get their foot in the door this way. They develop their skills, then work their way up to positions of greater responsibility at larger publications and networks.

4. Word of mouth is often the best way to get work in this field. Join professional associations, take workshops, and attend parties and events. Network as much as you can. Join Mediabistro (http://www.mediabistro.com), a group that caters to media professionals. They offer a variety of workshops, industry gatherings, and professional benefits and can help photojournalists connect with editors and writers.

5. Look for job listings online at JournalismJobs.com (http://www.journalismjobs.com), Monster (http://www.monster.com), Yahoo! Hotjobs (http://hotjobs.yahoo.com), as well as the classifieds at the New York Times on the Web (http://www.nytimes.com). Stay tuned to what is going on in the field by subscribing to magazines such as *Aperture* and *The Digital Journalist*. Regularly visit industry-related Internet sites such as Poynter Online (http://www.poynter.org) and World Press Photo (http://www.worldpressphoto.nl).

PRESS PHOTOGRAPHER

CAREER PROFILE

Duties: Photographs events and people for news coverage in newspapers, magazines, wire services; works locally, nationally, and internationally, depending upon assignments; works closely with photography directors, editors, and reporters; edits digital images, creates captions, and submits work to editors via the Internet

Alternate Title(s): News Photographer

Salary Range: $25,000 to $50,000

Employment Prospects: Fair

Advancement Prospects: Good

Best Geographical Location(s): Major cities and communities with newspapers and media centers

Prerequisites:

Education or Training—Two- or four-year degree, specialization in photography or journalism, with training in digital photography and photographic design software such as Adobe Photoshop

Experience—Two or three years of prior news photography, sports photography, or event photography helpful but not always required

Special Skills and Personality Traits—Strong interest in current events and news coverage; excellent visual-reporting skills; deadline-oriented; self-motivated and energetic; comfortable working under stress and in often chaotic, hectic environments; excellent verbal and written communication skills; organized; technologically savvy; adaptable; fast learner

CAREER LADDER

```
┌─────────────────────────────┐
│     Chief Photographer       │
└─────────────────────────────┘

┌─────────────────────────────┐
│      Press Photographer      │
└─────────────────────────────┘

┌─────────────────────────────┐
│    Freelance Photographer    │
└─────────────────────────────┘
```

Position Description

Press Photographers take photographs of breaking news for various media, including newspapers, magazines, and wire services. Depending upon their assignments, they cover local events or international issues. They photograph car accidents, fires, crime scenes, protests, rallies, charity events, sports, street fairs, political figures giving speeches, celebrities on the town, people at beaches and parks, and others. Their photographs are used to help illustrate written articles, or they may be published as stand-alone images, not needing much explanation beyond a short caption. Press Photographers may

also create images outside of the assignment, if they see something that they sense is newsworthy. These images may inspire photography directors and news editors to develop stories and photography projects.

Freelance Press Photographers often listen to police scanners so that they can be the first to hear about local stories that can make for headline news, such as a robbery in progress, a murder that has just occurred, or a fire in an apartment building with people needing to be rescued. They will gather their gear and race to the scene to photograph the events as they unfold. These spontaneous stories cannot be assigned and are often covered by freelance as opposed to staff Press Photographers.

Many Press Photographers use digital cameras and Wi-Fi technology to deliver their work. It is particularly helpful to photographers who are on location and need to send large image files quickly and efficiently. Many newsrooms also have file transfer protocol (FTP) sites that enable the transfer of digital files into password-protected Web servers.

Salaries

Press Photographers can earn annual salaries ranging from $25,000 to $50,000 or more, depending upon the size of the corporation, the newspaper's circulation, and the geographical location. Many Press Photographers work as full-time employees. Sometimes newspapers provide them with photographic equipment and company cars or reimbursement for travel. They often receive benefits that freelance photographers must pay for themselves, such as medical, dental, life, and equipment insurance. Press Photographers who work for large corporations such as the Associate Press and Reuters may be able to secure higher wages. A *stringer* is another type of Press Photographer. He or she usually works on assignment and has established a relationship with a news editor. Stringers are usually paid per photography project and do not receive staff employment benefits. Freelance news photographers are those who pitch unsolicited photographs for publication. They are paid only upon publication and are often paid rates based on the size of the space in which the photographs will be printed. The larger the print size, the more they will be paid.

Employment Prospects

The press photography field is competitive, but there should be good opportunities for employment with smaller publications across the country. Employment of photographers overall is expected to grow about as fast as the average for all occupations through 2012, according to the U.S. Department of Labor. As more magazines, journals, and newspapers move onto the Internet, more photographers will be needed to create digital images. Press Photographers will also find openings as other photographers move to less stressful positions, open their own studios, or retire.

Advancement Prospects

Normally after five or more years of daily newspaper experience, full-time Press Photographers can advance to become senior photographers. They can eventually take on more office-bound managerial responsibilities by becoming photography directors, overseeing other photographers, assigning projects, and working on layout. Press Photographers who have excellent writing skills and an interest in reporting can move in the photojournalism direction and become photographers/reporters and eventually senior correspondents.

Education and Training

A four-year degree in photography or journalism, with training in digital photography and color and image-enhancement systems (i.e. Adobe Photoshop), is recommended in this position. College graduates who worked on college newspapers as sports or campus event photographers are often solid candidates for entry-level photography positions at newspapers and media companies.

Experience, Skills, and Personality Traits

Many newspapers and media corporations prefer Press Photographers with one to two years of experience as photographers with daily publications. Those companies hiring more junior-level photographers will normally accept candidates with college degrees and portfolios that show their abilities to tell stories visually. Press Photographers must love the news. They must be passionate about what is happening in the world and clever about the ways they photograph stories. Press Photographers must be ready at any given moment to travel to news sites. There is a tremendous amount of stress in this job. They need to be able to react quickly and capture the stories while there is still something to tell. It requires a great deal of racing around, so flexibility, stamina, and patience are critical. Unless they have access to a company car, they must have their own form of reliable transportation and be prepared with the right photographic and computer equipment for on-location shoots. They must also have excellent interpersonal skills because they work with a variety of people, from reporters and photography directors to police and fire officials and others, as well as the general public. Professionalism, diplomacy, and sensitivity are key components in this position.

Unions and Associations

Press Photographers join the National Press Photographers Association, the American Society of Media Photographers, and the Professional Photographers of America for educational resources, employment referrals, networking opportunities, and discounts on photographic equipment and insurance.

Tips for Entry

1. Get an internship with a newspaper, news magazine, or wire service.
2. Before you start hunting for work, make sure your portfolio best represents your work in press photography and that you have a print and electronic portfolio on CD or online as options for prospective clients.

3. Check for job listings on the Internet at such Web sites as JournalismJobs.com (http://www.journalismjobs.com) and the National Press Photographers Association's site (http://www.nppa.org).

4. Visit the Web sites of media corporations and look through their employment sections for in-house positions. Such companies as Gannett, New York Times, Tribune, Knight Ridder, Media General, and others list photography jobs throughout the nation.

SPORTS PHOTOGRAPHER

CAREER PROFILE

Duties: Provides photographs of a wide variety of games and sports events and the athletes for newspapers, magazines, Web sites, and wire services; travels to various locations to cover games, practices, and training sessions; works closely with editors and reporters

Alternate Title(s): Athletics Photographer, Team Photographer

Salary Range: $20,000 to $50,000+

Employment Prospects: Good

Advancement Prospects: Fair

Best Geographical Location(s): Cities where professional games are played and where teams train

Prerequisites:

   Education or Training—Two- or four-year degree in photography; training in digital photography and design software programs

   Experience—Sports Photographer for college newspaper or yearbook; several years of prior experience as a photographer, preferably for daily newspaper or sports magazine; some prior experience as an athlete helpful but not required

   Special Skills and Personality Traits—In-depth knowledge of sports; able to take action shots at the right moments; motivated, energetic, and enthusiastic; thick-skinned and aggressive; works well in highly charged environments, with constant pressure; technologically skilled; attentive; extremely focused

CAREER LADDER

```
┌─────────────────────────────┐
│    Sports Photographer      │
└─────────────────────────────┘

┌─────────────────────────────┐
│    Freelance Photographer   │
└─────────────────────────────┘

┌─────────────────────────────┐
│   Photographer's Assistant  │
└─────────────────────────────┘
```

Position Description

Many consider sports photography to be a dream job because it has a number of positives. For one, most athletes and fans alike welcome Sports Photographers to help tell their stories and share their enthusiasm and energy. Photographers who are sports fanatics can get to know the players and coaches, particularly of their favorite teams. And the icing on the cake is that Sports Photographers take pictures of people living out *their* dreams, rising to the challenges, and enjoying themselves for the most part, regardless of how the game is going.

Sports Photographers are on the sidelines of games and take photographs of athletes, coaches, referees and umpires, stadium officials, and the fans. Their photographs are published in newspapers and magazines, such as the *New York Times* and the *New York Post, ESPN,* and *Sports Illustrated.* Their images also appear in online news outlets such as Reuters or Yahoo! and are sent to wire services such as the Associated Press and United Press International for worldwide distribution. Sports Photographers photograph baseball, basketball, football, hockey, soccer, tennis, swim and track meets, marathons, road races, skiing, snowboarding, skateboarding, surfing, boxing, martial arts, golf, and more. They attend games and training and practice sessions throughout the year and photograph in all types of weather. They photograph national events such as the Super Bowl and World Series and international events such as the Olympic Games and the Tour de France. Some Sports Photographers specialize in certain sports, such as track and field or football, and become known for their expertise in those arenas.

Sports Photographers work closely with editors and reporters. They use digital cameras with long telephoto lenses, laptops, and satellite phones and are able to transmit images immediately to their editors via a range of wireless technologies. In fact a growing number of stadiums have set up permanent high-speed networks that Sports Photographers can access for the fastest transmissions. With this technology, pictures can be posted onto sports Web sites within five minutes or less.

Salaries

Sports Photographers' annual salaries vary between $20,000 and $50,000 or more, depending upon the size and circulation of the publication or company for which they work. Large newspapers and major publications normally pay higher salaries, particularly to experienced photographers. Some companies allot certain amounts of money to Sports Photographers for cameras and equipment, but many photographers who are new to the field will initially have to cover these expenses themselves and provide their own equipment. While the salaries may be modest, Sports Photographers do enjoy such benefits as access to major sports events, often the best seats at games, the continual opportunity to be accidentally tackled by their favorite players and stars, as well as travel to different parts of the country and the world. Depending upon their contracts with companies, Sports Photographers can also augment their salaries by selling their images to stock agencies and licensing their work.

Employment Prospects

Sports photography is an incredibly competitive field because many people want this job. Very few staff Sports Photographer positions exist, and there are hundreds of applicants for those few opportunities that happen to arise. Newspaper mergers, consolidations, and closures have made the quest for employment more challenging. According to the Department of Labor, employment of reporters and other related positions is expected to grow more slowly than the average for all occupations through 2012. Employment of Sports Photographers draws a close parallel to that of newspaper and magazine reporters. Sports Photographers will have good chances of finding freelance work and opportunities, however, at online newspapers and magazines and at suburban newspapers and publications.

Sports Photographers travel heavily in their work, particularly between March and June. They work days, evenings, and weekends in a variety of capacities. They may be employees, stringers, or freelancers for newspapers or magazines. They may work for companies that sell sports photographs to the media or for companies that produce sports cards. They may also be employed as press photographers with a specialization in sports, or they may work for professional sports leagues or teams in the capacity of official photographer.

Advancement Prospects

Advancement comes primarily through rising toward the top of the field and photographing high-profile games and players and major sporting events. Sports Photographers who have excellent writing and reporting skills and some experience in journalism can move into other areas of sports coverage. They can become sports announcers or sports writers. They can start their own sports Web sites or magazines and hire other photographers to cover specific sports. Depending upon their agreements with the publications for which they have photographed, they can sell and license their images to stock photography agencies.

Education and Training

A two- or four-year degree in photography, or communications with training in photography, is recommended. Many Sports Photographers photographed sports and events for their college newspapers and yearbooks. Training in digital photography and photographic design software is critical to the position. Photographers can also take sports photography workshops, often offered by individuals already in the field.

Experience, Skill, and Personality Traits

Sports Photographers often develop a love for this field from their college-day experiences photographing games and athletes for their school newspapers and yearbooks. Photographers who are passionate about sports and deeply knowledgeable about the games and players they are covering are more likely to take better action shots. Once the game starts, they need to be completely tuned into what is going on. They have to follow the ball or the puck, the runs, the scores, the baskets, the flags on the field, all of it. This job requires complete immersion, focus, and the ability to know the right moment to take the shot. Some publications and companies may also require Sports Photographers to write captions to accompany the images, so strong writing skills will be beneficial. Sports Photographers work indoors and outside, so they must be flexible and prepared both physically and equipment- and gear-wise to deal with all types of conditions. Additionally, Sports Photographers—freelancers in particular—must be able to purchase all of the equipment and gear they need to do this job effectively and deliver quality images at professional standards.

Unions and Associations

Staff Sports Photographers for metropolitan newspapers and national magazines may be required to become union members in unions such as the Communication Workers of America, depending upon the structure of the publications. Sports Photographers may also belong to the National Press Photographers Association and Professional Photographers of America, which offer conventions, educational seminars, membership publications, employment referrals, and other benefits.

Tips for Entry

1. Internships are an excellent way to get started in the sports photography field. Get an internship at a newspaper, sports magazine, or Web site or with a wire service such as Associated Press. Be patient, flexible, and keep a positive attitude. Your work may be entry level, but you will have the unique opportunity to be at games and observe firsthand how the job is done.

2. Subscribe to and read the magazines and newspapers that publish sports photographs. Subscribe to Robert Hanashiro's newsletter *Sports Shooter* and visit the Web site http://www.sportsshooter.com to learn more about the business. Hanashiro is a staff Sports Photographer for *USA Today*.

3. Attend local school games on your own and practice photographing the players and fans. You can go to soccer matches, high school basketball games, or little league games and get a sense of the type of equipment you will need and the skills required to take shots of the players in action. You can also use these photographs to get paying work from local newspapers.

PHOTOGRAPHY BUSINESS AND RELATED JOBS

CAMERA DESIGNER

CAREER PROFILE

Duties: Designs cameras and photographic equipment for camera manufacturers, such as Canon, Nikon, and so on; works closely with design and engineering teams and clients, reviews camera designs, alters designs to enhance and improve product performance or appearance, and creates new designs to meet customer needs; creates designs by hand, as sketches, and uses clays, plastics, and other materials to create models of the products; uses computer-aided design (CAD) software

Alternate Title(s): Camera Engineer, Industrial Designer

Salary Range: $28,820 to $82,130+

Employment Prospects: Good

Advancement Prospects: Good

Best Geographical Location(s): Major industrial manufacturing areas

Prerequisites:

Education or Training—Bachelor of Science in industrial design or engineering; coursework in photography, sketching, advertising, and marketing

Experience—Three or more years of experience as an apprentice to a camera designer

Special Skills and Personality Traits—Knowledgeable about CAD software; creative; mathematical; excellent problem solver; able to work well on a team and independently; clear communication skills; good listener; detail-oriented and organized; strong interest in photography, cameras, and camera features; excellent design sensibilities and aesthetic taste

CAREER LADDER

```
┌─────────────────────────────────────┐
│  Senior Designer / Design Supervisor │
└─────────────────────────────────────┘

┌─────────────────────────────────────┐
│          Camera Designer             │
└─────────────────────────────────────┘

┌─────────────────────────────────────┐
│     Apprentice Camera Designer       │
└─────────────────────────────────────┘
```

Position Description

Camera Designers work closely with camera and photographic equipment manufacturers to enhance and improve camera and equipment designs, as well as to create new products to help grow the customer base. Camera Designers may change such aspects as the product's color and shape, the locations of specific features or their size, shape, and color. They can also impact the cost of the product and the efficiency of production by altering the types of materials used in creating the product. They may also be asked to review and take into account findings from market research and customer surveys when creating their designs. Camera Designers take into account the end use, whether the camera will be used by the layperson for snapshots of a family picnic or by a dentist for pictures of a molar. They may specialize in particular camera brands and models or types of cameras and photographic equipment. Designers can change every aspect of a camera, thereby affecting how photographers use and experience the cameras. For instance, Canon cameras focus in completely different ways from how Nikons focus, due to design decisions. Designers have more influence than many people realize.

Camera manufacturers hire Camera Designers to make products easier to use and more appealing to clients, with the main purposes being to meet customers' needs and increase sales. They may create completely new cameras or rework original designs to improve certain features. Camera Designers either work independently or as members of design teams. Clients provide product specifications and other data to support the designs they seek. Each Camera Designer approaches the work differently. Some may start by creating lists of ideas, then sketching out their thoughts by hand. Others may go directly to computers and create spreadsheets of design specifications and proposed production materials and use computer-aided design software (CAD) or computer-aided industrial design software (CAID) to create their designs. Tools of their trade can range from pens, pencils, inks, and watercolors for sketches, to clay, plastic, and wood for models. Some designers may be responsible for also providing costs for various design features and materials, which they usually first discuss with project leaders to secure approvals. Camera Designers will test their designs and make adjustments as needed. They may also be responsible for presenting their designs and product models, as well as budgets and schedules, to clients.

Camera Designers who work independently are responsible for managing all aspects of their business. In addition to promoting their services and negotiating and securing contracts, they may hire and oversee staff, handle accounts receivable and payable, make sure appropriate tax forms are filed, and maintain computer equipment and photographic and CAD software.

Salaries

Camera Designers can earn annual salaries ranging from as low as $28,820 to $82,130 or higher, depending upon their years of experience in the field and the types of manufacturers for whom they work. In 2002, industrial and commercial designers earned an average of $52,260 per year, according to the U.S. Department of Labor's *Occupational Outlook Handbook,* with about half earning between $39,240 and $67,430. Freelance Camera Designers normally work for various clients, usually under nondisclosure agreements, as the information is proprietary. They base their fees on estimated time frames to accomplish the work and usually charge one set price for the entire project.

Employment Prospects

Employment of Camera Designers is expected to grow about as fast as the average, or by about 10 to 20 percent, for all occupations through 2012, according to the U.S. Department of Labor. There is an increased interest in products that are convenient, ergonomic, and easy to use. Aiding this rise is the proliferation of digital cameras and continually improving technology. More consumers are using digital cameras and digital photographic equipment, and, as a result, more Camera Designers will be needed to improve and enhance camera designs.

Advancement Prospects

Staff Camera Designers can advance by taking on more complex projects and overseeing larger staff. Manufacturers can promote them to senior Camera Designers and heads of camera design divisions. Freelance Camera Designers may advance by increasing their client base, hiring more staff, and teaching in design and engineering schools. Some may enhance their skills and marketability by taking classes and securing more advanced degrees in specific areas of design and engineering.

Education and Training

Camera Designers must have, at minimum, a bachelor of science degree in industrial design or electrical engineering, depending upon design specialization. Some companies may require master's degrees. Coursework in advertising, marketing, sketching, and photography is highly recommended. On-the-job training as an apprentice to a camera designer is also highly recommended, as is training in CAD and CAID software.

Experience, Skills, and Personality Traits

Several years of experience as a camera designer apprentice or assistant are a solid background for this position. Camera Designers need to understand how cameras work from the photographer's perspective in order to improve designs and usability, so photography experience or experience working with photographers is extremely beneficial. The ability to work well on teams as well as independently is critical. To succeed in this field, strong written and verbal communication skills, coupled with excellent design, mathematical, and engineering abilities are essential. Camera Designers are patient, diligent, flexible, and curious. They love to experiment and come up with the most aesthetically pleasing products that perform best. If a design must be scrapped, they are ready and willing to get back to the drawing board and start over until they get it right.

Unions and Associations

Camera Designers can become members of the Industrial Designers Society of America (IDSA) and the International Council of Societies of Industrial Design for educational resources, networking opportunities, international news and events, and more. Women designers can join the Association of Women Industrial Designers for news about industrial and product designs, membership newsletters and magazines, and workshops and conferences. Camera Designers can also find useful information about contests, design tips and techniques, manufacturing issues, and peer interviews, on IDFuel (http://www.idfuel.com), an industrial design Weblog.

Tips for Entry

1. Get an internship or apprenticeship with a camera manufacturer. You can find job listings directly on camera manufacturer Web sites and by checking postings on such employment placement sites as Yahoo! Hotjobs (http://hotjobs.yahoo.com) and the New York Times on the Web (http://www.nytimes.com).

2. Stay tuned into what is going on in the area you plan to specialize in and keep abreast of the product design world overall by joining professional associations, such as the IDSA, and reading trade publications, such as *Design Diffusion, ID Magazine,* and *Industrial Equipment News.*

3. Create a portfolio of design work that is tailored to the companies to which you apply and the products you are most interested in designing. Make sure you have your work in a variety of formats, from electronic files to a traditional print portfolio. You never know which format you may be asked to submit, and it is better to be prepared in advance than scrambling to get it together at the last minute.

PHOTO EDITOR

CAREER PROFILE

Duties: Creates the overall look of photographs in books, magazines, periodicals, and Web sites; chooses photographers, assigns projects, reviews photographs, requests adjustments, selects final photos, and makes sure deadlines are met and invoices paid

Alternate Title(s): None

Salary Range: $44,522 to $59,298+

Employment Prospects: Good

Advancement Prospects: Good

Best Geographical Location(s): Major cities, such as Atlanta, Boston, Chicago, Dallas, Los Angeles, Miami, New York, San Francisco, and Washington, D.C.

Prerequisites:

Education or Training—Bachelor's degree in photography recommended; training in photographic design software beneficial (i.e., Adobe Photoshop and Illustrator).

Experience—Several years of experience as assistant photo editor recommended; editorial or magazine photography background an advantage

Special Skills and Personality Traits—Good visual eye; strong knowledge of lighting and composition; strong interest in and familiarity with the publications' editorial philosophy and goals

CAREER LADDER

```
┌─────────────────────────────────────┐
│           Photo Editor              │
└─────────────────────────────────────┘

┌─────────────────────────────────────┐
│  Magazine or Editorial Photographer │
└─────────────────────────────────────┘

┌─────────────────────────────────────┐
│      Assistant Photographer /       │
│      Assistant Photo Editor         │
└─────────────────────────────────────┘
```

Position Description

Photo Editors work closely with art directors and editorial directors, as well as with writers, reporters, copy editors, and executive staff, to create the overall look of publications and Web sites. Advertising agencies, magazine and book publishing companies, newspapers, photo stock agencies, greeting card companies, and many others retain Photo Editors to help them select the photographic images that are most effective in promoting and selling their services.

Photo Editors attend editorial and art department staff meetings to discuss projects and bounce ideas around. They discuss editorial content, themes (if any), and the look and feel that is being sought. If they have photographers and certain images in mind, they share their thoughts with the head of the project, which may be the editorial director, creative director, art director, or the publisher. Once a direction and specifics are agreed upon, Photo Editors choose the photographers for specific assignments, based on their specialties. For instance, if their client is a fashion magazine, they will select fashion photographers to cover certain stories for the publication. If it is a sports magazine and the article is about football, they will choose a sports photographer who is known for excellent football coverage. In their role as Photo Editors, they do not take photographs but rely on their photography backgrounds in making decisions about the photographers and the images they use. They negotiate photographers' fees on behalf of their clients, provide photographers with contracts and any releases or permissions that may be needed for shoots, and set deadlines for final submission of work.

Photographers submit their work to the Photo Editors, who review the images to make sure the requirements of the assignment have been met. If anything needs to be reshot, they contact the photographer to discuss the issues, terms, and time frame. Photo Editors may ask photographers to adjust images, composition, or lighting by using Adobe Photoshop or whatever photographic design software they may have. Or, Photo Editors may adjust the images themselves, enhancing light, cropping shadows, and deleting or adding objects. Photo Editors tasked with creating realistic images are careful not to stray too far from the original. If they are under time constraints, Photo Editors may secure photos from stock agencies. Most agencies have online photo libraries. Photo Editors can peruse by subject, choose, and purchase images that match the style and size required within a matter of minutes.

Photo Editors may work with assistants and a publication's creative staff and will be responsible for delegating and overseeing their work. Depending upon the size of the company for which they work, they may also be responsible for maintaining photography libraries (online and hard copies), keeping track of invoices and paperwork, and ordering and maintaining supplies, photographic design software, and equipment.

Salaries

Photo Editors' salaries can vary widely, depending upon the types of clients for which they work and their budgets. Major media, such as advertising agencies and corporations, typically pay higher salaries than publishing and editorial companies. In 2003, according to Salary.com, the median annual income for Photo Editors ranged from less than $44,522 to more than $59,298. Full-time, salaried Photo Editors usually have such benefits as group health insurance, disability, and stock options, as well as paid vacation and sick time, and bonuses. Freelance Photo Editors have the potential to earn higher wages, providing they have solid backgrounds and strong self-promotion and networking skills. But they will have to allot monies for business expenses and health insurance.

Employment Prospects

The job outlook for editors overall is fairly bright. Employment is expected to increase by about 10 to 20 percent through 2012, which is as fast as the average for all professions, according to the *Occupational Outlook Handbook*. The Photo Editor field interests far more people than there are jobs to fill, however, so keen competition will continue. The good news is that magazine publications are on the rise, as are corporate and organizational newsletters and Web sites, all of which will require Photo Editors to choose and manage the photography. Photo Editors can secure work with government agencies and nonprofit organizations, to help with their publications and Web sites, as well as take on freelance jobs through, or work on staff with, stock photo agencies.

Advancement Prospects

Photo Editors who work for large publications can advance by becoming senior and eventually chief Photo Editors, managing and overseeing staff and taking on more complex responsibilities. Freelance Photo Editors can advance by expanding their client base, diversifying their business, and writing for various publications, as well as by speaking and lecturing at schools and events hosted by professional associations.

Education and Training

A bachelor's degree in photography, with coursework in advertising and publishing, provides a solid educational background for Photo Editors. Some knowledge of graphic design is also beneficial. Photo Editors will work in different media and must be technologically savvy to meet clients' needs. It is to their advantage if they are well versed in photographic design software, such as Adobe Photoshop, Illustrator, Apple iPhoto, among others, and if they keep abreast of new and developing technology.

Experience, Skills, and Personality Traits

Several years of experience as an assistant photo editor with a publishing company or corporation is looked upon favorably. A commercial photography background or some professional photography experience is extremely helpful. Photo Editors can refer to their photography experiences when choosing photographers for assignments and discussing the intricacies of the projects. Photo Editors who understand the basics of design and have a grasp of the printing and publishing process stand out in the field. Knowledge of photography and photographic techniques is required, as is the ability to visualize and plan photos and layouts that work with the publication and achieve the clients' goals. Photo Editors spin many plates and must be organized and able to keep track of schedules and details to successfully meet deadlines and prevent everything from crashing. They work closely with various people, from staff members to outside consultants, thus excellent, clear communication skills are frequently called upon. They must be good managers and be equally adept at working with teams as well as working independently.

Unions and Associations

Photo Editors join such associations as the American Society of Media Photographers and Professional Photographers of America for employment referrals and career-related resources. Photo Editors who work in editorial can also join such groups as the National Press Photographers Association and Editorial Photographers for access to conferences, membership directories, networking opportunities, and more.

Tips for Entry

1. Do your research first on this field to see if your skills and interests match. Speaking with people who are

actually doing the job is one of the best ways to learn more about the work before taking the plunge. You can search for Photo Editors in your area by surfing the Web. Use an Internet search engine and the keywords "Photo Editor." Visit their Web sites, read the FAQ sections, and look at their work and the client lists. Contact the ones you are most interested in learning more about and see if you can set up a brief, informational meeting. Make sure to bring a list of questions with you and always write a thank-you note afterward.

2. Get an internship or a job in the photography department of a magazine or Web site. Trial by immersion is another great way to learn more about the business and to see where you best fit.
3. Keep up with industry trends and news. Read trade magazines, go to museums and gallery shows, and network with photographers. The Photo Editor's job is to help publications stay competitive by having unique and interesting looks, so staying inspired and creative is as important as doing the work itself.

PHOTO RESEARCHER

CAREER PROFILE

Duties: Searchs for and selects photos for various media and clients, including textbooks, magazines, trade books, design firms, corporations, advertising agencies, film and video production companies, Web sites, and others; provides photography editing services

Alternate Title(s): Photo Editor

Salary Range: $30,000 to $65,000

Employment Prospects: Good

Advancement Prospects: Good

Best Geographical Location(s): Major metropolitan areas, such as Atlanta, Boston, Chicago, Miami, New York, Philadelphia, San Francisco, and Washington, D.C.

Prerequisites:

Education or Training—Bachelor's degree in photography helpful, with coursework in advertising, art history, English literature, and publishing

Experience—Several years of experience in book or magazine publishing as an assistant photo researcher; museum, gallery, or stock photo agency experience also helpful

Special Skills and Personality Traits—Strong interest in and knowledge of photography, photography history, and photographers; excellent research and organizational skills; detail- and deadline-oriented; able to work well on a team as well as independently; computer savvy, able to work with different software programs; well versed in copyright laws; strong verbal and written communication skills; diligent; thorough; and patient

CAREER LADDER

```
┌─────────────────────────────────┐
│  Senior Photo Researcher /       │
│  Photo Research Director         │
└─────────────────────────────────┘

┌─────────────────────────────────┐
│  Photo Researcher                │
└─────────────────────────────────┘

┌─────────────────────────────────┐
│  Assistant Photo Researcher /    │
│  Assistant Photo Editor          │
└─────────────────────────────────┘
```

Position Description

Photo Researchers work part time or full time for photo libraries or agencies, museums and galleries, or for publishers and advertising agencies. They may also work as independents, developing and maintaining a client base while managing their own businesses. Photo Researchers work closely with art directors and art buyers to locate photographic images that meet the needs of specific projects. They will put together various photographs, based on the clients' directions, with creative directors or publishers making the final decisions regarding which images they will

use. Photo Researchers source these images through online photographic libraries, as well as by searching in-house prints and negatives. They may provide the images to clients by e-mail, transparencies, or CDs.

Photo Researchers first meet with clients to learn the types of images they need and how and where the photographs will be used. They help select photographs for book covers, magazine articles, company literature such as brochures and newsletters or even Web sites, and advertising campaigns. One example of an assignment may be to help the creative director of a fitness magazine locate historic photographs of gyms to accompany an article about the history of working out and the evolution of physical fitness. The Photo Researcher needs to have a series of questions addressed before beginning the search. How many photos are needed? What size will they be in the article? Should they be in portrait or landscape format? Will they be in color or black and white? What specific things about the gyms or fitness activities should they be searching for, such as types of exercises or equipment? Should the photographs be of gyms from any particular area of the country or world?

Photo Researchers who work on staff with magazine or book publishing companies, or for large stock agencies such as Getty Images, can source images from in-house photographic libraries. They will look at scores of images before deciding upon the photographs that meet all of their clients' criteria. In addition to discerning images based on photographic and artistic merits, they must also take into account licensing and copyright issues. For some Photo Researchers, a large part of the job may be administrative. Many photo libraries, publishers, and agencies require specific forms and reports to keep track of the images, particularly if they are originals and if they are of great value. Licensing rights and fees, and contract negotiations, are also critical parts of this type of work and can add to the complexity of the job.

Other job responsibilities may include creating and generating contracts, negotiating fees with stock agencies and libraries on the behalf of clients, using digital photographic software to enhance photographs (when permitted and licensed), refiling or returning photographic images once the project is completed, and invoicing clients. Some Photo Researchers with more experience may oversee and manage staff. Freelancers are also responsible for maintaining their businesses, which can entail everything from advertising and promoting their services, to handling their own bookkeeping and making sure their office equipment functions properly.

Salaries

Salaries for Photo Researchers vary, depending upon the types of clients for which they work and the project budgets. Advertising companies with national advertising campaigns will typically allot higher wages for Photo Researchers than nonprofit associations with company brochure projects. Photo Researchers usually earn annual wages ranging from $30,000 to $65,000 or more. Full-time Photo Researchers have the advantage over freelancers in that they are provided with such benefits as health insurance, disability, paid vacations, sick time and personal days, bonuses and raises, and stock options and retirement plans.

Employment Prospects

Photo Researchers often work in similar industries as writers and editors, and a parallel can be drawn regarding employ-ment prospects. According to the U.S. Department of Labor, employment of writers and editors is expected to grow about as fast as the average for all occupations through the year 2012, and the same can be said for Photo Researchers. As the demand for various publications increases, such as newspapers, magazines, books, and zines, the demand for photographic images to enhance these publications will similarly increase. Additionally, each year more businesses and organizations are expanding their promotional efforts and needing Photo Researchers to help them select appropriate photos to include in their brochures and Web sites. The public's interest in museums and art is also on the rise, as cited in the *Occupational Outlook Handbook,* and Photo Researchers will be needed for various advertising and promotion campaigns, as well as for exhibitions and display.

Advancement Prospects

Freelance Photo Researchers can advance by expanding into other industries. For instance, if they have worked primarily in book or magazine publishing, they may explore working with advertising clients. They may also expand by growing their businesses and hiring more staff that specialize in certain areas. With years of experience, Photo Researchers can move up to become heads of photography research departments within publishing companies, libraries, museums, galleries, or stock agencies. They can contribute articles on the subject to trade publications and lecture at schools and professional associations.

Education and Training

A bachelor's degree from an arts or liberal arts school is a solid educational background in this field. Photo Researchers usually have degrees in any number of areas, from English literature or photography, to political science or art history. More experienced Photo Researchers may have advanced degrees in library science or archive administration. An apprenticeship or previous work experience as an assistant photo researcher or editor is highly recommended.

Experience, Skills, and Personality Traits

Several years of experience as an assistant photo researcher are generally a solid background for Photo Researchers. Those who enjoy this work the most are passionate about photography and extremely knowledgeable about photographers and photographic images. They have a good grasp of photo history as well as current trends in the industry. A large part of the work can be administrative, so strong organizational skills and the ability to manage paperwork is a must.

Photo Researchers who are clear communicators with excellent interpersonal skills will do well in this field. The job entails working closely with clients, listening carefully to their needs, and effectively meeting those needs and deadlines. Clients may also change their minds midway during projects. Photo Researchers need to be problem solvers with vast amounts of patience and creativity to get the work done on time and keep clients coming back with new assignments.

To save time, Photo Researchers need to keep track of where they found specific images and where to locate them again, if needed. Exceptional research skills and sharp minds and memories are absolute requirements. Additionally, Photo Researchers need to have a solid grasp of licensing issues and copyright laws and be able to educate their clients in these arenas as well. To advance within the field, strong management and team-building abilities will also be needed.

Unions and Associations

Photo Researchers may join the American Society of Picture Professionals, Professional Photographers of America, the American Society of Media Photographers, and the National Press Photographers Association for professional resources and employment referrals.

Tips for Entry

1. Referrals and word of mouth are often the best ways to get work in the photo research field, so network as much as you possibly can. Go to gallery show openings, museum events, conferences, parties, and any and all events that your prospective clients will attend.

2. Read the publications of the clients with whom you are interested in working, to familiarize yourself with the subject matter and artistic styles, as well as the photographers they have used in the past. If you want to work for magazine publishers, subscribe to the magazines they publish. If you are leaning toward building a career with advertising agencies, study their past and current advertising campaigns. Many Photo Researchers work in a variety of media, so be sure to cover all of the bases if you are opting for an all-encompassing path.

3. Get a job as an assistant photo researcher. Volunteer for a short time, if that is the only way to get your foot in the door. Working firsthand with a trained and experienced Photo Researcher is the best education and an excellent way to determine if this work suits you. Find work in the photo research departments of galleries, museums, or publishers. Search the companies' Web sites directly, as well as employment sites such as MuseumJobs (http://www.museumjobs.com), MuseumEmployment (http://www.museum-employment.com), or the New York Times on the Web (http://www.nytimes.com).

PHOTO GALLERY MANAGER

CAREER PROFILE

Duties: Manages a gallery exhibiting and selling photographs of past and contemporary photographers; advertises to and networks with museum curators, private collectors, interior designers and decorators, and cultural institutions; arranges exhibition and sales contracts with photographers and photographers' representatives; oversees and manages gallery staff and freelance consultants

Alternate Title(s): None

Salary Range: $50,000 to $100,000+

Employment Prospects: Good

Advancement Prospects: Fair

Best Geographical Location(s): Major cities and towns where photographers, artists, and collectors live and work (i.e., New York, Los Angeles, Santa Fe)

Prerequisites:

Education or Training—Four-year degree in photography or art history; coursework in small business management; master's degree may be beneficial

Experience—Five years of experience as a fine arts or commercial photographer; several years of experience in photo or art gallery

Special Skills and Personality Traits—Knowledgeable about photography, photographic styles and techniques, film development and printing processes, and past and current photographers; entrepreneurial; versed in industry practices; skilled in negotiation and sales ethical; reliable and responsible; excellent verbal and communication skills; diplomatic;

CAREER LADDER

```
┌─────────────────────────────────┐
│       Photo Gallery Owner        │
└─────────────────────────────────┘

┌─────────────────────────────────┐
│      Photo Gallery Manager       │
└─────────────────────────────────┘

┌─────────────────────────────────┐
│   Photo Gallery Assistant /      │
│    Freelance Photographer        │
└─────────────────────────────────┘
```

Position Description

Photo Gallery Managers exhibit and sell photographs in galleries and oversee permanent collections. They are responsible for helping with or overseeing the matting and hanging of exhibitions. They keep inventory of photographs that are on site, in storage, and in the process of being shipped. They coordinate exhibition schedules with photographers and photographers' representatives. Photo Gallery Managers also make sure that photographs, particularly old images, are exhibited in appropriate environments to prevent damage. They also ensure that all archival images are packed in appropriate materials and stored in safe environments.

Photo Gallery Managers are approached directly by photographers or pursue those whose work they want to exhibit. They negotiate contracts with photographers on behalf of photo gallery owners. They help set prices for photographs and are responsible for sales to collectors, curators, and the general public. Depending upon the staff structure of the gallery, managers may come up with the ideas for shows and choose specific photographers to exhibit based on photographic techniques, styles, color and lighting, and themes. They may work with exhibition designers and photographers on exhibitions and help promote the shows. Photo Gallery Managers work with graphic designers to create promotional literature (i.e., flyers, postcards, brochures) and advertisements for shows and events. They also oversee the writing and placement of press releases and the management and maintenance of the gallery's Web site. They manage and oversee gallery staff, freelance consultants (such as grant writers, bookkeepers, and accountants), office cleaners, and others.

Salaries

Photo Gallery Managers can earn salaries ranging from $50,000 to $100,000 or more. Earnings will vary, depending upon the desirability of the photographs in the marketplace and whether the photographers are up-and-comers, respected veterans in the field, or masters from long ago. Photo Gallery Managers may earn commissions on their sales, thus those who are excellent negotiators and have reputations for being professional and ethical have the potential to secure higher wages.

Employment Prospects

Photo Gallery Managers have good opportunities to find work. According to the U.S. Department of Labor's *Occupational Outlook Handbook,* the general population has been showing an increased interest in art and art museums, and this is an interest that is expected to continue to grow through 2012. Large, major cities that feature an abundance of galleries and museums, such as New York and Philadelphia, as well as smaller cities that artists and collectors flock to, such as Santa Fe, will always need Photo Gallery Managers to oversee collections and draw in new and interesting photography and photographers.

Advancement Prospects

With years of experience, Photo Gallery Managers can move up to either own the galleries they work for, once the owners retire or sell, or they can open their own galleries. If they already are in the dual-role position of manager/owner, they can always open other galleries in other towns and cities. They can also expand into new areas of photography, exploring different styles or focusing on a wider variety of themes and issues. Photo Gallery Managers with strong speaking skills and an urge to share information to help elevate the industry can speak at industry conferences and panel discussions, as well as teach at photography associations and technical and art schools. They can also write articles and columns for industry publications and write books either about the industry or about particular photographers and photographic styles.

Education and Training

A bachelor's degree in photography or art history is usually a solid educational foundation for Photo Gallery Managers. Small business management coursework and training in word-processing and data-management programs is recommended.

Experience, Skills, and Personality Traits

Some galleries may prefer managers with several years of prior experience in gallery management or administration. Managers with professional photography experience may also have the advantage in their job hunts. Photo Gallery Managers need to be able to juggle projects and people. Their job is multifaceted, from soliciting photographers and conceiving photography shows, to networking and maintaining relationships with curators and collectors, to making sure gallery staff receive their paychecks on time. Successful managers have a combination of all of the following skills and traits: clear, forward thinking; creative and innovative; resourceful; self-motivated; detail- and deadline-oriented; excellent interpersonal skills; strong leadership abilities; energy; enthusiasm; passion for photography; savvy business managers.

They must be able to speak the language of photographers one minute and the language of curators and collectors the next. As a representative of the gallery and often the first impression people have of the organization, Photo Gallery Managers must be professional and presentable. They will often field inquiries from the press and formulate statements for publication. Clear communication skills are essential. They must always know what is happening in the industry, who the top in-demand photographers are, what is being sold where and for how much, who the collectors are, and what the current industry business practices are.

Unions and Associations

Photo Gallery Managers can become members of the Art Dealers Association of America, once they have been endorsed and accepted, and enjoy a wide variety of professional benefits to further their careers. They can join the Photo Marketing Association International for news about national and international gallery shows as well as educational resources, and they can also join Professional Photographers of America for access to networking opportunities and other career-enhancing benefits.

Tips for Entry

1. Visit photo galleries near you to see the types of photographs exhibited, the mountings and exhibition design, how the galleries are set up, the staff size and job responsibilities, and other features. Speak with gallery managers or owners to find out how they started their businesses.

2. Network at events that photographers attend. Go to photography association meetings and conferences, take workshops, and visit photography shows and exhibitions.

3. Get your foot in the door by taking an internship in a photo gallery. The best way to learn how this business works is by full immersion. Find job listings through employment placement sites, association Web sites, and classifieds in trade publications. This is your opportunity to get a taste of everything, from staff management styles to photography selection to show conception and design.

PHOTOGRAPHER'S AGENT

CAREER PROFILE

Duties: Represents photographers to art directors, curators, publishers, corporate public relations executives, interior decorators, for-profit and nonprofit social organizations, museum publicists, government officials, political parties, collectors, philanthropic groups, unions, and other organizations that use photography; negotiates contracts and fees on behalf of photographers; creates estimates and handles billing; helps photographers create portfolios tailored to specific clients and coordinates or creates photographers' promotional and marketing campaigns; manages own business, including self-promotion through mailings and Web site

Alternate Title(s): Photographer's Representative

Salary Range: $30,000 to $75,000+

Employment Prospects: Fair

Advancement Prospects: Good

Best Geographical Location(s): Major cities, such as Atlanta, Boston, Chicago, Los Angeles, New York, Philadelphia, and San Francisco

Prerequisites:

Education or Training—Four-year college degree, with coursework in photography and business management

Experience—Several years of experience in a photo gallery; firsthand experience either as a photographer or as a photographer's assistant beneficial

Special Skills and Personality Traits—Extremely knowledgeable about photography and photographers; well aware of contract terms and industry practices; excellent negotiation and sales skills; strong interpersonal and communication skills; professional, organized, and presentable; resourceful and creative

CAREER LADDER

```
┌─────────────────────────────────┐
│         Agency Owner            │
└─────────────────────────────────┘

┌─────────────────────────────────┐
│     Photographer's Agent        │
└─────────────────────────────────┘

┌─────────────────────────────────┐
│  Professional Photographer /    │
│  Assistant Photographer's Agent │
└─────────────────────────────────┘
```

Position Description

Photographers sign up with a Photographer's Agent typically when they have reached a certain juncture in their careers and it is time for a new direction or when they have simply had enough of handling the business side of things and would rather devote their time to what they do best, which is taking photographs. A Photographer's Agent works independently or in partnerships with other agents. He or she represents those photographers who have reputations that most suit his or her business and whose styles match current and prospective clients' needs.

A Photographer's Agent helps forge relationships on the behalf of photographers with prospective clients. Agents help promote and market photographers by researching the market and identifying the advertising agencies, publishing houses, corporations, and other organizations that can use and benefit from a particular photographer's work. Agents create postcards and direct mailings, always in collaboration with photographers to make sure their approach is what the photographers want. Agents advise photographers about their portfolios, discussing which pieces best represent them and which work well together as a collection for viewing. They also guide photographers toward other avenues of promotion, such as through competitions and trade publications (i.e., *Workbook, American Showcase,* and *The Black Book*) that showcase the work of different photographers and are often used by art directors and clients to locate the right photographer for a job. Agents handle all of the details, from reviewing contracts to filling out and submitting registration forms with accompanying fees and artwork. Agents also usually have their own Web sites, in which they showcase samples of their photographers' work.

Agents set up meetings with clients and present their photographers' work. While they may represent many photographers, to avoid overwhelming clients, they first determine the clients' style, past campaigns, and current needs and tailor the presentations by showing the work of either one or only several photographers. Agents are responsible for negotiating the terms of the contracts. They review clients' agreements or create their own agreements on behalf of the photographers. They advise photographers about which terms are acceptable and which need to be adjusted. They act as liaisons between the photographers and the clients, overseeing the work of the photographers and making sure quality of work and deadlines are met according to agreements and that fees are paid as scheduled.

A Photographer's Agent is responsible for invoicing clients, making sure photographers are paid, making sure commissions are received, and keeping records of all transactions. Agents create contracts with their photographers that spell out terms of service based on standard business practices, including commission percentages, promotional work that will be done, and terms of separation should they decide to part ways.

Agents also run their own businesses as well as those of their photographers. They must develop their brand images through creative Web sites, promotional literature, resourceful networking and advertising, writing and placing articles in appropriate industry publications, and participating in panel discussions and speaking engagements.

Salaries

A Photographer's Agent receives a percentage of commissioned jobs, with the industry standard being 25 to 35 percent, according to the Graphic Artists Guild's *Handbook of Pricing & Ethical Guidelines.* Depending on the number of photographers an agent represents, the desirability of the work in the marketplace, and years of experience in the

field, Photographer's Agents can earn annual salaries ranging from $30,000 to $75,000 or more. Agents also enhance photographers' salaries as well as their own by pursuing opportunities for reuse and licensing agreements. They may also offer side services on a fee-per-service basis, without representation, such as portfolio reviews.

Employment Prospects

Not every photographer wants or needs a Photographer's Agent, so prospects for employment can be random and difficult to predict. Additionally, according to the Department of Labor's *Occupational Outlook Handbook,* digital photography has made it easier for people to access photographs on their own. A Photographer's Agent who is good at pitching his or her business and following through on the services has the best prospects of securing talented photographers and matching them with reputable clients.

Advancement Prospects

Seasoned agents who work in larger agencies with other agents can advance to become owners of or partners in the agencies. Agents who already own their own agencies can open their doors to other agents who represent styles and types of photographers that are different from the original collective. A Photographer's Agent can boost his or her businesses by speaking about the business of being a representative or about photography issues, such as copyright and other contract terms, at trade conferences and panel discussions. Agents can teach at art and technical schools, write articles for print publications and Web sites, as well as participate in online forums.

Education and Training

A four-year degree in photography is beneficial to a Photographer's Agent but not required. An undergraduate degree in any arts-related subject, with coursework in and exposure to photography, is equally useful in this field. Agents must be fluent in the language of contracts and can learn and keep abreast of terms by reading industry publications and Web sites and subscribing to literature from such associations as the Society of Photographers and Artists Representatives and Volunteer Lawyers for the Arts. Agents must also understand how to run a small business and can learn useful skills through continuing education courses at local universities as well as through professional associations for entrepreneurs.

Experience, Skills, and Personality Traits

Three to five years of experience as an assistant to a Photographer's Agent is an excellent way to learn about this business firsthand. Agents need to be knowledgeable about photography and photographers and have a good grasp of how the business works. They must have a strong under-

standing of contracts and contract terms and be smart negotiators who know how to close deals that are beneficial to
their photographers as well as to their clients. As essential
liaisons, they need to have exceptional written and verbal
communication skills, as well as organizational abilities to
keep all of the paperwork straight. To succeed and thrive in
this business, a Photographer's Agent must be professional,
have excellent presentation skills, self-motivation and deter-
mination, strong ethics, and good judgment. To maintain
good working relationships with their photographers and
their clients, agents must be accessible, responsible, and
reliable.

Unions and Associations

Agents can join the Society of Photographers and Artists
Representatives for industry news, resources, and networking opportunities. Because they have a two-tiered approach
to business, meaning they must secure photographers to represent as well as locate clients to hire these same photographers, they will do well to join associations to which
prospective clients belong, as well as those to which photographers belong. It may behoove them to join their local

Chamber of Commerce, Advertising Photographers of
America, the American Society of Media Photographers,
and Professional Photographers of America.

Tips for Entry

1. Find a Photographer's Agent, either through searching
   the Internet, contacting a local photo gallery, or by
   looking through photography books such as *American
   Showcase, The Black Book,* and *Workbook.* Make a
   list of the agents whose work interests you and contact them to see if you can set up a date to discuss the
   representation field.
2. Get a job in an agent's office as an assistant. Treat the
   job as you would an important class. Take notes, ask
   questions, and make sure you understand the answers.
   Education by immersion is the best way to get a jump
   start in the business.
3. Network as much as you possibly can. Attend industry events and conferences. Go to gallery openings
   and photo shows. Much of this business is not only
   based on a Photographer's Agents' intelligence and
   savvy but also on who knows whom.

PHOTOGRAPHIC ADMINISTRATOR

CAREER PROFILE

Duties: Handles administration of photographic libraries and collections for corporations, associations, and educational institutions; liaises between clients and photographers for photography assignments; handles a variety of administrative tasks in relation to office and staff management and business transactions; creates budgets, cash and expense reports; attends board and staff meetings

Alternate Title(s): Photography Manager

Salary Range: $25,000 to $50,000+

Employment Prospects: Good

Advancement Prospects: Good

Best Geographical Location(s): Boston, Chicago, Los Angeles, New York, Philadelphia, Rochester, San Francisco, Seattle, and Washington, D.C.

Prerequisites:

Education or Training—Bachelor's degree in art history, photography, or other liberal arts specialization; master's may be required; coursework in small business management; trained in Microsoft Word, Excel, and database-management programs

Experience—Several years of prior management experience in corporate or association photography environment

Special Skills and Personality Traits—Knowledgeable about photography and photographers; excellent verbal and written communication skills; team player as well as independent worker; strong interpersonal skills; organized; reliable and responsible; able to work in structured environment; computer savvy; strong management and leadership abilities

CAREER LADDER

```
┌─────────────────────────────────────────┐
│     Director of Photography Department    │
└─────────────────────────────────────────┘

┌─────────────────────────────────────────┐
│       Photographic Administrator          │
└─────────────────────────────────────────┘

┌─────────────────────────────────────────┐
│          Photography Manager              │
└─────────────────────────────────────────┘
```

Position Description

Photographic Administrators work in the photography departments of universities, museums, associations, and corporations and handle all administrative tasks related to photographic work and photography archives. They liaise with boards of directors, committees, members, volunteers, professors, students, staff, photographers, teachers, and the general public. They also work in the photography and communications departments of federal and city agencies and handle requests for photographic services. Photographic Administrators may also work in photography agencies and match clients to photographers for specific projects. They will listen carefully to the client's description of the work needed and the style of photography desired. They will research the agency's photography database, study the photographers' backgrounds, and match the appropriate photographer or photographers to the job.

Photographic Administrators may work in public relations and communications firms, where they will oversee a small staff dedicated to meeting clients' requests for photographic images for advertisements, press releases, newspaper and magazine articles, corporate brochures, and Web sites. They are responsible for maintaining control of in-house labor costs and outside supplier fees. If press agents request certain pictures, they oversee these transactions as well, making sure terms of usage are clear and appropriate permissions and releases have been secured.

Photographic Administrators work closely with a variety of people, from board members and staff, to volunteers and consultants. They may coordinate production and work schedules and oversee photography department Web sites, business transactions, invoices, agreements, and accounts receivable and payable, as well the maintenance and management of office equipment and supplies. They attend regular staff meetings with boards of directors and meet with teachers to discuss possible workshops for future educational programs. They are also responsible for creating department budgets and expense reports. Photographic Administrators normally have their fingers in many pies. Their work can range from mundane, daily tasks to the more interesting work attached to organizing and hosting events and exhibitions.

Photographic Administrators provide backup for appropriate personnel. They may help research and locate new temporary offices for new departments of the company. They may help plan for office and equipment renovations, as well as overall company growth. They are the in-office support for the board of directors, always accessible by phone, e-mail, and in person to field inquiries about financial records, board history, membership records, business transactions, and agreements with sales vendors. Photographic Administrators provide board members with regular weekly, monthly, or quarterly reports on the status of business operations. They work closely with board members in creative budgets and project proposals. Photographic Administrators may also work on staff at major newspaper and magazine publishing companies. They will help editors and researchers locate photographs and coordinate transactions.

Photographic Administrators are also expected to review all materials and pitches from prospective service and equipment providers. They will meet with vendors, manufacturers, computer and printer consultants, and others to learn and discuss all aspects of the products and services that they are offering. They compare findings in order to make intelligent, budget-conscious recommendations to board members and department executives about purchases and services. Once the purchase is approved, Photographic Administrators will negotiate prices and manage transactions from purchase to fulfillment.

Salaries

Photographic Administrators are normally full-time employees who can earn annual salaries ranging from $30,000 to $50,000 or more, depending upon their years of experience and the size and budget of the organization. Small associations, educational institutions, and museums will typically pay lower salaries, while large, well-funded organizations and government agencies usually pay higher wages.

Employment Prospects

Arts administrator positions are expected to grow at about the same speed as other jobs, or by about 10 to 20 percent, through 2010, according to the U.S. Department of Labor's *Occupational Outlook Handbook*. Photographic Administrators with strong management experience, excellent connections in the field, and innovative ideas will find more opportunities for work.

Advancement Prospects

With several years of experience, Photographic Administrators can advance to become senior administrators, taking on more responsibilities and overseeing more staff. They can transfer their skills to other jobs, such as photographer's agent or an administrative role within a photography agency or stock house. They can also write articles for association and trade newsletters, as well as lecture and teach.

Education and Training

A four-year degree is usually required to be a Photographic Administrator. Some organizations may require advanced degrees. Specializations can vary, but administrators should have coursework in photography and small-business management. Knowledge of photography, photographers, and photographic techniques may be useful in some administrative positions. On-the-job management training can also be beneficial.

Experience, Skills, and Personality Traits

Photographic Administrators usually have several years of experience as managers in commercial photography studios, stock image agencies, or photography stores. They are typically well connected in the field and understand, either through prior experience as photographers or through their work backgrounds, standard industry practices. They have excellent written and verbal communication skills. They know how to organize and prioritize their work. They are independent workers and team players, able to work with a wide variety of people, including department staff, boards of directors, volunteers, teachers, photographers, clients, and the general public. Photographic Administrators have a solid knowledge of word-processing programs, such as Microsoft Word and Excel, as well as database-management software. They are also comfortable with numbers and managing money. They are able to juggle many projects and demands at once and still meet deadlines. Photographic Administrators are also adept at working under pressure while keeping cool heads and professional demeanors.

Unions and Associations

Photographic Administrators may join such associations as the National Society of Association Executives, Photo Marketing Association International, Professional Photographers of America, and others for workshops and conferences, networking events, and other career-enhancing benefits.

Tips for Entry

1. Get an internship in the photography department of a museum, university, or corporation. Learn the basics of photographic administration from the ground up.

2. Search for employment opportunities with museums and associations through the Web sites of such groups as the American Association of Museums (http://www.aam-us.org) and The Foundation Center (http://fdncenter.org).

3. Create a list of city agencies that have photography departments. Check their Web sites for employment listings and contact the human resources departments to find out how to apply.

PHOTOGRAPHIC RETOUCHER

CAREER PROFILE

Duties: Retouches photographic images by computer and by hand to improve color and lighting and moves, resizes, or crops images, for magazine, newspaper, and book publishers, photography studios and photographers, advertising agencies, production houses, Web sites, and others; may manage film development and oversee printing processes; maintains image databases

Alternate Title(s): Imaging Specialist

Salary Range: $30 to $100 per hour

Employment Prospects: Good

Advancement Prospects: Fair

Best Geographical Location(s): Atlanta, Boston, Chicago, Denver, Las Vegas, Los Angeles, Minneapolis, New York, Philadelphia, Portland, Seattle, and Washington, D.C.

Prerequisites:

Education or Training—Two- or four-year degree in art, with coursework in photography, graphic design, painting, drawing, and printing processes; training in design software such as Adobe Photoshop and QuarkXPress required

Experience—Several years of experience as an intern in photography studio, production house, or advertising agency beneficial

Special Skills and Personality Traits—Excellent eye-hand coordination; knowledgeable about color, lighting, and composition; fluent in photographic design software programs; strong verbal and written communication skills; able to follow directions and make suggestions for changes; professional; diplomatic; deadline-oriented; organized

CAREER LADDER

```
┌─────────────────────────────────┐
│        Senior Retoucher         │
└─────────────────────────────────┘

┌─────────────────────────────────┐
│     Photographic Retoucher      │
└─────────────────────────────────┘

┌─────────────────────────────────┐
│  Assistant or Junior Retoucher  │
└─────────────────────────────────┘
```

Position Description

Photographic Retouchers improve and enhance photographic images by hand or with design software such as Adobe Photoshop, Illustrator, and QuarkXPress. Publishers, advertising agencies, photography studios, and others commission retouchers to correct color and lighting, crop out shadows and objects, and resize shapes to improve the overall composition of the image. Some independent clients may even hire Photographic Retouchers to scan damaged photographs, fix the problem areas, and create new and improved shots for their personal archives.

Before starting work, Photographic retouchers meet with clients to discuss how the images will be used, the reasons for retouching, and the specific changes that must be made.

They review the images and discuss all aspects, from color and composition to objects that may need to be deleted, and what the end results should look like. Photographic Retouchers scan the images and save the original, untouched versions as digital files in their computers. If the clients have only a vague idea of the changes they want, Photographic Retouchers offer suggestions and recommendations based on their experience in the field.

Many people now have digital cameras and are able to retouch images themselves using photographic design software on their home computers. There are still many others, however, who prefer to have professional retouchers handle their personal photographs, particularly those that are extraordinarily old and require extensive restoration. Depending upon the age and condition of the photograph, and the client's specifications, Photographic Retouchers may work directly on the original photograph, using special brushes and paints to restore tones and colors faded due to years in direct sunlight or repair cracks, chips, and other damage caused by decades spent crumpled in an attic. They may also scan the image to retouch colors, contrasts, and light digitally and create new and improved photographs.

Salaries
Freelance Photographic Retouchers usually charge $30 to $100 per hour, depending upon their years of experience in the field and the budgets of their clientele. For complicated work or rush jobs requiring evening and weekend hours, retouchers charge higher hourly rates, as is industry standard. Freelance wages will also depend upon the intended usage of the image. For example, if a top advertising agency plans to use the image in multiple ways (i.e., in print publications, on billboards, on the Internet, in mass direct-mail campaigns), Photographic Retouchers usually charge more. The 11th edition of the Graphic Artists Guild's *Handbook of Pricing & Ethical Guidelines,* which provides examples of Photographic Retoucher rates, cites that the national/general consumer market and Web companies pay more—at $65 to $200 per hour—than the regional/trade, which is $60 to $150 per hour. The guild's rates are based on 2001 surveys of industry professionals around the country.

Employment Prospects
Retouchers work as freelance contractors or on staff in retouch and design departments of publishing companies, advertising agencies, and postproduction facilities. The best opportunities will be for freelance digital retouching work, which Photographic Retouchers can find by exploring a variety of paths, from networking through professional associations to searching and securing work via online employment sites. Retouchers who work with advertising companies may have a slight advantage. According to the U.S. Department of Labor, the advertising industry will con-

tinue to grow due to intense international and domestic competition in consumer products and services. More advertisements will be needed to meet this increasing demand and thus more images will need to be improved and enhanced by skilled technicians.

Advancement Prospects
Retouchers who are employed full time can advance to become senior or lead retouchers within the retouching department. They may hire and manage other image specialists and oversee their work. After years of honing their skills and establishing a reputation in the business for quality, professional work, Photographic Retouchers can also advance by starting their own postproduction agencies. They can write educational articles for trade association and educational publications, and they can teach at vocational institutions and art schools.

Education and Training
A two-year degree from a technical or vocational school may be sufficient in this field. Some companies may prefer a bachelor's degree in art, with training in graphic design, painting and drawing, and photographic design software such as Adobe Photoshop. Retouchers must be fluent in color-correction techniques and be able to look at images and see what can be improved, so courses in color are also critical.

Experience, Skills, and Personality Traits
Most Photographic Retouchers have prior experience either as assistants or apprentices in photography studios or postproduction houses. Photographic Retouchers must have an excellent eye for details and be extremely knowledgeable about color and all of the techniques involved in correcting color. While they may not be directly involved in the printing process, they need to have a good idea of how the images and colors will look in print in order to go about their work. They must be fluent in photographic design software on both PC and Mac platforms. Strong verbal and written communication skills are important, as is an ability to listen closely to the clients' specifications. Photographic Retouchers often work under intense deadline pressure, so they must be able to stay focused, manage their time well, and deliver quality work to meet clients' needs.

Unions and Associations
There are no known associations or unions dedicated solely to Photographic Retouchers. Retouchers may join such associations as the American Society of Media Photographers, Professional Photographers of America, and Advertising Photographers of America for various benefits. They

can also join organizations that cater to graphic and digital artists, such as the Association of Graphic Artists and the American Institute of Graphic Artists.

Tips for Entry

1. Visit the Web site RetouchPRO (http://www. retouchpro.com) to participate in online forums for retouchers, read about new techniques and technologies, and learn about upcoming classes.
2. Get an internship or apprenticeship in the retouch department of an advertising agency or with a production studio that has in-house retouch capabilities.
3. Find job listings through the Internet, on such Web sites as the New York Times on the Web (http://www. nytimes.com), Monster (http://www.monster.com), Yahoo! HotJobs (http://hotjobs.yahoo.com), Craigslist (http://www.craigslist.org/about/cities.html), and others. You can also find job openings by visiting the Web sites of advertising agencies, magazine publishers, photography studios, postproduction houses and labs, and others.
4. It is important to keep up with what is going on in the digital retouching industry. Technology and software changes and improves constantly. To stay sharp, regularly read industry and trade magazines, take workshops, and network with others in the field.

PHOTOGRAPHIC SALES REPRESENTATIVE

CAREER PROFILE

Duties: Promotes and sells photographic products and equipment to retail stores and professional and commercial photography labs; covers certain geographical territories; researches and creates lists of prospective clients; meets with and visits small-business owners and large retail outlets to discuss sales prospects; conducts product demos and dealer training sessions; attends and works at trade shows; prepares budgets and sales reports

Alternate Title(s): Manufacturer's Representative, Photographic Equipment Salesperson

Salary Range: $30,000 to $80,000+

Employment Prospects: Good

Advancement Prospects: Good

Best Geographical Location(s): Cities and regions with high populations and busy photographic industries

Prerequisites:

Education or Training—Two- to four-year degree, with coursework or training in photography beneficial; B.A. in marketing may be required by some manufacturers

Experience—Three of more years of experience in sales; depending upon product, several years of experience as a photographer

Special Skills and Personality Traits—Knowledgeable about photographic products and manufacturers; confident and outgoing; self-motivated; responsible and reliable; deadline-oriented, goal-driven, and comfortable working under stress; able to travel; flexible and adaptable; enthusiastic, upbeat personality; honest; ethical; excellent written and verbal communication skills; ability to work independently and with a team

CAREER LADDER

```
┌─────────────────────────────────────┐
│        Vice President of Sales        │
└─────────────────────────────────────┘

┌─────────────────────────────────────┐
│  Regional or National Sales Manager   │
└─────────────────────────────────────┘

┌─────────────────────────────────────┐
│  Photographic Sales Representative    │
└─────────────────────────────────────┘
```

Position Description

Photographic Sales Representatives work for manufacturers and sell photographic products to small photography stores, retail chains, photography labs, and directly to photographers. They may work for companies that produce camera and film, photographic lighting systems, or tripods and photographic gear. They may even sell custom presentation products and picture frames to photographers. Photographic

Sales Representatives are normally assigned geographical locations, or "territories," which they travel throughout to develop and maintain relationships with customers. Depending upon their territory, they may travel 25 to 50 percent of the time.

Photographic Sales Representatives are responsible for expanding business by developing new customers and maintaining relationships with current clientele. They are given target sales goals and commission incentives. They gather information about prospective customers by attending trade shows, reviewing past lists of leads, searching equipment rental records, business directories, Web sites, advertisements, direct mail inquiries, and a variety of other sources. They create lists of these prospective clients and initiate contact by cold calls, e-mail, and, eventually, personal visits.

In addition to actually conducting sales, Photographic Sales Representatives may be responsible for reviewing and improving the sales team's process of prospecting, selling, and closing deals. This may entail testing and revamping sales scripts, if used, as well as conducting training sessions to orient teams to new processes and work through any kinks. Photographic Sales Representatives provide technical, marketing, and product training support internally as well as externally. When they visit photography stores, they also speak with the sales associates about the products and demonstrate to them how they work and the advantages over other products. They get salespeople excited so that the salespeople can, in turn, share their knowledge and enthusiasm with customers. Photographic Sales Representatives may offer salespeople special deals on products or giveaways. They conduct in-store demonstrations for storeowners, sales associates, and customers. They make in-person visits to photographers' studios to demonstrate products and to allow photographers to test equipment and provide feedback.

Salaries

Photographic Sales Representatives are usually full-time employees who earn annual salaries plus commissions. Earnings can range from $30,000 to $80,000 or more, depending upon years of experience, the manufacturer, and quantity of products sold. Staff sales representatives also receive such benefits as a 401(k); medical, dental, and life insurance; vacation and sick leave; use of company cars; and frequent flier mileage. They also receive reimbursement for transportation, hotels, meals, and wining and dining customers. Some companies provide Photographic Sales Representatives with cash bonuses, all-expense paid vacations, or other incentives for outstanding sales achievements.

Employment Prospects

Demand for Photographic Sales Representatives should grow about as fast as the average for all occupations, or by about 10 to 20 percent, through 2012, according to the U.S. Department of Labor. With the constant development and improvement of photographic equipment and supplies, customers will continue to need Photographic Sales Representatives to show them how to use the products. Sales representatives will find the most employment opportunities in small wholesale and manufacturing firms. More of these companies are depending upon sales representatives to help them control costs and expand client bases by marketing

their products directly. Photographic Sales Representatives who have excellent knowledge of the products, the industry, technical expertise, and a proven track record in sales will be in high demand.

Advancement Prospects

Photographic Sales Representatives who meet their sales goals, develop effective sales processes that achieve results, and who successfully manage accounts and meet customers' needs have good opportunities to advance. With several years of experience, they can move up to become regional directors or national directors. With five or more years of experience, they can advance to become vice presidents of sales departments.

Education and Training

Most manufacturers hire Photographic Sales Representatives who have four-year degrees. Educational backgrounds can vary in this field; a bachelor's degree in marketing, with photography experience, often suffices. Many Photographic Sales Representatives hone their sales skills by taking continuing education workshops in sales and marketing through business schools or professional associations. They keep up with industry trends and issues by reading trade publications and joining professional associations for membership newsletters and magazines.

Experience, Skills, and Personality Traits

Many companies require their Photographic Sales Representatives to have several years of prior experience in sales. Sales representatives must have strong customer service skills and be adept at developing rapport with people quickly. For more senior-level positions, manufacturers want to see demonstrated records of past sales successes. Sales representatives must be able to maintain relationships either in person, by telephone, or through e-mail and therefore need to have strong written and verbal communication skills. There may be a great deal of travel involved in this type of work, so having a flexible attitude, enthusiasm, and energy can ease the challenges. Photographic Sales Representatives must be highly organized and able to prioritize workloads to achieve sales goals. They must be able to meet and exceed these goals and work well under a great deal of pressure. Those who thrive under the stress of deadlines do extremely well in this field. In addition to being versed in the products and the company they represent, they must also be computer savvy and very familiar with Microsoft Word, Excel, e-mail, the Internet, and order-and-billing software.

Unions and Associations

There are no associations specifically dedicated to Photographic Sales Representatives. Sales representatives can belong to the Manufacturers' Agents National Association for general sales-representative benefits, such as the monthly *Sales Agency* magazine; an online directory of members and manufacturers; lobbying efforts in Washington, D.C., in defense of professional standards and ethics; contract guidelines; career counseling; educational seminars; and more. Photographic Sales Representatives may also join Professional Photographers of America, Advertising Photographers of America, American Society of Media Photographers, and others, for networking and educational opportunities.

Tips for Entry

1. Learn standard business practices, negotiating tactics, contract language, and more by subscribing to such newsletters as *Guide to Agreements, Sales Rep's Advisor,* and *Sales Rep's Strategies,* published by the Alexander Communications Group.
2. Find job listings through such employment placement Web sites as RepLocate (http://www.replocate.com), Sales Vault (http://www.salesvault.com), JustClosers (http://www.justclosers.com), Work (http://www.work.com), Monster (http://www.monster.com), Yahoo! Hotjobs (http://hotjobs.yahoo.com), CareerBuilder (http://www.careerbuilder.com), and many others.
3. Create a list of photographic equipment and product manufacturers that interest you. Visit their Web sites and check their employment listings section. Contact the human resources departments to see if there are sales opportunities in territories you are familiar with or that are feasible for you to cover.
4. Ask the sales associates in photography stores and retail chains near you who the store's sales representatives are and the manufacturers with whom they work. Explain that you are interested in this type of work and ask if you can have the sales representatives' contact information. E-mail or call them to learn more about how they got into the field and if there are any current openings.

PHOTOGRAPHIC TECHNICAL WRITER

CAREER PROFILE

Duties: Provides consumer-oriented, technical writing about photography equipment and accessories for national publications directed to novice photographers; writes product reviews, how-to features, profiles of personalities in the field, and travel articles; may teach at universities

Alternate Title(s): Photography Writer, Writer

Salary Range: $30,270 to $80,900

Employment Prospects: Good

Advancement Prospects: Good

Best Geographical Location(s): Anywhere throughout the United States

Prerequisites:

Education or Training—Four-year degree in liberal arts (i.e., photography, communications, journalism, or English); coursework in photography

Experience—Four to five years of experience as a professional photographer, and some experience as a computer and digital consultant or retoucher; several years of experience writing and editing technical articles; one to three years of experience in a photography equipment store

Special Skills and Personality Traits—Well versed in digital photography and design software programs (i.e., Adobe Photoshop and Illustrator); extremely knowledgeable about photography, cameras, camera accessories, and computers; excellent written and verbal communication skills; able to translate technical content into layperson's terms

CAREER LADDER

```
┌─────────────────────────────────────┐
│              Editor                  │
└─────────────────────────────────────┘

┌─────────────────────────────────────┐
│  Photographic Technical Writer       │
└─────────────────────────────────────┘

┌─────────────────────────────────────┐
│     Photographer / Associate         │
│   Photographic Technical Writer      │
└─────────────────────────────────────┘
```

Position Description

Photographic Technical Writers share their knowledge of the industry by writing instructional manuals and guidelines to accompany photographic equipment, as well as articles about photography for industry and consumer publications. They translate technical language into content that is easy to read. Technical writers cover all of the bases in their instructions. They understand every single bit about cameras as well as computers and know how to clearly explain this knowledge in simple terms so that everyone can grasp it. Technical writers provide an overview of the camera's features and accessories and give step-by-step lessons in how best to use them. They clearly educate consumers about how to frame shots and when to use macro, auto, and manual settings. They spell out the distinctions in lighting and exposure. Once the pictures are completed, they tell users how to save or delete them, as well as how to connect digital cameras to computers and synch up with design software programs. Photographic Technical Writers also share the problems that may arise with equipment and offer troubleshooting solutions.

Photographic Technical Writers also write product descriptions for catalogs, create parts lists, sales promotion literature, and proposals for projects. Trade and consumer magazines often commission Photographic Technical Writers to review products. Technical writers may attend trade shows and experience firsthand the premarket releases of innovative equipment. They can then provide insights about these new-and-improved or revolutionary products in roundup articles. Photographic Technical Writers also write for the FAQ, service, and instructional areas of product Web sites. Some are even able to contribute graphic design and layout skills.

Writers also cover the photography industry for magazines such as *American Photo, Outdoor Photographer,* and *PCPhoto Magazine.* Articles may cover news and current trends in photography, special techniques for different types of shooting, interviews with prominent photographers, reviews of popular locations, and much more. Depending on a magazine's editorial slant, these articles may be aimed at professionals or amateurs, and Photographic Technical Writers must adjust the tone of their writing accordingly.

Photographic Technical Writers can work either on staff with magazines or on a freelance basis. Those on staff usually participate in regularly scheduled editorial meetings, brainstorming story ideas, potential contributors, artwork, photographs, or layout for upcoming issues. They also fill in for other writers when needed. Freelance Photographic Technical Writers can work from home, on site at various publications and product headquarters, and anywhere on the road with their laptops. They take assignments from editors as well as pitch unsolicited story ideas and articles. Both freelance and staff technical writers are responsible for researching products, conducting interviews, ensuring that their information is accurate and original and that quotes are accurately conveyed.

Salaries

Photographic Technical Writers can earn salaries ranging from $30,270 to $80,900. The *Occupational Outlook Handbook* cites that in 2002, the median annual earnings for writers in computer systems design and related services were $51,730. Entry-level technical writers earned median annual salaries of $41,000 that same year, according to the Society for Technical Communication. Mid-level, nonsupervisory technical writers earned higher median salaries of $49,900, and senior-level, nonsupervisory writers garnered $66,000.

Employment Prospects

According to the *Occupational Outlook Handbook (OOH),* employment of writers overall is expected to grow by about 10 to 20 percent, or about as fast as the average for all occupations. Technical writers overall will find the best opportunities for employment. Technical writers and writers with expertise in specialized areas will be in greater demand due to continued expansion of scientific and technical informa-

tion and the need to communicate it to others. The *OOH* states that, "Developments and discoveries in the law, science, and technology generate demand for people to interpret technical information for a more general audience. Rapid growth and change in the high technology and electronics industries result in a greater need for people to write users' guides, instruction manuals, and training materials. This work requires people who are not only technically skilled as writers, but also familiar with the subject area."

Advancement Prospects

Staff Photographic Technical Writers can advance to become editors or managing editors, depending on their expertise and years with the publication. Freelance Photographic Technical Writers can advance by teaching or by participating in panel discussions at trade shows and events hosted by professional associations. Photographic Technical Writers can also expand their businesses by providing consultant services.

Education and Training

A four-year degree in liberal arts is required in the technical writing field. Photographic Technical Writers can have undergraduate degrees in communications, journalism, English, or photography. Whatever the degree, they must have experience in the area of photography they are writing about.

Experience, Skills, and Personality Traits

Photographic Technology Writers must have a consummate knowledge of photography, photographic equipment, styles, techniques, brands, features, and computers and design software. Writers who are highly sought after have prior experience as photographers, design and computer consultants, or as retouchers. They are curious individuals, always researching products and ideas, learning what is out there and what is to come. They stay inquisitive and know how to convey what they learn in ways that are logical and readable. Writers in general need to have strong ethics and know when and when not to publish something. Freelance Photographic Technical Writers in particular need to be self-disciplined and self-motivated, as their days will not be structured like those of staff writers. Technology writers, overall, need to be extremely familiar with electronic publishing, graphics, and design software programs.

Unions and Associations

Photographic Technical Writers can join the Association for Technical Communication and the National Writers Union for access to employment listings, salary information, special interest groups, educational opportunities and conferences, publications, discounts on group health insurance, and other services.

Tips for Entry

1. Technical writers first and foremost need to know how to write. Take writing classes if you are still in college. If you have graduated already, you can still take continuing education writing classes at local universities and colleges.

2. The first step in being a professional technical writer is getting published. Start submitting articles that are geared to general consumer audiences to local newspapers. Make sure you are familiar with the style of the newspaper and that your content matches the audience's needs. Also be sure the topics you cover have not already been recently covered and, if so, that you have a completely different slant.

3. Join a writer's association. Often the best way to find work in this field is through networking. Writer's associations often have employment listings that members can subscribe to as either part of their membership or for discounted rates.

4. Join your local Chamber of Commerce and other professional organizations. Enlist yourself as a speaker about digital photography and any specifics in relation to the field at an upcoming meeting or luncheon. Turn your speech into a handout and include your name and contact information. Prepare a press release about your talk as well as a follow-up article about it and submit it to local media for coverage and publicity.

PHOTOGRAPHIC EQUIPMENT TECHNICIAN

CAREER PROFILE

Duties: Maintains and repairs cameras and film and video equipment; meets with clients to discuss problems and expected turnaround times; keeps track of orders and invoices; sells other products; manages staff

Alternate Title(s): Camera Technician

Salary Range: $16,480 to $50,340

Employment Prospects: Fair

Advancement Prospects: Good

Best Geographical Location(s): Major metropolitan areas, such as Atlanta, Boston, Chicago, Dallas, Houston, Los Angeles, Miami, New York, San Francisco, Seattle, and Washington, D.C.

Prerequisites:

Education or Training—B.A. in photography helpful but not required; specialized training in photographic equipment maintenance and repair required

Experience—One to two years of apprenticeship in photo-equipment repair division of a camera store or with camera manufacturer or dealer recommended

Special Skills and Personality Traits—Technologically and mechanically agile; patient; excellent eye for details; excellent hand-eye coordination; problem solver; reliable; deadline-oriented

CAREER LADDER

```
┌─────────────────────────────────────────┐
│    Supervisor of Technician Department    │
└─────────────────────────────────────────┘

┌─────────────────────────────────────────┐
│    Photographic Equipment Technician      │
└─────────────────────────────────────────┘

┌─────────────────────────────────────────┐
│         Apprentice or Trainee             │
└─────────────────────────────────────────┘
```

Position Description

More people than ever before are using cameras and photographic equipment, thanks to lowered prices and wider access to products and services. The hobbyist as well as the professional photographer turns to the Photographic Equipment Technician for help in maintaining and caring for complicated, expensive, and unique equipment. Photographic Equipment Technicians are responsible for maintaining and fixing cameras and film and video equipment. They keep them functioning well by testing them and making minor adjustments as needed. Technicians will first speak with customers to learn what the specific issues are. They will troubleshoot first, asking if the customer has tried alternatives, finding out what the conditions were when the camera

was used, and if this has ever happened before. They will also discuss rates and solidify the expected turnaround time.

To discern problems, Photographic Equipment Technicians will take cameras and other film and video equipment apart to examine all of the parts to see if anything is worn, out of place, or defective. Even for the most complex inner mechanics, the tools of their trade can be as rudimentary as wire cutters, pliers, and screwdrivers, as well as a jeweler's loupe for close examination. Technicians use electronic test equipment, such as optical measuring instruments, to check the camera's shutter speed and make sure the focus is working accurately. They also check the operating speed of motion picture cameras and light-meter readings. Manufacturers' blueprints and repair manuals serve as guides throughout the tests. Most modern cameras have automatic focus and aperture settings as well as built-in light meters. When things go wrong, only the trained technician has the skills to patiently and carefully address the problems.

Camera maintenance is another important part of the Photographic Equipment Technician's job. To work properly, cameras need to be kept extremely clean and well lubricated. Photographic Equipment Technicians use air pressure and vacuum devices to remove dust and fine particles. For hardened dirt, they use ultrasonic cleaning equipment. They also use chemical solvents and tissue paper to clean lenses and apply fine lubricants to equipment with syringes or cotton swabs. Some technicians may create parts to replace those that are worn or not working correctly. They will use milling machines, grinders, small instrument-maker's lathes, and other equipment.

Salaries

The median salary for Photographic Equipment Technicians was $31,390 in 2002, according to the U.S. Department of Labor. The lowest paid 10 percent earned $16,480, while the highest paid 10 percent earned $50,340 or more a year. Self-employed technicians have earnings that vary widely. In the right location, independent technicians can build up businesses that give them earnings higher than those of technicians who work for manufacturers or shops. Some Photographic Equipment Technicians enhance their salaries by continuing to work as freelance photographers.

Employment Prospects

The outlook is not particularly bright for Photographic Equipment Technicians. According to the *Occupational Outlook Handbook,* a decline in employment growth in the photographic equipment repair field is expected over the next several years, due to several factors. Prices for cameras have dropped, yet the cost for labor remains high. For many people, it is more affordable to purchase a new camera than it is to have certain repairs done. Digital photography, however, has introduced a wide range of sophisticated and expensive equipment into the marketplace, making it more worthwhile to maintain the equipment than to replace it. Successful technicians are often those whose knowledge and expertise covers a range of photographic equipment brands and models. The more versatile the technician is, the more clients he or she can help. Competition will be fierce because there are few jobs and still more candidates applying for the positions. Technicians may find more opportunities in large camera and photographic equipment shops, as well as with major camera manufacturers and dealers. Those specializing in film and video equipment may find some opportunities with film- or television-production companies.

Advancement Prospects

With time, freelance Photographic Equipment Technicians advance by growing their client base. They become adept at working with a wider variety of old and current camera brands and models, by continually taking classes and finessing their skills. Photo Equipment Technicians may also grow their shops by expanding their products and selling *add-ons,* such as film, photo accessories, and photographic equipment, to their customers. Experienced technicians may train others, teach classes at technical schools and institutions, and contribute articles to trade publications.

Education and Training

Specialized training in photographic equipment maintenance and repair is required in this field. A bachelor's degree in photography is beneficial, and technical training is essential. Photographic Equipment Technicians may take courses online or in person at technical schools and institutions. Technicians will learn to repair various cameras and equipment as well as gain a more thorough understanding of electronics. Courses that pertain to specific camera brands and models, as well as on-the-job training, round out the education and make for better-qualified technicians. Those who work on staff with camera manufacturers and importers often receive in-house training on that company's specific products.

Experience, Skills, and Personality Traits

Several years of experience as an apprentice or trainee with a Photographic Equipment Technician is the best way to gain firsthand exposure to the job. Photographic Equipment Technicians must be comfortable working alone and have patience and focus to accomplish their goals. This is by no means a glamorous position, and only those who truly enjoy solving problems thrive in the field. The job is stationary and sedentary, often requiring long hours examining small parts. Successful technicians know how to address some of the consequences of the work: eye strain, physical aches, and general tedium. Handling the small camera parts requires steady hands and calm, patient demeanors. Excellent vision and mechanical aptitude are also heavily relied upon. Independent Photographic Equipment Technicians must also be able to work with customers, listening closely to their needs, asking questions, and communicating the steps they plan to take and the time frame required. They must also have good business-management skills, particularly if they are running their own companies.

Unions and Associations

Photographic Equipment Technicians can join such groups as the National Association of Photo Equipment Technicians and the Society of Photo-Technologists International for professional conferences, employment referrals, and networking and educational opportunities.

Tips for Entry

1. Find the larger camera and photographic equipment stores in your area and speak with the on-site camera

repairperson. He or she may have useful information to share and can shed further light on the field for you.

2. Take photographic equipment courses to hone your skills and keep fresh on the latest technology. Technology schools and institutions provide educational opportunities as well as valuable connections for employment referrals.

3. Join a professional association, such as the National Association of Photo Equipment Technicians. Keep up with what is going on in the industry by reading all of the literature and networking whenever possible.

4. Stay immersed in the field by reading trade publications such as *Photo District News, Popular Photography,* and others.

PHOTOGRAPHY STORE MANAGER

CAREER PROFILE

Duties: Manages photography stores and oversees sales and stock of photographic equipment and accessories; supervises repair work; interviews, hires, trains, and supervises sales associates and other store employees; makes sure the store is clean and organized; oversees expenses and receipts; responds to customer inquiries

Alternate Title(s): Sales Manager

Salary Range: $18,380 to $100,000+

Employment Prospects: Fair

Advancement Prospects: Good

Best Geographical Location(s): Major metropolitan areas

Prerequisites:

Education or Training—Bachelor's degree in liberal arts, photography, or retail preferred

Experience—Several years of experience as a camera-store sales associate beneficial

Special Skills and Personality Traits—Strong knowledge of photographic equipment, cameras, and brands; excellent management and interpersonal skills; reliable; responsible; clear communicator; organized; well versed in store policies; energetic; diplomatic; customer-service oriented

CAREER LADDER

```
┌─────────────────────────────────┐
│        Regional Director         │
└─────────────────────────────────┘

┌─────────────────────────────────┐
│   Photography Store Manager      │
└─────────────────────────────────┘

┌─────────────────────────────────┐
│ Photography Store Sales Associate│
└─────────────────────────────────┘
```

Position Description

Photography Store Managers oversee all aspects of a photography store's operation. They work long hours to ensure that everything is running smoothly and all employees are performing well. They are responsible for reviewing employment applications, interviewing and hiring, as well as training and monitoring the staff's performance. When an employee is making frequent mistakes or his or her conduct is inappropriate, it is the store manager's job to meet with this employee, discuss the situation, and choose an appropriate course of action that is in keeping with the store's policy. On the flip side, the Photography Store Manager rewards employees who perform well with bonuses, pay raises, and promotions. Store managers delegate assignments to workers, such as unpacking, shelving, and listing new inventory or organizing and cleaning the stock room.

When sales associates are unable to resolve a client's problem or if a difficult customer comes along, they often refer the individual to the store manager. It is the store manager's job to represent the store well by maintaining a professional, diplomatic demeanor and putting on his or her best customer service face. Additionally, store managers must be able to keep the peace among employees who may not always get along with each other. Managers must know how to resolve conflicts to mutual satisfaction and keep the team spirit alive.

Tracking store inventory is another key part of a Photography Store Manager's job. They must keep records of all photographic equipment and accessories in order to review sales and plan how much stock to order next and when to order. They review inventory deliveries to make sure the order is accurate and the merchandise is undamaged, then usually have staff record, price, and display or shelve the products. Depending upon the store's size and employee structure, Photography Store Managers may also oversee the bookkeeping and accounting, data processing, advertising, sales, and shipping. Store managers usually have more singularly focused jobs if they work in larger stores. Those who work for smaller stores will have more diverse duties, ranging from hands-on camera sales to actually developing film.

Salaries

Photography Store Managers' earnings vary, depending upon the size of the store, the job responsibilities, and the type of clientele the store serves. In 2002, the median annual earnings of all sales managers were $29,700, according to the U.S. Department of Labor. Annual salaries ranged from less than $18,380 to $55,810 or more. Sales managers who oversee an entire region for a retail chain can earn upward of $100,000. The more skilled and experienced the store manager, the more wages he or she is able to garner. Large national photo retailers may pay higher salaries to attract and secure top-notch employees. Photography Store Managers may also receive store merchandise discounts, with some stores extending the benefits to the managers' families. Salaried managers may also receive such benefits as medical insurance, paid vacation and sick leave, and retirement benefits.

Employment Prospects

Employment of retail managers overall will grow more slowly than the average for all occupations through 2012, according to the U.S. Department of Labor. Competition is expected to remain fierce, particularly because many retailers have been curbing costs by streamlining operations and reducing management staff. Photography Store Managers with advanced degrees and relevant experience in respected and established stores will have greater odds of securing employment. Some managers will be able to find work due to staff turnover and employees retiring from their positions. Managers can also get a foot in the door by taking a temporary step back. Employment of retail sales personnel is expected to grow about as fast as the average over the next few years. Stores may opt to extend business hours to attract more customers or may need to replace staff. If a managerial position is currently not available in the store that most interests the store manager, a management background will enable the individual to quickly move up from a sales position. Individuals who are especially knowledgeable about photographic products and camera brands and accessories and who are able to clearly describe and demonstrate features to customers will also be able to secure work and advance in a short time.

Advancement Prospects

Photography Store Managers who work for large retail chains may advance to become directors of certain areas or regions, overseeing a number of stores. They may relocate to larger stores in other cities and take on more responsibilities and manage larger staffs. Advancement depends upon the managers' skills, years of experience, and the types of stores with which they have been employed. Managers with advanced degrees and more training may also have greater advancement opportunities. With years of experience, store managers can open their own photography stores.

Education and Training

A bachelor's degree, while not required, provides Photography Store Managers with a well-rounded and solid educational background for this type of work. More stores, in fact, prefer managers to have college degrees. Studies can be in photography, liberal arts, or business, with coursework in business and marketing, accounting, English, advertising, and computer science. Some managers attend school while they work part time or full time in photo stores.

Experience, Skills, and Personality Traits

Photography Store Managers should have at least several years of experience as sales associates in camera and photographic equipment stores. Excellent management and leadership skills are essential in order to create cohesive, well-functioning and productive staff teams. Store managers also need solid communication skills to work well with fellow employees and to interact and provide good service to customers. Diplomacy, professionalism, a good appearance, patience, and energy all come in handy in this field. The retail industry often requires long hours and Photography Store Managers are usually expected to be flexible to work any and all hours. The work can be stressful, particularly when dealing with difficult staff members or clients. Store managers need to be able to juggle tasks and resolve conflicts. Stamina and a certain degree of physical fitness will also serve store managers well because the job requires them to be on their feet throughout most of the day. In addition to enjoying working with people, store managers need to be interested in and savvy about camera brands and features, photographic equipment, and photo accessories. Managers with outgoing personalities who are knowledgeable about photography equipment and cameras, organized and professional, and able to inspire respect and motivation from their employees usually do extremely well in this career.

Unions and Associations

Photography Store Managers can find useful educational information on the photography sales industry through such organizations as National Retail Federation and Photo Marketing Association International. Professional Photographers of America also provides access to educational resources and networking opportunities. Joining the local

Chamber of Commerce is also an excellent way to increase the store's sales and forge beneficial relationships with business owners and managers within the community.

Tips for Entry

1. Work in retail first before you decide to pursue this career. Take a job as a sales associate in a camera store or electronics retailer, such as Best Buy or Circuit City. Even a part-time job in a small store will give you firsthand exposure to the business. You will gain solid experience working directly with customers, fielding inquiries and handling sales, processing payments, and more. If you decide the photo retail track is for you, you will have a solid foundation to move up the career ladder.

2. Check job listings through all avenues: national and local newspapers, the back pages of trade publications, store Web sites, online employment Web sites—such as Yahoo! Hotjobs (http://hotjobs.yahoo.com), Monster (http://www.monster.com), and the New York Times on the Web (http://www.nytimes.com)—and placement agencies that specialize in retail.

3. Learn as much as you can about photographic products and accessories, as well as the latest technologies, by reading trade publications, attending photo trade shows, and networking at professional association conferences.

4. Hone your management skills by taking workshops and reading books offering management tips and advice.

PHOTOGRAPHIC LABORATORY WORKER

CAREER PROFILE

Duties: Develops exposed film, both color and black and white, by using printing machines or creating chemical baths; trims film, mounts slides, and sorts and packages completed photographs for clients; other responsibilities vary, depending upon the type of laboratory and its staff structure

Alternate Title(s): Photographic Process Worker, Darkroom Technician

Salary Range: $14,110 to $40,000+

Employment Prospects: Poor

Advancement Prospects: Fair

Best Geographical Location(s): Major cities and metropolitan areas, such as Atlanta, Boston, Chicago, Dallas, Denver, Houston, Los Angeles, Miami, New York, San Francisco, and Seattle

Prerequisites:

Education or Training—Two-year degree from technical school or institution required; four-year degree, with specialization in photography, helpful; training in digital photographic technologies recommended

Experience—One to two years of experience as a film developer in a photo lab beneficial

Special Skills and Personality Traits—Strong knowledge of photographic processes; manual dexterity; good color perception; clear communication skills with good interpersonal skills; patient

CAREER LADDER

```
┌─────────────────────────────────┐
│   Senior Darkroom Technician    │
└─────────────────────────────────┘

┌─────────────────────────────────┐
│  Photographic Laboratory Worker │
└─────────────────────────────────┘

┌─────────────────────────────────┐
│         Film Developer          │
└─────────────────────────────────┘
```

Position Description

Photographic Laboratory Workers use various chemical or water baths to develop exposed film. A series of steps are involved in created photographic images. Lab workers start the process by mixing developing and fixing solutions, then placing the film in the developer, stop bath, and fixer, creating a negative image. They time the film's immersion in the chemical bath based on the type of developer that is being used, as well as the effects that are specified for each print. After they remove the film from the developer, they remove all of the chemicals by immersing the film into water and then finally place it inside a drying cabinet.

Projection printers may assist lab workers by projecting film to transfer images from negatives onto photographic paper. (The light passes through the negative while a magnifying lens projects the image onto the paper.) The projection printers and lab workers can adjust the image by enhancing the contrast or removing certain details once they reach the printing process. Lab workers and technicians may also work closely with master developers, particularly if they work for large commercial laboratories with a more organized and traditional staff structure.

In larger operations, automatic print developers oversee machines that develop film and fix, wash, and dry prints.

They monitor and adjust temperature controls and review and refer quality challenged prints to quality control workers. Color-print operators manage color-print machines, loading negative film and placing photographic paper into the developer. Finished prints and processed negatives are placed in envelopes for customers. Other workers include automatic mounters for the color transparency slicing and slide-mounting machines, paper-process technicians, takedown sorters, photo checkers and assemblers, and digital imaging technicians. Precision photographic process workers, who work directly on negatives, include airbrush artists, colorists, and photographic spotters. For many of these, the titles are self-explanatory.

Specialized laboratories that handle custom work may employ retouchers to enhance and alter prints, as well as hand mounters, photograph finishers, print controllers and washers and inspectors, cutters and splicers, automatic developers, and film-processing utility workers.

Salaries
The median annual salary for Photographic Laboratory Workers in 2002 was $20,220, according to the U.S. Department of Labor. For workers overall, annual earnings ranged from $14,110 to $36,250. More experienced lab workers who move on to supervisory or management positions can earn upward of $40,000 per year. Most lab workers are full-time employees who may receive such benefits as health insurance, disability, and paid vacations and overtime.

Employment Prospects
Photographic Laboratory Workers can expect slower than average growth in their field through 2012, according to the U.S. Department of Labor. Experienced lab workers will have better odds of securing work, and those jobs will most likely open up because of workers who are retiring or relocating. There are few positions to be found, and those that exist are difficult to secure. While digital photography has reduced the need for traditional photographic processing, there are still a number of professional photographers and hobbyists who will continue to use conventional cameras or sophisticated disposable cameras and, consequently, still need photo lab work. Consumers who use digital cameras may also not be interested in purchasing and learning how to use digital photographic software and thus will rely on Photographic Laboratory Workers to process and retouch their photographic images. Individuals who are experienced using computers and digital technology will also find more opportunities for work.

In 2002, Photographic Laboratory Workers held about 28,000 jobs, with one out of four working in one-hour mini-labs and photo-finishing labs. Portrait studios and commercial laboratories that specialize in processing professional photographers' work employed one in six of all lab workers.

About 16 percent of all Photographic Laboratory Workers worked for general merchandise stores, and 10 percent were employed in the motion picture, printing, and publishing industries. Favorable times of year to find work are during the late spring and throughout summer, particularly for school graduations and vacations, and during winter holidays.

Advancement Prospects
With years of experience, Photographic Laboratory Workers can advance to become senior or head darkroom technicians or move up to management or supervisory jobs. Knowledgeable and entrepreneurial technicians can open up and manage their own photographic laboratories. They can also expand their skills and add to their résumés by teaching classes in technical schools and participating in conferences hosted by professional associations. Many lab workers freelance as photographers while holding down their day jobs in the laboratories. Those who are more focused on becoming commercial photographers can eventually move up and out by starting their own commercial photography studios.

Education and Training
Most Photographic Laboratory Workers have at least two-year degrees from technical institutes or from arts schools with photographic technology programs. Coursework in chemistry and math is also beneficial. Many lab workers train as assistants or apprentices to more experienced technicians. Training can last anywhere from several weeks to several months, and, once completed, fledgling lab workers will be permitted to start printing and developing film on their own.

Experience, Skills, and Personality Traits
Photographic Laboratory Workers usually get their feet in the door by first working as film developers. A strong interest in photography and knowledge of photographic techniques and processes are essential to this type of work. Photographic Laboratory Workers need to have mechanical aptitude, excellent vision, knowledge of color, and the ability to see true color. Experience in developing procedures is a good background for development work. Photographic Laboratory Workers must have excellent communication skills and be able to work well with both customers and fellow staff members. They must have a strong eye for detail, be reliable and responsible, and be always interested in learning about new technologies and development processes. The work can be tedious, so patient and calm individuals who enjoy seeing the results of their hard efforts will thrive in this field.

Unions and Associations
The Association of Professional Color Imagers, American Society of Media Photographers, Professional Photogra-

phers of America, and Advertising Photographers of America provide members with educational resources and networking opportunities. Photographic Laboratory Workers can also find useful information through membership to the American Institute of Graphic Artists.

Tips for Entry

1. If you are still in school, join a photography club. You will get invaluable experience shooting and developing your own photographs and learning how to adjust lighting and composition.
2. Pursue all avenues in your job hunt. Look for job listings in print newspapers and on Web employment sites, such as Yahoo! Hotjobs (http://hotjobs.yahoo.com), Monster (http://www.monster.com), and the New York Times on the Web (http://www.nytimes.com). You can also find listings on store Web sites.
3. Speak with Photographic Laboratory Workers to learn more about their job responsibilities and what they like most and least about their work. See if you can schedule informational meetings with them. Tell them that a mere 10 minutes of their time can make a world of difference in your career path. Be sure to create a list of questions before you meet. To show your appreciation, treat them to a cup of coffee or a soda or even lunch if they are spending their break with you.

RETAIL SALES ASSOCIATE, PHOTOGRAPHY

CAREER PROFILE

Duties: Assists photography store customers in understanding performance features of cameras and photography equipment and guides them toward purchases; works in small stores, large camera and electronic centers, convenience stores with camera counters; may work with companies that offer online services

Alternate Title(s): Electronics Sales Associate, Product Specialist, Wireless Retail Salesperson

Salary Range: $20,000 to $60,000

Employment Prospects: Good

Advancement Prospects: Good

Best Geographical Location(s): Major cities and suburban areas

Prerequisites:

Education or Training—High school diploma required; two-year degree, with specialization in photography, helpful; trained in digital photography

Experience—Some experience as a freelance photographer helpful; one or more years of experience in retail sales

Special Skills and Personality Traits—Extremely knowledgeable about digital photography systems and accessories; knowledgeable about computers, cell phones, PDAs, and other electronic equipment; approachable and friendly; excellent communication and interpersonal skills; responsible and reliable; able to multitask; energetic and capable of working at a fast pace

CAREER LADDER

```
┌─────────────────────────────────┐
│       Department Manager        │
└─────────────────────────────────┘

┌─────────────────────────────────┐
│  Assistant Department Manager   │
└─────────────────────────────────┘

┌─────────────────────────────────┐
│     Retail Sales Associate      │
└─────────────────────────────────┘
```

Position Description

Retail Sales Associates may work in small, individually owned photography stores or large electronics chains, such as Best Buy and Circuit City. They guide customers in the purchase of cameras, lights, light stands, tripods, and all other photographic equipment. They field customer questions, find out the types of pictures the customer plans to take with the camera as well as how much the customer is willing to spend, and directs the customer to the cameras that fit his or her needs.

Retail Sales Associates know how cameras work and often demonstrate the various features. They may show customers how to synch up digital cameras to computers and download images or show them the types of photographic design software they can use to enhance color, crop shots, and change image size. They may also demonstrate scanning and printing options that work best with the cameras, by printing images and pointing out image and color qualities. When a customer is ready to purchase the camera, Retail Sales Associates look in the store's database to confirm it is in stock. They create the purchase order in the computer by getting the customer's name, address, payment information, terms of warranty, and other information. Many stores provide sales associates with commissions, so they always include their initials or employee ID numbers on the order forms.

Retail Sales Associates specialize in cameras and photographic equipment, but they are also representatives of the store. They are sometimes the first impression a customer may have of the store, and therefore their main job is customer service. Customers will often ask questions about subjects beyond the photography department, and sales associates will need to know how to answer them. They must be familiar with the store's chain of command in case they need to refer a customer with a problem or complaint to the appropriate manager or director. They must also be knowledgeable about store policies, current store sales and special offers, the locations of other departments, and where other products can be found.

Salaries

Retail Sales Associates who work full time can earn salaries ranging from $20,000 to $60,000. Many work at a base salary and earn commissions for their sales. They often augment their incomes by advising customers about the benefits of enhanced photographic systems and guiding them toward purchasing computers, printers, and photographic design software and literature. Retail stores often provide their full-time electronics sales associates with attractive benefits packages, which may include medical, dental, and life insurance; retirement plans; disability; paid vacations and holidays; sick leave; and tuition reimbursement; as well as discounts on store merchandise, cell phone and Internet plans, and other services.

Employment Prospects

Thanks to the advent of digital photography and continual innovations in technology, there is no shortage of opportunities for the technically proficient Retail Sales Associate. Technology chains stores such as Circuit City, Best Buy, CompUSA, and Staples are constantly seeking knowledgeable, qualified sales associates and product specialists. Prospective employees can find job listings directly on these stores' Web sites as well as through Internet employment placement sites.

Advancement Prospects

Advancement comes at a faster pace in camera-computer sales than in most other retail sales areas in the country today. The growth of computers in the home and the relationship of digital cameras to those computers have made electronics stores high-profit centers around the world. Sales associates with two or three years of retail experience

can advance to become assistant department managers or, depending upon the store and staff structure, move directly into department manager positions. Associates with outstanding sales performance often advance the fastest into store leadership positions.

Education and Training

A high school diploma and extensive knowledge of technology may be sufficient for some electronics and photography retail centers. Sales associates who have at least a two-year degree in photography, however, will have better educational backgrounds, which can help them advance faster in this field. Sales associates who take workshops and train in sales techniques and business management often can improve their opportunities of securing employment.

Experience, Skills, and Personality Traits

Most Retail Sales Associates have at least one or more years of prior retail sales experience. While some may focus specifically on photographic equipment, many are also knowledgeable about cell phones, computers, and consumer electronics. Successful sales associates have winning personalities; they are confident, outgoing, and know how to tune into people's needs and purchasing styles. They know how to "read" people and sense the appropriate time to approach and assist. Sales associates also know how to phrase their questions and, based on the answers, which products to point customers toward. Dealing with the general public is no easy task. It requires stamina and full attention. Not all customers will be pleasant and easy to help. Every so often the difficult customer will appear, demanding immediate attention. Sales associates need to be skilled in diplomatically handling this type of customer. To keep their jobs and move up in the field, they must know how to stay poised and professional while still attempting to meet this customer's needs. This skill requires a great deal of self-discipline and restraint.

Unions and Associations

There are no associations specifically dedicated to Retail Sales Associates. Sales associates can learn about the business and keep abreast of technological developments by regularly reading industry publications, such as *Professional Photographer, Petersen's Photographic, American Photo, Digital Photo Pro,* and others. They can also join professional photography associations (i.e., Professional Photographers of America), either as full or associate members, for access to educational and networking opportunities.

Tips for Entry

1. Create a list of the large photography and electronics centers near you. Visit their Web sites to see if they

have job openings or visit the stores directly and inquire in person. Be sure to have your résumé and references with you so that you can immediately and accurately complete the store's application for employment.

2. Keep up with technology by reading trade publications and taking workshops. Some retail stores offer free or very affordable classes to customers to introduce them to digital cameras, computer equipment, and other electronics.

3. Check job listings on placement sites such as Yahoo! Hotjobs (http://hotjobs.yahoo.com) and Monster (http://www.monster.com) and scan your local newspaper's help-wanted section.

STOCK PHOTO AGENCY OWNER/MANAGER

<table>
<tr>
<td>

CAREER PROFILE

Duties: Provides photographic images of a wide variety of subjects (i.e., television personalities, movie stars, musicians, politicians) for rental to magazine, newspaper, and book publishers, advertisers, television-program creators, and others; negotiates usage agreements and rates with photographers as well as stock buyers; oversees creation and maintenance of stock library; secures photographers from all over the world for assignments; conducts photo research; oversees and manages staff

Alternate Title(s): None

Salary Range: $50,000 to $250,000+

Employment Prospects: Fair

Advancement Prospects: Fair

Best Geographical Location(s): Major entertainment and publishing hubs, such as Boston, Chicago, Hollywood, Las Vegas, Los Angeles, Miami, New York, Seattle, San Francisco, and Washington, D.C.

Prerequisites:

Education and Training—Two- or four-year degree in photography; coursework in small-business management, marketing, and advertising

Experience—Several years of experience as a freelance commercial photographer; three or more years of experience working in photography agencies

Special Skills and Personality Traits—Passionate and knowledgeable about photography and photographers; marketing and sales savvy; entrepreneurial; strong management abilities; ethical

</td>
<td>

CAREER LADDER

```
┌─────────────────────────────────────┐
│          Franchise Owner             │
└─────────────────────────────────────┘

┌─────────────────────────────────────┐
│  Stock Photo Agency Owner/Manager    │
└─────────────────────────────────────┘

┌─────────────────────────────────────┐
│           Photographer               │
└─────────────────────────────────────┘
```

</td>
</tr>
</table>

Position Description

Stock Photo Agency Owner/Managers offer rentals of photographic images as well as other photographic services to clients for publication in books, magazine articles, CD and DVD covers, zines, calendars, posters, T-shirts, and more. They negotiate stock photo usage and sales agreements with photographers and with buyers. A critical part of their job is maintaining a current client base, attracting new customers, keeping current stock photographers happy, and enlisting fresh photographers and images. Stock Photo Agency Owner/Managers work with graphic and Web designers to create the agency's promotional and marketing campaigns, through stock image directories and catalogs, Web site databases and e-mail newsletters and advertisements, CDs, and postcards. Owner/managers also hire and retain photographers for clients who need new photographs and photographic services as opposed to stock images.

Stock photo agencies are either exclusive, meaning the photographer's image can only appear in one publication and with one client, or nonexclusive, meaning photographers can sell the same images to other agencies, usually with some caveats to the agreements. Stock photo agencies typically offer photographers several options for selling their images: through online databases, by request from clients, and through online portfolios, in which the agency offers a space on the Web site and clients buy directly from photographers without the agency receiving commission. Some agencies, such as Getty Images, offer clients the option to purchase either rights-managed or royalty-free images.

Photography, artwork, music, and more may be used and reproduced in any number of ways but only in accordance with the terms of agreement between the original creator, the stock agency, and the buyer. Transactions involving photographic prints, slides, or digital reproduction can take place by Internet or fax. Buyers can also have images delivered to FTP (file transfer protocol) servers or saved on CD-R (CD-Recordable, which is a nonreusable disc.) Original artwork is usually picked up in person or express-mailed with proper insurance. Rental and licensing fees will depend upon how the image will be used. The wider the distribution and variety of media in which the image will appear, the higher the fee. A one-time publication of the image in a national magazine with a circulation in the millions will cost more than a small reproduction in a town newspaper. Once a picture has had national exposure, its value diminishes for a few years until it is out of public memory.

Owners of small stock-photo agencies now compete with the likes of the Library of Congress, which offers prints for under $50, and the National Archives, with its own historic files and relevant photographs. The New York Public Library has a collection of more than 2 million photographs covering topics primarily in New York. Additionally, media corporations now offer their own stock libraries through their Web sites. The New York Times, United Press, Associated Press, Reuters, and others feature enormous collections of news photographs. Stock photo houses may have images of most presidents but few photos of other political subjects and issues. These photos are readily available on media Web sites.

Stock Photo Agency Owner/Managers are not only responsible for keeping abreast of industry standards and ethics, overseeing contracts, setting price structures, and creating direct marketing and promotional campaigns to attract new customers but also handling the everyday administrative and management tasks involved in running a business. They hire and manage staff. They make sure office equipment is maintained and office supplies are stocked. They regularly meet and work with freelance consultants such as graphic designers, Web designers, writers, and computer technicians. They set employment policies, review and

decide upon benefit packages and incentives, and oversee bookkeeping, tax payments, and accounts receivable and payable.

Salaries
A Stock Photo Agency Owner/Manager's annual salary can range from $50,000 to $250,000 or more. Earnings will depend upon the size of the photo library, the quality of the images, the caliber of the photographers, and the focus of the subject matter. Images of television and film stars, movie directors, politicians and political events, singers, bands, concerts, sports stars and games, and royalty are always in demand. High-quality shots and images featuring hard-to-find perspectives and content can generate higher incomes.

Employment Prospects
Stock Photography Agency Owner/Managers have major competition because of the more diversified ways people can now access stock images via the Internet. Challenging them more is the fact that stock houses have consolidated over the years, to the point where corporations have taken over. For instance, Microsoft leader Bill Gates purchased stock image house Corbis, the world's largest collection of photographs in nine countries on three continents. Stock Photo Agency Owner/Managers who can come up with new, innovative ideas and partnerships that embrace photographer's rights, and who are passionate about the subject of the photographs and the photographers, may have better lasting power than those who are simply in it for the money.

Advancement Prospects
Stock Photo Agency Owner/Managers advance by adding more photographs and photographers to their agencies. They expand their businesses by opening new agencies in other cities and franchising their business. They advance their careers by speaking at association meetings and conferences, lecturing at universities and technical schools, and writing articles for trade publications.

Education and Training
A two- or four-year degree in photography, with coursework in small business management, industry practices and ethics, and marketing and negotiating tactics, is recommended for this position. Five or more years of experience as a commercial photographer, with training in digital photography and design software, is beneficial.

Experience, Skills, and Personality Traits
Several years of experience as a professional photographer and five or more years of on-the-job training at a photo

agency is recommended for this position. If the stock photo house focuses its library on a particular subject (i.e., music and entertainment), having a passion for and strong knowledge of that subject matter will be an excellent asset. Stock Photo Agency Owner/Managers need to be tuned into the photography industry and fluent in industry standards and contract language. Negotiating and selling skills are an inherent part of the job. Because they juggle many projects and people throughout the day, solid organizational and communication skills, as well as the ability to prioritize and meet deadlines, are essential. Stock Photo Agency Owner/Managers are self-motivated, enthusiastic, and ethical individuals with a deep appreciation for photographers and photography.

Unions and Associations

Stock Photo Agency Owner/Managers may belong to the Photo Marketing Association International, Advertising Photographers of America, American Society of Media Photographers, and Professional Photographers of America for networking opportunities, educational workshops and conferences, opportunities to promote their businesses, and discounts on professional services.

Tips for Entry

1. Do an Internet search of stock photo agencies. Read the FAQs or "about us" sections of their Web sites.

Sometimes the owners include their biographies and explain what interested them most in this type of work. This is an excellent way to learn more about the individuals who comprise this field. You can find out what makes them successful and see if you have any of the same traits.

2. Read everything you can about the stock photography business and take workshops. It is critical that you understand the rules and regulations regarding copyright and trademark laws and that you have a firm grasp on business standards and ethics in this field. Read magazines such as *Photo District News* and publications by photography associations such as the American Society of Media Photographers. You can also find valuable information about stock image usage in the Graphic Artists Guild's *Handbook of Pricing and Ethical Guidelines.*

3. Visit Stockphoto Network (http://www.stockphoto. net) for educational resources and online networking opportunities and Corbis (http://pro.corbis.com) to review a major stock archive.

4. Get an internship or entry-level position in a respectable stock-photo agency. This way you will see what the business is like firsthand and know if this is a field you want to pursue.

PORTRAIT PHOTOGRAPHY

BABY AND CHILD PHOTOGRAPHER

CAREER PROFILE

Duties: Photographs infants and children for family portraits; creates headshots for modeling and casting agencies, representatives, publishers, etc.; creates estimates; books appointments; oversees staff; handles accounts receivable and payable

Alternate Title(s): Children's Photographer, Portrait Photographer

Salary Range: $25,000 to $75,000+

Employment Prospects: Good

Advancement Prospects: Fair

Best Geographical Location(s): Major cities with large suburbs, such as Chicago, Los Angeles, New York, Philadelphia, and Washington, D.C.

Prerequisites:

Education or Training—Four-year degree in photography, with coursework in computer design software (Adobe Photoshop, Illustrator)

Experience—Two to three years of experience as an assistant photographer in a portrait studio or with a commercial studio

Special Skills and Personality Traits—Strong knowledge of composition and lighting; excellent communication skills; agile at working with babies, children, and adults; flexible; creative; patient; warm, inviting personality that puts people at ease

CAREER LADDER

```
┌─────────────────────────────────┐
│     Full-Service Studio Owner     │
└─────────────────────────────────┘

┌─────────────────────────────────┐
│   Baby and Child Photographer     │
└─────────────────────────────────┘

┌─────────────────────────────────┐
│      Assistant Photographer       │
└─────────────────────────────────┘
```

Position Description

Baby and Child Photographers create photographic images of babies and children for their parents and families, as well as for a variety of commercial clients such as publishers and advertisers. Most Baby and Child Photographers work independently and own their own portrait studios, or they may share studio space with other photographers to reduce costs and enhance their brand image. Some will work exclusively with babies and children, taking photographs on site in the studio as well as in homes, schools, parks, and at special events, such as birthday parties, Little League games, and graduations. To stay competitive and keep work flowing, however, many photographers have realized that offering multiple services and working in cross disciplines can be more advantageous than specializing in a particular niche. While they work with babies and children, they may also offer adult portraits, special event and wedding photography, etc.

Baby and Child Photographers usually have low start-up costs and have modest but practical furnishings in their studios. A rocking chair, some eye-catching and appropriate toys, clean blankets and quilts, and other simple props can often suffice. If working exclusively with digital camera equipment, a darkroom is unnecessary. Their studio reception area can double as a sales center for low-cost picture frames and countertop printouts of digital images, photo repairs, and duplications.

Freelance Baby and Child Photographers are responsible for all aspects of their business, including hiring and overseeing staff, scheduling appointments, purchasing photography equipment and film, making sure the studio is clean, maintaining office supplies and equipment, managing accounts receivable and payable, as well as networking and marketing their services. They may hire specialists, such as bookkeepers, accountants, and representatives, to address some of these tasks, or they may choose to do much of the work themselves until they are well established in the industry.

Salaries

Most Baby and Child Photographers are freelance and can, therefore, earn annual salaries that range anywhere from $25,000 to $75,000 or more, depending on experience, type of clientele, and the region in which they work. Less experienced photographers who are new to the business may earn lower salaries in their first few years. Seasoned photographers with steady clientele and strong reputations in the field will command higher rates. Photographers who work in major cities or suburbs with large populations will have greater opportunities to earn higher wages. Portrait photographers usually enhance their incomes by taking adult portraits and passport photos, doing wedding photography, and selling frames and photographic goods. They may also enhance their salaries by licensing their work.

Employment Prospects

Baby and Child Photographers will find greater employment opportunities in major cities and in larger studios, which offer a host of services. These city studios employ portrait photographers for children and adults. They will send photographers to executive offices in the city to take photographs of employees for annual reports, brochures, Web sites, and other publications. Portrait photographers will also travel to homes and estates in the suburbs to take individual shots of babies, children, and parents, as well as group photos of entire families. Some portrait photographers may work for department stores as well. While there are no statistics about employment in this specific discipline, the *Occupational Outlook Handbook* predicts that as the population grows, so, too, will the need for portrait photographers.

Advancement Prospects

Freelance Baby and Child Photographers may expand their businesses by offering even more services, such as adult portraits, full-length wedding gown photography, commercial product photography, and weekend work at weddings. Staff photographers typically advance by having increased management responsibilities. Some move up to become studio owners when owners retire or sell their business. Portrait photographers can also teach photography to community groups and to high school, college, and continuing education students. They can also write articles for industry publications and Web sites.

Education and Training

A two- or four-year degree in photography is recommended, with training in design software such as Adobe Photoshop and Illustrator. Like all professional photographers, Baby and Child Photographers need to stay tuned into technological developments in the industry and can do so by reading trade publications, visiting Web sites, and attending conferences and product demos.

Experience, Skills, and Personality Traits

A portrait photographer's job is to capture an individual at his or her natural best. This is no easy task and is harder still for the Baby and Child Photographer. Babies and children are still developing individuals and rely heavily on their parents for reassurance, safety, and comfort. Baby and Child Photographers must first and foremost be interested in working with these age groups. They must be sensitive to young people and know how to ease anxieties when they arise, and they can rest assured they will arise. They know when to soothe and speak quietly and when to bring in high energy and animation. They are adept at working with adults, also, and at communicating clearly about the portraits they plan to create. Kids and parents will have good days and bad. If they are having a bad day, it is up to photographers not to add to the stress by finding ways to keep things calm and focused. They may also have to deal with anxious and doting parents. Individuals with endless supplies of patience in addition to solid technical skills will do well here.

Baby and Child Photographers must be playful too. They need to know which toys and props are appropriate and how to play with kids of all ages. At times they may work with large groups for such things as school or sports team portraits. Their ability to handle these groups in a professional, calm, yet warm manner will come in handy. Baby and Child Photographers often have at least one to three years of experience as assistant photographers or studio assistants in portrait or commercial studios.

Unions and Associations

Baby and Child Photographers may join such associations as the American Society of Media Photographers, Professional Photographers of America, and Wedding and Portrait Photographers International for educational and networking opportunities, job listings, conventions, magazines and newsletters, and discounts on various products.

Tips for Entry

1. Visit small portrait studios in your area. Introduce yourself to the owners and ask if there are any job opportunities. Remember to keep track of business cards, contact names, and dates of meetings. Following up with a written thank-you note always leaves a good impression.
2. Jobs can be found through various avenues. Be sure to frequently check advertisements in trade publications, local newspapers, and Web sites.
3. Intern or volunteer with a studio. It is a great way to get a foot in the door, meet photographers and other professionals, learn how studios are set up, and see the methods by which portraits are created.

BOUDOIR PHOTOGRAPHER

CAREER PROFILE

Duties: Creates private portraits of women or men for their significant others; meets with clients to discuss attire and accessories, styles, and moods of photographs; may provide framing as part of portrait package; creates estimates; handles accounts receivable and payable

Alternate Title(s): Glamour Photographer, Portrait Photographer, Theatrical Photographer

Salary Range: $25,000 to $40,000+

Employment Prospects: Good

Advancement Prospects: Good

Best Geographical Location(s): New York, Washington, D.C., Atlanta, Chicago, Las Vegas, Los Angeles, Miami, and San Francisco

Prerequisites

    Education or Training—Associate's or bachelor's degree from a technical photography school or from a liberal arts school, with specialization in photography; digital camera and design software training

    Experience—Several years of freelance or staff experience as a professional photographer at a portrait studio or in theatrical photography; freelance experience photographing children, adults, and weddings

    Special Skills and Personality Traits—Personal warmth; flexible nature; creative; professional and mature manner, with poise and dignity in a boudoir setting; excellent communication skills; able to work with a variety of people; sensitive; diplomatic

CAREER LADDER

```
┌─────────────────────────────────────┐
│     Photography Studio Owner         │
└─────────────────────────────────────┘

┌─────────────────────────────────────┐
│      Boudoir Photographer            │
└─────────────────────────────────────┘

┌─────────────────────────────────────┐
│    Portrait Photographer /           │
│    Wedding Photographer              │
└─────────────────────────────────────┘
```

Position Description

Women and men hire Boudoir Photographers when they want to have intimate, provocative portraits created to give as gifts to their husbands, wives, boyfriends, and girlfriends. Actors, artists, musicians, and other professionals in the entertainment business may also hire Boudoir Photographers to create portraits for marketing and promotional purposes. These clients entrust Boudoir Photographers to provide safe, clean environments in which they can feel comfortable enough to be themselves when posing. Clients first meet with Boudoir Photographers to review portfolios and determine if the style of the portraits is what they are looking for. Boudoir Photographers typically present samples depicting various clothing arrangements and accessories, diverse body types, varying degrees of undress, and other more, or less, suggestive poses.

Boudoir Photographers are usually freelancers and have the flexibility to create and adjust their studio environment to suit each client's need. They use various colors, textures, and lighting to create moods and visuals that will best suit each portrait. Props can include couches, chairs, pillows, and drapery.

Boudoir Photographers discuss all aspects of the portraits with clients prior to the appointment and allow them to decide what they are most interested in and with what they are most comfortable. Clients choose either their own attire or select clothing and accessories from a wardrobe provided by the Boudoir Photographer. When the actual sitting occurs, Boudoir Photographers are sensitive to their clients' comfort levels and frequently ask them how they are doing and if they are comfortable with the style and with the poses. Although clients may have chosen and agreed to certain things beforehand, checking in with them during the shoot is a critical aspect of this practice.

Digital photography has helped the boudoir photography business grow. Whereas on-film boudoir photograph negatives need to be processed in labs, digital images stay safely in one place at the boudoir photography studio. With digital photography, clients do not have to worry about their private portraits being viewed by film lab technicians and possibly others; the digital system bypasses any public exposure of proofs or finished prints. Boudoir Photographers can retouch digital images using software programs such as Adobe Photoshop and Illustrator. Another boon to the business is that with digital, Boudoir Photographers never run out of film. Digital also lightens the load on the Boudoir Photographer's back if traveling to location shoots. All equipment can be carried in a shoulder bag and in one carrying case.

Salaries

Boudoir Photographers are usually freelancers and can typically earn annual salaries ranging from $25,000 to $40,000 or more. Factors influencing earnings may include the budgets of the clientele with which the Boudoir Photographer works, the number of sittings he or she is able to secure each week, the geographical location of the studio or shoots, and overhead costs. Boudoir Photographers can enhance their incomes by having studios that can be quickly rearranged to suit other types of portrait photography, such as babies, children, or corporate executives.

Employment Prospects

Boudoir Photography is largely an offshoot of wedding photography and studio portraiture and can offer good employment prospects. According to the *Occupational Outlook Handbook,* the demand for portrait photographers will grow as the population increases. Photographers who are well networked with artists, actors, performers, and others in the entertainment field will have the word-of-mouth advantage that is needed to secure work. Photographers who have solid backgrounds in portrait photography and who have established reputations for their quality work, as well as their professional and ethical conduct, will also have better chances of finding consistent and steady work.

Advancement Prospects

There is no specific career ladder for the boudoir photography field. The Boudoir Photographer who establishes a name for himself or herself can expand by hiring staff and catering to different clientele. He or she can also expand the business geographically, by opening specialized or full-service studios in other cities.

Education and Training

The foundation for a Boudoir Photographer is usually a two- or four-year degree, with a specialization in photography. Because more studios have been moving into digital photography, coursework and/or on-the-job training in digital cameras and design software (i.e. Adobe Photoshop, Illustrator) is highly recommended.

Experience, Skills, and Personality Traits

Boudoir Photographers usually have several years of prior experience in portrait photography. Fashion and beachwear portraits with live models is also a suitable training ground for boudoir photography. Like all portrait photographers, Boudoir Photographers must have exceptional people skills. They must have approachable, friendly manners and be excellent communicators. It is of utmost importance that the individuals who work in this field are adept at making people feel comfortable. Professionalism and honesty are also keys to being successful in this particular niche. Boudoir Photographers need to be extremely focused on the job at hand and simultaneously imaginative. They must know how to combine all of the elements, from props and types of clothing, colors and textures, to appropriate poses and lighting, to create special portraits that appeal to clients.

Unions and Associations

There are many associations with benefits for the Boudoir Photographer. The Professional Photographers of America is not only the publisher of the leading publication, *Professional Photographer* but also offers classes and workshops through a professional school, as well as an annual trade fair with seminars and demonstrations. The more business-oriented Photo Marketing Association International is the largest association, with an annual convention and trade fair, as well as business guidance seminars, lectures, equipment demonstrations, and more. Boudoir Photographers can also join Wedding and Portrait Photographers International for access to educational and networking opportunities and other resources.

Tips for Entry

1. Create a portfolio of sample images that best represent this style of photography. Add boudoir photography to your Web site, brochure, and other promotional literature.
2. Do an Internet search for "Boudoir Photographer," via Google or other search engines. Contact the studio owners located in your area to set up informational interviews and to see if they have any freelance or staff work they can offer.
3. Advertise in as many venues as are appropriate. Test the market by first placing small advertisements in local newspapers. If you plan to work with actors and other performers, advertise in trade publications such as *Backstage* and on industry-specific Web sites.
4. If you are currently working as a portrait photographer, tell your clients that you also do boudoir photography. Ask them to tell their friends and anyone they know who might be interested in this type of portrait. Give them your brochures to share. As previously mentioned, word of mouth is often the best form of advertising.

PET PHOTOGRAPHER

CAREER PROFILE

Duties: Creates indoor and outdoor photographic portraits of family pets, primarily dogs and cats; photographs horses for owners and breeders; may photograph animals for advertisers and publishers; may specialize in capturing photographs of show animals for breeders and others; researches breeds; creates sets and scouts locations, when needed; creates estimates; schedules shoots; manages accounts receivable and payable

Alternate Title(s): Animal Photographer (i.e., Dog Photographer, Cat Photographer, Equine Photographer)

Salary Range: $35,000 to $50,000+

Employment Prospects: Good

Advancement Prospects: Fair

Best Geographical Location(s): Major urban and suburban areas

Prerequisites:

  Education or Training—Four-year degree, with specialization in photography recommended but not required

  Experience—Several years of freelance assistant and professional photography experience helpful; animal handling or show experience helpful

  Special Skills and Personality Traits—Creative; flexible; calm and patient; passionate about animals and skilled in working with them; in-depth knowledge of animal breeds; strong knowledge of digital photography and photography design software (i.e. Photoshop); solid grasp of lighting, color, and composition

CAREER LADDER

```
┌─────────────────────────────────┐
│  Full-Service Studio Owner or    │
│         Book Author              │
└─────────────────────────────────┘

┌─────────────────────────────────┐
│        Pet Photographer          │
└─────────────────────────────────┘

┌─────────────────────────────────┐
│ Assistant Photographer / Pet Handler │
└─────────────────────────────────┘
```

Position Description

Pet Photographers create photographs of animals for their owners. While dogs are most commonly captured, Pet Photographers may also photograph cats, birds, rabbits, ferrets, hamsters, and other pets. Animal breeders often hire Pet Photographers to take pictures of their animals for advertising purposes. Horses that are prize breeds or race hopefuls will be photographed for investors and owners. Experienced horse photographers are well versed in the horse racing world. They know which poses to take that best capture the special features of each horse. Pet Photographers may also specialize in the show world, photographing dogs or cats that have been meticulously groomed to show specifications. They, too, understand which aspects of the animals to focus on that are particular to their breed, such as ears, tail, coat, nose, stance, and so on.

Before the shoot, owners or handlers will spend time either playing with the animals or calming them, depending on the type of shots planned. They will remain on hand throughout the photography session. Pet Photographers are also adept at working with animals. To get animals to pose and look in certain directions, Pet Photographers may employ various tricks and devices, such as the EyeLiner Focusing Device, which may also be used when photographing children. EyeLiner, a two-way mirror mounted in front of the camera lens, gets animals to focus on the lens. One of the mirrors features an image that animals will be interested in, such as a treat or a toy. Animals will look directly at the image, not realizing they are looking directly into the camera lens. A Pet Photographer may also do something as simple as creating a trail of food leading to the spot where they want to photograph the animal.

Pet Photographers may use design software, such as Adobe Photoshop or Illustrator, to create an array of backgrounds, graphics, and illustrations. They may have a custom-built studio or an outdoor space. Pet Photographers also scout and choose locations and may travel to homes. They usually have a table, bench, and other support and backgrounds. For instance, puppies may need pillows for support, while larger dogs may be kept relatively inactive on platforms. Active animals may be photographed in parks or other public sites, and birds may be photographed on stands in front of uncluttered backgrounds. A kitchen table covered with a poster of a bright color is a good base for a close-up portrait of a cat and smaller animals.

Salaries

Pet Photographers' salaries can range from $35,000 to $50,000 or more, depending on specialization, years of experience, and reputation in the business. Photographers who work with show animals may earn higher incomes, as may those who work exclusively with celebrities' pets and animals owned by the wealthy. Pet Photographers are usually freelance, although some work either part- or full-time with pet stores, such as PETCO. Burgeoning Pet Photographers can show their photographs in shops and develop a small following. In the first year or two of their career, Pet Photographers can arrange one to three sittings per week to secure minor start-up income. Pet Photographers can also increase their income by renting booths at shows and providing on-site digital photography services. According to several veterans in the field, once they establish themselves in the business and hone their skills, Pet Photographers can charge day rates ranging anywhere from $500 to $1,500.

Employment Prospects

Pet Photographers who are just starting out have great opportunities to offer services to independent portrait studios. They can suggest to studio owners a trial phase of pet photography as a profitable, add-on service. To save further expense and time, they can use a digital camera and create 4″ × 6″ color proofs right at the sitting. Starting a pet photography department within a portrait studio is simple; all that is needed is a small bench and small props for the animals (i.e. hats, ties, anything holiday-related).

Pet Photographers who prefer steadier income may seek employment with PETCO, one of America's largest pet industry chains. PETCO has divided the country into regions covered by traveling professional Pet Photographers. Customers register four to six weeks in advance of the photographer's scheduled visit to their local PETCO.

Advancement Prospects

While there is no specific career path for Pet Photographers, after five to 10 years, many choose to grow their businesses by adding more staff and services and expanding and enhancing their Web sites. Some may take on business partners and branch out by photographing breeds other than those they may have originally worked with. Pet Photographers can author books, either photographic or how-to, as well as write and publish their photographs in various publications. Some may choose to license their work to greeting card companies or other manufacturers (i.e., for mugs, calendars).

Education and Training

A four-year degree in photography is recommended. Studio photography experience is helpful, and classes in training and working with animals can also be helpful.

Experience, Skills, and Personality Traits

Pet Photographers first and foremost need to be passionate and deeply interested in animals. They must have a natural way with animals and be able to combine this interest with their technological skills to best capture the animals for the intended audience. Flexible, patient, calm yet energetic individuals fit best in this role. Strong knowledge of the breeds being photographed and the ability to research those breeds, when needed, is critical. A solid grasp of lighting, composition, framing, and color is also required.

Unions and Associations

Pet Photographers can join such associations as the Professional Photographers of America for networking opportunities, educational resources, trade fairs, conventions, the publication *Professional Photographer,* and more. They can also join associations and clubs that pertain to the types of animals and breeds they are photographing, such as the American Dog Owners Association, the American Association of Cat Enthusiasts, the Thoroughbred Owners and Breeders Association, and many others.

Tips for Entry

1. Create a portfolio. If you are not yet working professionally, you can still find ways to photograph animals. Volunteer to photograph the pets of people you know, such as family members, friends, or neighbors.
2. Post your photography services in as many venues as possible, such as the bulletin boards of pet stores, veterinary offices, local community centers, and in local newspapers and trade magazines.
3. Attend national dog or cat shows and watch professional photographers at work. Take notes and, if possible, see if you can set up informal meetings with them at later dates.
4. If you are not strong in digital photography, take a class. You can also learn a great deal by reading such magazines as *Digital Photographer* and *Digital Pro Photographer.*

PORTRAIT PHOTOGRAPHER

CAREER PROFILE

Duties: Photographs individuals and groups at various events and for various purposes, including at proms, conferences, corporate gatherings, and sports events; photographs authors for book jackets, entertainers for headshots, and individuals for professional bios; sets appointments with clients; chooses and sets up lights, backgrounds, cameras, film, and shot angles and distances; works with assistants, makeup artists, stylists, and other creative staff.

Alternate Title(s): Commercial Photographer, Lifestyle Photographer, Wedding Photographer

Salary Range: $45,047 to $63,121+

Employment Prospects: Good

Advancement Prospects: Fair

Best Geographical Location(s): Major cultural and corporate centers, such as Atlanta, Boston, Chicago, Dallas, Houston, Los Angeles, Miami, New York, Philadelphia, San Francisco, Seattle, and Washington, D.C.

Prerequisites:

Education or Training—Bachelor's degree in photography beneficial; training in photographic design software (i.e., Adobe Photoshop and Illustrator) recommended; training in digital photography recommended

Experience—Three to five years of experience as an assistant photographer in portrait or commercial studio

Special Skills and Personality Traits—Strong knowledge of lighting, composition, and framing; knowledgeable about color; good visual eye; excellent hand-eye coordination; enjoys working with people; energetic and friendly; reliable and responsible; deadline-oriented; creative; organized; technically and technologically savvy

CAREER LADDER

```
┌─────────────────────────────┐
│    Portrait Studio Owner     │
└─────────────────────────────┘

┌─────────────────────────────┐
│    Portrait Photographer     │
└─────────────────────────────┘

┌─────────────────────────────┐
│   Assistant Photographer     │
└─────────────────────────────┘
```

Position Description

Portrait Photographers take photographs of individuals and groups in various settings and for diverse purposes. Some Portrait Photographers specialize in particular areas such as baby and child photography, boudoir photography, wedding photography, or yearbook photography. Individuals may hire general Portrait Photographers to create pictures for their personal bios or résumés. Families may hire Portrait Photographers to create portraits for photo albums and wall hangings. Portrait Photographers may work inside their studios, creating backdrops, choosing certain lights and film speeds, and setting up specific cameras at different angles to best capture each individual's features. They may also travel to locations and work off site, such as at corporate offices to take photographs of employees for annual reports and promotional literature or to homes to photograph families in front of fireplaces. Actors, musicians, and other performers also hire Portrait Photographers when they need *headshots,* pictures of themselves that they send to agencies and submit to casting directors when they are trying out for roles. Athletic teams may employ Portrait Photographers for team pictures or individual shots of athletes for programs and yearbooks.

Portrait Photographers meet first with clients to discuss the types of photographs needed, the style of photograph (i.e., glamorous, direct), and how the photographs will be used. They may suggest styles of clothing and colors people should wear, based on their hair color, skin tones, and the types of photograph that will be created. Certain colors will contrast better in black-and-white film as opposed to color, so this can play a big part in how the pictures will appear. Portrait Photographers will also frame pictures and arrange people to create balanced shots, directing them to look in certain directions or position their hands or bodies in certain ways.

Portrait Photographers shoot in film as well as in digital. Most photographers take test shots first, using Polaroid cameras, to check the shots and adjust cameras and lights if needed, before going to actual film. They may share these shots with clients to secure approvals. Portrait Photographers may also develop and print photos. They may scan film or work digitally and use photographic design software, such as Adobe Photoshop, to manipulate images and crop shadows or enhance lighting and color.

Portrait Photographers who run their own studios hire and manage staff for shoots. They also may hire employees to handle the day-to-day business tasks involved in running a business. They select and purchase cameras and photographic equipment and accessories and maintain office supplies and stock as well as office equipment. Independent Portrait Photographers also allot time for advertising and promotional campaigns and networking to draw in new clients. They negotiate fees, create contracts, secure permissions as needed, and invoice clients. Depending upon the size of their business, they may also handle the overall bookkeeping for their company.

Salaries

Portrait Photographers' salaries vary depending upon the size of the portrait studio and the types of clientele and projects. According to Salary.com, photographers can expect to earn annual median incomes of $53,526. Portrait Photographers with years of experience and excellent reputations in the business will secure consistent work through referrals and earn higher wages. Photographers who specialize in wedding photography and those who create portraits of celebrities may also earn higher wages. Self-employed photographers must allot money from their incomes for medical insurance, equipment purchase and maintenance, and general business overhead costs, such as rent and utilities.

Employment Prospects

In 2002, about 130,000 photographers held jobs, with more than half self-employed. According to the U.S. Department of Labor's *Occupational Outlook Handbook,* most full-time photographers work in commercial or portrait photography studios, and employment of photographers overall is expected to increase about as fast as the average for all occupations through the year 2012. While demand for Portrait Photographers is expected to increase as the population grows, the field remains extremely competitive. Highly creative photographers with unique styles, who are well versed in technology as well as technically skilled, will have the advantage in the job hunt.

Advancement Prospects

Portrait Photographers who work full time for large studios can advance to become senior Portrait Photographers, taking on more complex projects and managing larger staffs. Independent photographers can branch out by hiring more staff or growing their businesses by opening more studios in other cities. They can write articles for trade and commercial publications and teach portrait photography in art and technical schools.

Education and Training

While not required, a bachelor's degree in photography, with coursework in advertising, marketing, and publishing, is an excellent background for this type of work. Certification or a degree in photography from a technical school is equally valid and beneficial. To stay competitive, Portrait Photographers need to keep up with advances in technology. At the very least, training in digital photography and photographic design software is essential, as an ever-growing number of portrait and commercial studios have moved in the digital direction.

Experience, Skills, and Personality Traits

Many Portrait Photographers get their start in the business by working for several years as apprentices or assistants in portrait photography studios. On-the-job training is invaluable in this field and an excellent way to hone skills as well as forge career-lasting relationships. Some start out as part-time employees in studios or even in photography and camera stores.

Portrait Photographers must have a balance of technical and technological knowledge and an ability to interact well with people and put them at ease. Only the best have this combination. They have an excellent eye for composition and framing, know exactly which cameras and equipment to choose, and know the types of backdrops to use to get the best shots. They are able to relax people so they can capture their true spirit on film. They also know how to manage staff, working well with clients, assistants, creative staff, and others. Successful Portrait Photographers know how to run their businesses effectively, keep appointments, and create photographs that meet their clients' needs. They are organized, able to prioritize, and able to juggle many tasks while still meeting deadlines.

Unions and Associations

Portrait Photographers join Advertising Photographers of America, American Society of Media Photographers, Professional Photographers of America, and Wedding and Portrait Photographers International for educational and networking opportunities, employment referrals, industry conferences, magazines and newsletters, and discounts on career-related services and products.

Tips for Entry

1. Get a paying job or internship with a portrait studio. Find job listings in the back pages of trade publications, the employment sections of local newspapers, and on employment placement Web sites, such as Yahoo! Hotjobs (http://hotjobs.yahoo.com) and Monster (http://www.monster.com).

2. If you cannot find a paying gig at the studio of your choice and can afford to, volunteer. Get your foot in the door by offering your services for free for a limited basis, and do your best to impress the studio owner. This is your chance to show what you are made of and how indispensable you are to the company. Work hard and efficiently and be smart and friendly.

3. Create a list of portrait studios near you. Use an Internet search engine, such as Google (http://www.google.com) to see if they have Web sites and, if they do, look through their sites to see the type of work they do and review their client list. Check off the studios that interest you and contact them to see if they need any help. See if you can set up an informational interview, at the very least, to learn more about the business and find out if they have any advice or suggestions for your next steps.

4. Create a portfolio of work that best represents you and is also tailored to the style of work of the studios you approach. Make sure you have your work available in various formats (i.e., digital, transparency, CD, print) and always ask first which format the studio prefers before submitting.

YEARBOOK PHOTOGRAPHER

CAREER PROFILE

Duties: Provides a range of photographs of students, faculty, and facilities for schools, students, and parents; takes traditional poses of individuals, entire classes, school sports teams, committees, and other after-school groups; photographs students in candid shots; photographs faculty, campus, classrooms, equipment, and buildings and other school-related subjects

Alternate Title(s): Commercial Photographer, Portrait Photographer, School Photographer

Salary Range: $45,000 to $60,000

Employment Prospects: Fair

Advancement Prospects: Limited

Best Geographical Location(s): Major urban and suburban areas with many schools

Prerequisites:

Education or Training—Bachelor's degree in photography, with coursework in art and journalism; trained in digital photography and photographic design software

Experience—Two or more years of experience in a commercial or portrait photography studio

Special Skills and Personality Traits—Knowledgeable about lighting and composition; adept at working with students and faculty; strong communication skills; flexible and patient; organized; reliable

CAREER LADDER

```
Magazine Photographer
```

```
Yearbook Photographer
```

```
Freelance Commercial/
Portrait Photographer
```

Position Description

The role of the professional, salaried Yearbook Photographer is not to be confused with that of the high school student volunteering to take photographs for the yearbook. The Yearbook Photographer is actually a paid representative of a printing company, readying the next yearbook for numerous high schools and colleges around the country. He or she may also be a freelance portrait photographer, experienced in photographing individuals and groups.

Yearbook Photographers work on location at schools, outside on campuses, inside auditoriums and classrooms, as well as at their own portrait studios. Photographers may spend several days at schools, creating portraits as well as capturing student life. They will photograph sports activities, committee meetings, bands and orchestras, drama clubs, debate teams, teachers in action, study halls, cafeterias, buses arriving and leaving school, bookshops, proms, dances, and more. Photographers will also photograph

building facades, statues, arches, courtyards, and other areas that may hold sentimental memories for students.

Yearbook Photographers meet initially with school officials to discuss photographic needs, key personnel the photographer will interact with, and to tour the school to get a grasp of the layout and possible location shots. They also coordinate with the school's student photographers for those areas and events the students are best suited to cover. Yearbook Photographers typically create and work from a checklist of departments to interact with and possibly photograph: athletics, science, math, art, language, history, computer, and more. They also cover theater, newspaper, publicity, the kitchen and cafeteria, security, and campus historian (if one exists).

They learn in advance about special activities that may make for excellent photographic opportunities. Yearbook Photographers usually visit the yearbook office to check files of past photographs to see if anything from the past might enlighten current students. They peruse previous yearbooks and photographic files to acclimate to each school's style. If a school has a publicity director, they meet to discuss the areas of the school they should cover. A quick look at a scrapbook and past press releases with attached photos may yield photos with humor, Halloween fun, graduation-day pranks, or the renovation of an old school building.

The athletic department is the best hiding place for action photos on the football field, in the gymnasium, of awards ceremonies, and the hallway of trophies. Many interesting photographs may sometimes be found at or near the school's theater. Images of stage scenes, set construction, costuming, rehearsal moments, and portraits of actors who followed professional careers in theater, music, opera may be in the files, on the walls, or at the ticket box.

Portrait days are set aside and advertised well in advance to students. Students are given the studio location, details about what they should wear and how they should groom, as well as the various types of photography packages and price ranges available to them. Photographers send students preview shots. They select the poses they like and send their order forms and payments to the photographers. Yearbook Photographers retouch images and enhance color by using photographic design software such as Adobe Photoshop. Depending on the size of their studio and staff, they may either develop film in their own labs or send film to labs for development. Yearbook Photographers also cover graduation ceremonies. They create cap-and-gown portraits, take action shots of students receiving their diplomas and of caps being tossed into the air, and photograph guest speakers and postgraduation celebrations.

Salaries

Yearbook Photographers can earn salaries ranging from $45,000 to $60,000 or more, depending upon the number of schools they photograph for each year and their years of experience in the field. Yearbook Photographers who dedicate their services solely to school photography usually enhance their incomes by increasing their staff and opening studios in other locations. Some offer their photographs to schools for free, an agreement that can assure years of repeat business. They earn their wages in sales of photographs and package deals to students and their families. Many photographers run full commercial and portrait photography studios and also provide photography for weddings, special events, and various types of portraits. Yearbook Photographers on staff with a yearbook printer or publisher may earn a set salary with benefits.

Employment Prospects

Employment of photographers overall is expected to grow by about 10 to 20 percent, or as fast as the average for all occupations, according to the Department of Labor's *Occupational Outlook Handbook*. As the population grows, demand for portrait photographers in general should also grow. A growing number of high schools, colleges, universities, and printing establishments are hiring Yearbook Photographers. Yearbook printers and publishers may have more than one Yearbook Photographer, and if they are national suppliers, they will retain regional staff photographers. Yearbook Photographers who

focus solely on this type of work do not often stay long in the field. They become weary of traveling to and from schools and frequently move on to freelance or staff magazine photography and other commercial work. Departing and retiring Yearbook Photographers pave the way for new photographers every year.

Advancement Prospects

If working on staff with a printer or publisher, Yearbook Photographers can advance to become photo editors for all of the yearbook projects and to serve as liaisons with clients in campus yearbook offices. More office-based work reduces burnout and assures photographers and their employers more years of quality service and employment. Yearbook Photographers may also advance by growing their own commercial and portrait studios and moving on to photojournalism, sports photography, magazine photography, and other mediums. They can also become digital photography and photographic design software consultants within yearbook printing and publishing companies.

Education and Training

There are no specific educational requirements for Yearbook Photographers. A two- or four-year degree in photography, however, with coursework in journalism and art, is a beneficial foundation for this type of work.

Experience, Skills, and Personality Traits

Most Yearbook Photographers have prior work experience as wedding photographers or portrait photographers for commercial studios. They are highly skilled in digital photography, lighting, and composition. Most important, they enjoy working with people and are adept at making people feel comfortable and at ease. They know how to direct people and manage individuals and crowds, without being perceived as arrogant or aggressive. They must be organized and reliable and capable of meeting deadlines. A sense of humor helps. Yearbook Photographers should enjoy working around students.

Unions and Associations

Yearbook Photographers join Professional Photographers of America and Wedding and Portrait Photographers International for educational resources, employment referrals, and networking opportunities.

Tips for Entry

1. Do an Internet search of publishers and printing companies that feature yearbooks among their services. Track down the names of the photographers and see if you can speak with them about their work.
2. Look at your own yearbook and the yearbooks of friends and family members. Identify the publication source and use a search engine to track down their contact information if it is not included. Get in touch with the art department to learn more about who they work with and to learn about employment opportunities.
3. Secure an internship or apprenticeship in a commercial or portrait studio that does school photography.

APPENDIXES

APPENDIX I
TWO-YEAR ASSOCIATE DEGREE AND
CERTIFICATE PHOTOGRAPHY PROGRAMS

ALABAMA

Calhoun Community College
P.O. Box 2216
Decatur, AL 35609
Phone: (256) 306-2718
http://www.calhoun.edu

ARIZONA

Chandler-Gilbert Community College
2626 East Pecos Road
Chandler, AZ 85225
Phone: (480) 732-7089
Fax: (480) 732-7090
http://www.cgc.maricopa.edu

Collins College
1140 South Priest Drive
Tempe, AZ 85281
http://www.collinscollege.edu

CALIFORNIA

Academy of Art University
79 New Montgomery Street
San Francisco, CA 94105
Phone: (415) 274-2200 or
  (800) 544-ARTS
E-mail: admissions@academyart.edu
http://www.academyart.edu

**American InterContinental
  University–Los Angeles**
12655 West Jefferson Boulevard
Los Angeles, CA 90066
Phone: (800) 846-1994
http://www.aiuniv.edu

**Brooks Institute of Photography–Santa
  Barbara**
801 Alston Road
Santa Barbara, CA 93108
Phone: (805) 966-3888 or (888) 304-
  3456 (toll-free)
http://www.brooks.edu

California Institute of the Arts
24700 McBean Parkway

Valencia, CA 91355
Phone: (661) 255-1050
E-mail: admiss@calarts.edu
http://www.calarts.edu

Miami Ad School San Francisco
415 Jackson Street
Suite B
San Francisco, CA 94111
Phone: (415) 837-0966
Fax: (415) 837-0967
http://www.miamiadschool.com

Otis College of Art and Design
9045 Lincoln Boulevard
Los Angeles, CA 90045
Phone: (310) 665-6800 or (800) 527-OTIS
Fax: (310) 665-6821
E-mail: admissions@otis.edu
http://www.otis.edu

Pacific Union College
One Angwin Avenue
Angwin, CA 94508-9707
Phone: (800) 862-7080
Fax: (707) 965-6311
E-mail: enroll@puc.edu
http://www.puc.edu

Santa Monica College
1900 Pico Boulevard
Santa Monica, CA 90405-1628
Phone: (310) 434-4217
Fax: (310) 434-3651
http://www.smc.edu

COLORADO

The Art Institute of Colorado
1200 Lincoln Street
Denver, CO 80203
Phone: (303) 837-0825 or (800) 275-
  2420
E-mail: aicadm@aii.edu
http://www.aic.artinstitutes.edu

Colorado Mountain College
P.O. Box 10001
Glenwood Springs, CO 81602

Phone: (970) 945-8691 or
  (800) 621-8559
Fax: (970) 947-8324
E-mail: joinus@coloradomtn.edu
http://www.coloradomtn.edu

CONNECTICUT

Gibbs College Norwalk
10 Norden Place
Norwalk, CT 06855-1436
Phone: (203) 838-4173
http://www.gibbsnorwalk.edu

Paier College of Art
20 Gorham Avenue
Hamden, CT 06517
Phone: (203) 287-3032
Fax: (203) 287-3021
http://www.paierart.com

DELAWARE

Delaware College of Art and Design
600 North Market Street
Wilmington, DE 19801
Phone: (302) 622-8000
Fax: (302) 622-8870
E-mail: info@dcad.edu
http://www.dcad.edu

DISTRICT OF COLUMBIA

Corcoran College of Art and Design
500 17th Street NW
Washington, DC 20006
Phone: (202) 639-1801, ext. 1800
http://www.corcoran.edu

FLORIDA

**American InterContinental
  University–Fort Lauderdale**
2250 North Commerce Parkway, #100
Weston, FL 33326
Phone: (800) 846-1994
http://www.aiuniv.edu

International Academy of Design &
    Technology–Tampa
5225 Memorial Highway
Tampa, FL 33634
Phone: (813) 884-0007
http://www.academy.edu

Miami Ad School
955 Alton Road
Miami Beach, FL 33139
Phone: (305) 538-3193
Fax: (305) 538-3724
http://www.miamiadschool.com

GEORGIA

**American InterContinental
    University–Atlanta (Buckhead)**
3330 Peachtree Road NE
Buckhead, GA 30326
Phone: (800) 846-1994
http://www.aiuniv.edu

**American InterContinental
    University–Atlanta (Dunwoody)**
6600 Peachtree-Dunwoody Road
Dunwoody, GA 30328
Phone: (800) 846-1994
http://www.aiuniv.edu

The Art Institute of Atlanta
6600 Peachtree-Dunwoody Road
Atlanta, GA 30328
Phone: (800) 275-4242
E-mail: aiaadm@aii.edu
http://www.aia.aii.edu

The Creative Circus
812 Lambert Drive
Atlanta, GA 30324
Phone: (404) 607-8880 or
    (800) 728-1590
Fax: (404) 875-1590
http://www.creativecircus.com

North Georgia College
Dahlonega, GA 30597
Phone: (706) 864-1423
Fax: (706) 864-1429
http://www.ngcsu.edu

ILLINOIS

Harrington College of Design
200 West Madison Street
2nd Floor
Chicago, IL 60606
Phone: (312) 939-4976
http://www.interiordesign.edu

MARYLAND

Anne Arundel Community College
101 College Parkway
Arnold, MD 21012
Phone: (410) 647-7100
http://www.aacc.cc.md.us

MASSACHUSETTS

**Center for Digital Imaging Arts at
    Boston University**
282 Moody Street
Waltham, MA 02453
Phone: (781) 209-1700 or
    (800) 808-CDIA
Fax: (781) 209-1701
E-mail: info@digitalimagingarts.com
http://www.digitalimagingarts.com

Gibbs College–Boston
126 Newbury Street
Boston, MA 02116
Phone: (617) 369-9905
http://www.gibbsboston.edu

Hallmark Institute of Photography
241 Millers Falls Road
Turners Falls, MA 01376
Phone: (413) 863-2478
Fax: (413) 863-4118
E-mail: info@hallmark.edu
http://www.hallmark-institute.com

Holyoke Community College
303 Homestead Avenue
Holyoke, MA 01040
Phone: (413) 552-2491
Fax: (413) 534-8975
http://www.hcc.mass.edu

Montserrat College of Art
23 Essex Street
P.O. Box 26
Beverly, MA 01915
Phone: (978) 921-4242
Fax: (978) 921-4241
E-mail: admiss@montserrat.edu
http://www.montserrat.edu

New England School of Photography
537 Commonwealth Avenue
Boston, MA 02215-2005
Phone: (617) 437-1868
Fax: (617) 437-0261
http://www.nesop.com

MICHIGAN

Grand Rapids Community College
143 Bostwick NE
Grand Rapids, MI 49503-3295

Phone: (616) 234-3544
http://www.grcc.cc.mi.us

Oakland University
307 Wilson Hall
Rochester, MI 48309-4401
Phone: (248) 370-3375
Fax: (248) 370-4208
E-mail: thenews@oakland.edu
http://www.oakland.edu

MISSISSIPPI

Antonelli College–Hattiesburg Campus
1500 North 31st Avenue
Hattiesburg, MS 39401
Phone: (601) 583-4100
http://www.antonellic.com

Antonelli College–Jackson Campus
2323 Lakeland Drive
Jackson, MS 39232
Phone: (601) 362-9991
http://www.antonellic.com

MISSOURI

**Saint Louis Community
    College–Florissant Valley**
3400 Pershall Road
Saint Louis, MO 63135
Phone: (314) 595-4200
http://www.stlcc.edu/fv

**Saint Louis Community
    College–Meramec**
11333 Big Bend Boulevard
Saint Louis, MO 63122
Phone: (314) 984-7500
http://www.stlcc.edu/mc

NEW HAMPSHIRE

McIntosh College
23 Cataract Avenue
Dover, NH 03820
Phone: (603) 742-1234 or (800) 624-6867
http://www.mcintoshcollege.edu

New Hampshire Institute of Art
148 Concord Street
Manchester, NH 03104
Phone: (603) 623-0313
E-mail: aabbott@nhia.edu
http://www.nhia.edu

NEW JERSEY

Gibbs College–Montclair
630 West Mount Pleasant Avenue
Route 10

Livingston, NJ 07039
Phone: (973) 369-1360 or (866) 442-2765
Fax: (973) 369-1446
http://gibbsnj.edu

Union County College Coop
1033 Springfield Avenue
Cranford, NJ 07016
Phone: (908) 709-7000
http://www.ucc.edu

NEW MEXICO

Taos Art School
P.O. Box 2588
Taos, NM 87571
Phone: (505) 758-0350
Fax: (505) 758-4880
E-mail: tas@laplaza.org
http://www.taosartschool.org

NEW YORK

**Alfred School of Art and Design at
Alfred University**
2 Pine Street
Alfred, NY 14802
Phone: (607) 871-2441
Fax: (607) 871-2490
http://art.alfred.edu

Briarcliffe College–Bethpage
1055 Stewart Avenue
Bethpage, NY 11714
Phone: (516) 918-3600 or (888) 333-
1150
http://www.bcbeth.com

Briarcliffe College–Patchogue
225 West Main Street
Patchogue, NY 11772
Phone: (631) 654-5300 or (866) 235-5207
http://www.bcpat.com

Cazenovia College
22 Sullivan Street
Cazenovia, NY 13035
Phone: (800) 654-3210
E-mail: admission@cazenovia.edu
http://www.cazenovia.edu

**The Cooper Union for the
Advancement of Science & Art**
30 Cooper Square
New York, NY 10003
Phone: (212) 353-4120
E-mail: admissions@cooper.edu
http://www.cooper.edu

Fashion Institute of Technology
Seventh Avenue at 27th Street
New York, NY 10001
Phone: (212) 217-7665
http://www.fitnyc.suny.edu

Katharine Gibbs School–New York
50 West 40th Street
New York, NY 10138
http://www.gibbsny.edu

Sage College of Albany
140 New Scotland Avenue
Albany, NY 12208
Phone: (518) 445-1778 or
(888) VERY-SAGE
http://www.sage.edu/sca

OHIO

Antonelli College
124 East Seventh Street
Cincinnati, OH 45202
Phone: (513) 241-4338
Fax: (513) 241-9396
http://www.antonellic.com

Clark State Community College
570 East Leffel Lane
Springfield, OH 45505
Phone: (937) 325-0691
http://www.clark.cc.oh.us

**Ohio Institute of Photography and
Technology**
2029 Edgefield Road
Dayton, OH 45439
Phone: (937) 294-6155 or (800) 846-3040
http://www.oipt.com

Ohio Wesleyan University
61 South Sandusky Street
Delaware, OH 43015
Phone: (740) 368-2000
http://www.owu.edu

Sinclair Community College
444 West Third Street
Dayton, OH 45402-1460
Phone: (800) 315-3000
E-mail: admit@sinclair.edu
http://www.sinclair.edu

OREGON

Oregon College of Art & Craft
8245 Southwest Barnes Road
Portland, OR 97225

Phone: (503) 297-5544 or (800) 390-0632
E-mail: admissions@ocac.edu
http://www.ocac.edu

Southern Oregon Art School
112 East 6th Street
Medford, OR 97501
Phone: (541) 779-7959
Fax: (541) 846-9344
http://www.southernoregonartschool.com

PENNSYLVANIA

Antonelli Institute
300 Montgomery Avenue
Erdenheim, PA 19038
Phone: (215) 836-2222 or (800) 722-
7871
Fax: (215) 836-2794
http://www.antonelli.org

The Art Institute of Philadelphia
1622 Chestnut Street
Philadelphia, PA 19103
Phone: (800) 275-2474
http://aiph.aii.edu

**International Academy of Design &
Technology**
555 Grant St.
Pittsburgh, PA 15219
Phone: (412) 391-4197 or (800) 447-8324
http://www.iadtpitt.edu

Keystone College
One College Green
La Plume, PA 18440
Phone: (877) 4COLLEGE (toll-free)
Fax: (570) 945-7916
http://www.keystone.edu

Penn State–Lehigh Valley
8380 Mohr Lane
Fogelsville, PA 18051
Phone: (610) 285-5000
http://www.lv.psu.edu

Oakbridge Academy of Art
1250 Greensburg Road
Lower Burrell, PA 15068
Phone: (724) 335-5336 or (800) 734-5601
Fax: (724) 335-3367
http://www.oaa.edu

Pennsylvania State University
201 Shields Building
P.O. Box 3000
University Park, PA 16804-3000

Phone: (814) 865-5471
Fax: (814) 863-7590
http://www.psu.edu

Pittsburgh Filmmakers, Inc.
477 Melwood Avenue
Pittsburgh, PA 15213
Phone: (412) 681-5449
http://www.pghfilmmakers.org

SOUTH DAKOTA

Dakota State University
820 North Washington
Madison, SD 57042
Phone: (888) DSU-9988 (toll-free)
E-mail: yourfuture@dsu.edu
http://www.dsu.edu

TENNESSEE

Nossi College of Art
907 Two Mile Parkway
Suite E6
Goodlettsville, TN 37072
Phone: (615) 851-1088
Fax: (615) 851-1087
http://www.nossi.com

Watkins College of Art and Design
2298 MetroCenter Boulevard
Nashville, TN 37228
Phone: (615) 383-4848
Fax: (615) 383-4849
http://www.watkins.edu

TEXAS

Collin County Community College–Central Park Campus
2200 West University Drive
P.O. Box 8001
McKinney, TX 75071
Phone: (972) 548-6790

Fax: (972) 758-3860
http://www.ccccd.edu

Our Lady of the Lake University
411 Southwest 24th Street
San Antonio, TX 78207
Phone: (210) 434-6711
http://www.ollusa.edu

VIRGINIA

Gibbs College
1980 Gallows Road
Vienna, VA 22182
Phone: (703) 556-8888
http://www.trade-schools.net/kgsdc

J. Sargeant Reynolds Community College
P.O. Box 85622
Richmond, VA 23285-5622
Phone: (804) 371-3000
Fax: (804) 371-3588
http://www.jsr.vccs.edu

WASHINGTON

The Art Institute of Seattle
2323 Elliott Avenue
Seattle, WA 98121
Phone: (206) 448-0900 or (800) 275-2471
http://www.ais.edu

Clark College
1800 East McLoughlin Boulevard
Vancouver, WA 98663
Phone: (360) 992-2000
http://www.clark.edu

Photographic Center Northwest
900 Twelfth Avenue
Seattle, WA 98122-4412
Phone: (206) 720-7222

Fax: (206) 720-0306
E-mail: pcnw@pcnw.org
http://www.pcnw.org

WEST VIRGINIA

Shepherd University
P.O. Box 3210
Shepherdstown, WV 25443-3210
Phone: (304) 876-5000 or (800) 344-5231
Fax: (304) 876-3101
http://www.shepherd.edu

WISCONSIN

Madison Area Technical College
3550 Anderson Street
Madison, WI 53704
Phone: (608) 246-6100 or (800) 322-6282
Fax: (608) 246-6880
E-mail: admissions@matcmadison.edu
http://matcmadison.edu/matc

Milwaukee Institute of Art & Design
273 East Erie Street
Milwaukee, WI 53202
Phone: (414) 291-8070 or (888) 749-MIAD (toll-free)
Fax: (414) 291-8077
http://www.miad.edu

WYOMING

Casper College
125 College Drive
Casper, WY 82601
Phone: (307) 268-2110 or (800) 442-2963
http://www.caspercollege.edu

Northwest College
231 West 6th Street
Powell, WY 82435
Phone: (307) 754-6000
http://www.northwestcollege.edu

APPENDIX II
FOUR-YEAR UNDERGRADUATE FINE ARTS PHOTOGRAPHY PROGRAMS

ALABAMA

Jacksonville State University
700 Pelham Road North
Jacksonville, AL 36265-9982
Phone: (800) 231-5291
http://www.jsu.edu

University of Alabama
Tuscaloosa, AL 35487-0270
Phone: (205) 348-6010
E-mail: admissions@ua.edu
http://www.ua.edu

University of Montevallo
Montevallo, AL 35115-6400
Phone: (205) 665-6000
http://www.montevallo.edu

University of North Alabama
UNA Box 5011
Florence, Alabama 35632-0001
Phone: (256) 765-4608 or
    (800) TALK UNA
http://www.una.edu

ALASKA

University of Alaska Anchorage
3211 Providence Drive
Anchorage, AK 99508
Phone: (907) 786-1800
http://www.uaa.alaska.edu

ARIZONA

Arizona State University
P.O. Box 870112
Tempe, AZ 85287-0112
Phone: (480) 965-3468
Fax: (480) 965-8338
http://www.asu.edu

Prescott College
220 Grove Avenue
Prescott, AZ 86301
Phone: (928) 778-2090 or
    (877) 350-2100 (toll-free)

E-mail: admissions@prescott.edu
http://www.prescott.edu

University of Arizona
Office of Admissions
P.O. Box 210040
Tucson, AZ 85721-0002
Phone: (520) 621-2211
http://www.arizona.edu

ARKANSAS

University of Central Arkansas
201 Donaghey Street
Conway, AR 72035
Phone: (501) 450-5000 or (800) 243-8245
E-mail: admissions@mail.uca.edu
http://www.uca.edu

CALIFORNIA

Academy of Art University
79 New Montgomery Street
San Francisco, CA 94105
Phone: (415) 274-2200 or (800) 544-
    ARTS
E-mail: admissions@academyart.edu
http://www.academyart.edu

Biola University
13800 Biola Avenue
La Mirada, CA 90639
Phone: (562) 903-6000
http://www.biola.edu

**Brooks Institute of Photography–Santa
    Barbara**
801 Alston Road
Santa Barbara, CA 93108
Phone: (805) 966-3888 or (888) 304-
    3456 (toll-free)
http://www.brooks.edu

California College of the Arts–Oakland
5212 Broadway
Oakland, CA 94618-1426
Phone: (510) 594-3600 or
    (800) 447-1ART

E-mail: enroll@cca.edu
http://www.cca.edu

**California College of the Arts–San
    Francisco**
1111 Eighth Street
San Francisco, CA 94107-2247
Phone: (415) 703-9500 or
    (800) 447-1ART
E-mail: enroll@cca.edu
http://www.cca.edu

California Institute of the Arts
24700 McBean Parkway
Valencia, CA 91355
Phone: (661) 255-1050
E-mail: admiss@calarts.edu
http://www.calarts.edu

California Polytechnic State University
San Luis Obispo, CA 93407
Phone: (805) 756-111
Fax: (805) 756-6321
http://www.calpoly.edu

California State University–East Bay
25800 Carlos Bee Boulevard
Hayward, CA 94542
Phone: (510) 885-3000
E-mail: adminfo@csuhayward.edu
http://www.csuhayward.edu

California State University–Fullerton
P.O. Box 34080
Fullerton, CA 92834
Phone: (714) 278-2011
http://www.fullerton.edu

**California State University–Long
    Beach**
1250 Bellflower Boulevard
Long Beach, CA 90840-3501
Phone: (562) 985-4111
http://www.csulb.edu

Chapman University
One University Drive
Orange, CA 92866

Phone: (714) 997-6815
http://www.chapman.edu

Otis College of Art and Design
9045 Lincoln Boulevard
Los Angeles, CA 90045
Phone: (310) 665-6800 or
  (800) 527-OTIS
Fax: (310) 665-6821
E-mail: admissions@otis.edu
http://www.otis.edu

Pacific Union College
One Angwin Avenue
Angwin, CA 94508-9707
Phone: (800) 862-7080
Fax: (707) 965-6311
E-mail: enroll@puc.edu
http://www.puc.edu

San Francisco Art Institute
800 Chestnut Street
San Francisco, CA 94133
Phone: (415) 771-7020
Fax: (415) 749-4590
http://www.sfai.edu

San Jose State University
One Washington Square
San Jose, CA 95192-0089
Phone: (408) 924-1000
Fax: (408) 924-4326
http://www.sjsu.edu

University of California–Los Angeles
1147 Murphy Hall, Box 951436
Los Angeles, CA 90095-1436
Phone: (310) 825-3101
Fax: (310) 206-1206
E-mail: ugadm@saonet.ucla.edu
http://www.ucla.edu

COLORADO

The Art Institute of Colorado
1200 Lincoln Street
Denver, CO 80203
Phone: (303) 837-0825 or (800) 275-2420
http://www.aic.artinstitutes.edu

Metropolitan State College of Denver
P.O. Box 173362
Denver, CO 80217-3362
Phone: (303) 556-2400
http://www.mscd.edu

Rocky Mountain College of Art & Design
1600 Pierce Street
Lakewood, CO 80214

Phone: (800) 888-ARTS
E-mail: admission@rmcad.net
http://www.rmcad.edu

University of Colorado–Denver
Campus Box 167
P.O. Box 173364
Denver, CO 80217-3364
Phone: (303) 556-5600
E-mail: admissions@cudenver.edu
http://www.cudenver.edu

University of Denver
2199 South University Boulevard
Denver, CO 80208
Phone: (303) 871-2000
http://www.du.edu

CONNECTICUT

Paier College of Art
20 Gorham Avenue
Hamden, CT 06517
Phone: (203) 287-3032
Fax: (203) 287-3021
http://www.paierart.com

University of Connecticut
875 Coventry Road
Storrs, CT 06269-1099
Phone: (860) 486-2000
http://www.uconn.edu

University of Hartford
200 Bloomfield Avenue
West Hartford, CT 06117
Phone: (860) 768-4100
http://www.hartford.edu

University of New Haven
300 Boston Post Road
West Haven, CT 06516
Phone: (203) 932-7000 or
  (800) DIAL-UNH
Fax: (203) 931-6097
http://www.newhaven.edu

DISTRICT OF COLUMBIA

Howard University
2400 Sixth Street NW
Washington, DC 20059
Phone: (202) 806-6100
Fax: (202) 806-9258
http://www.howard.edu

FLORIDA

Barry University
11300 Northeast Second Avenue

Miami Shores, FL 33161-6695
Phone: (305) 899-3100 or (800) 695-2279
E-mail: admissions@mail.barry.edu
http://www.barry.edu

Florida State University
Tallahassee, FL 32306-1170
Phone: (850) 644-6200
Fax: (850) 644-0197
E-mail: admissions@admin.fsu.edu
http://www.fsu.edu

New World School of the Arts
300 Northeast Second Avenue
Miami, FL 33132
Phone: (305) 237-3135
Fax: (305) 237-3794
http://www.mdc.edu/nwsa

Ringling School of Art and Design
2700 North Tamiami Trail
Sarasota, FL 34234-5895
Phone: (941) 351-5100 or (800) 255-7695
Fax: (941) 359-7517
E-mail: admissions@ringling.edu
http://www.rsad.edu

University of Florida
Gainesville, FL 32611
Phone: (352) 392-3261
http://www.ufl.edu

GEORGIA

The Art Institute of Atlanta
6600 Peachtree Dunwoody Road
Atlanta, GA 30328
Phone: (800) 275-4242
E-mail: aiaadm@aii.edu
http://www.aia.aii.edu

Kennesaw State University
1000 Chastain Road
Kennesaw, GA 30144
Phone: (770) 423-6300
E-mail: ksuadmit@kennesaw.edu
http://www.kennesaw.edu

Savannah College of Art and Design
P.O. Box 2072
Savannah, GA 31402-2072
Phone: (912) 525-5100 or (800) 869-7223
Fax: (912) 525-5986
E-mail: admission@scad.edu
http://www.scad.edu

University of Georgia
Athens, GA 30602-7287
Phone: (706) 542-3000

E-mail: undergrad@admissions.uga.edu
http://www.uga.edu

University of West Georgia
1601 Maple Street
Carrollton, GA 30118
Phone: (678) 839-5000
E-mail: admiss@westga.edu
http://www.westga.edu

ILLINOIS

Bradley University
1501 West Bradley Avenue
Peoria, IL 61625
Phone: (309) 677-2967
E-mail: admissions@bradley.edu
http://www.bradley.edu

Columbia College Chicago
600 South Michigan Avenue
Chicago, IL 60605
Phone: (312) 663-1600
Fax: (312) 344-8024
E-mail: admissions@colum.edu
http://www.colum.edu

Governors State University
1 University Parkway
University Park, IL 60466-0975
Phone: (708) 534-5000
E-mail: gsunow@govst.edu
http://www.govst.edu

Illinois State University
Normal, IL 61790-5620
Phone: (309) 438-2181 or (800) 366-2478
E-mail: admissions@ilstu.edu
http://www.ilstu.edu

Northern Illinois University
DeKalb, IL 60115
Phone: (815) 753-1000
http://www.niu.edu

University of Illinois at Chicago
Chicago, IL 60612
Phone: (312) 996-7000
http://www.uic.edu

INDIANA

Ball State University
2000 University
Muncie, IN 47306
Phone: (765) 285-8300 or
 (800) 482-4BSU
E-mail: askus@bsu.edu
http://www.bsu.edu

Herron School of Art
Indiana University Purdue
 University–Indianapolis
1701 North Pennsylvania Street
Indianapolis, IN 46202-1414
Phone: (317) 920-2416
Fax: (317) 920-2401
E-mail: herrart@iupui.edu
http://www.herron.iupui.edu

Indiana State University
200 North Seventh Street
Terre Haute, IN 47809-9989
Phone: (800)-GO-TO-ISU
http://www.indstate.edu

Indiana Wesleyan University
4201 South Washington Street
Marion, IN 46953
Phone: (765) 674-6901
http://www.indwes.edu

Saint Mary's College
Notre Dame, IN 46556-5001
Phone: (574) 284-4000
E-mail: admission@saintmarys.edu
http://www.saintmarys.edu

IOWA

Maharishi University of Management
1000 North Fourth Street
Fairfield, IA 52557
Phone: (800) 369-6480
Fax: (641) 472-1179
E-mail: admissions@mum.edu
http://mum.edu

University of Northern Iowa
1227 West 27th Street
Cedar Falls, IA 50614
Phone: (319) 273-2311
E-mail: admissions@uni.edu
http://www.uni.edu

KANSAS

Kansas State University
Manhattan, KS 66506
Phone: (785) 532-6250
Fax: (785) 532-6393
E-mail: kstate@k-state.edu
http://www.ksu.edu

KENTUCKY

Eastern Kentucky University
521 Lancaster Avenue
Richmond, KY 40475

Phone: (859) 622-1000
Fax: (859) 622-6509
http://www.eku.edu

Kentucky State University
400 East Main Street
Frankfort, KY 40601
Phone: (502) 597-6000
Fax: (502) 597-6409
http://www.kysu.edu

Murray State University
P.O. Box 9
Murray, KY 42071
Phone: (270) 762-3784 or
 (800) 272-4MSU
E-mail: admissions@murraystate.edu
http://www.murraystate.edu

Northern Kentucky University
Nunn Drive
Highland Heights, KY 41099
Phone: (859) 572-5220 or (800) 637-9948
Fax: (859) 572-6501
http://www.nku.edu

University of Louisville
Louisville, KY 40292
Phone: (502) 852-5555 or (800) 334-UofL
Fax: (502) 852-6791
http://www.louisville.edu

LOUISIANA

Louisiana State University
110 Thomas Boyd Hall
Baton Rouge, LA 70803
Phone: (225) 578-1175
E-mail: admissions@lsu.edu
http://www.lsu.edu

Louisiana Tech University
P.O. Box 3178
Ruston, LA 71272
Phone: (318) 257-3036 or
 (800) LATECH-1
http://www.latech.edu

University of Louisiana–Lafayette
104 University Circle
Lafayette, LA 70504
Phone: (337) 482-1000
http://www.louisiana.edu

MAINE

Heartwood College of Art
123 York Street
Kennebunk, ME 04043

Phone: (207) 985-0985
Fax: (207) 985-6333
E-mail: hca@heartwoodcollegeofart.org
http://www.heartwoodcollegeofart.org

Maine College of Art
97 Spring Street
Portland, ME 04101
Phone: (207) 775-3052 or (800) 639-4808
Fax: (207) 772-5069
E-mail: info@meca.edu
http://www.meca.edu

University of Southern Maine–Gorham
37 College Avenue
Gorham, ME 04038
Phone: (207) 780-4141 or
        (800) 800-4USM
Fax: (207) 780-5640
E-mail: usmadm@usm.maine.edu
http://www.usm.maine.edu

MARYLAND

Maryland Institute College of Art
1300 Mount Royal Avenue
Baltimore, MD 21217
Phone: (410) 669-9200
http://www.mica.edu

MASSACHUSETTS

**Art Institute of Boston at Lesley
    University**
700 Beacon Street
Boston, MA 02215
Phone: (617) 585-6600
http://www.aiboston.edu

Hampshire College, Department of Art
893 West Street
Amherst, MA 01002
Phone: (413) 549-4600
Fax: (413) 559-5631
E-mail: admissions@hampshire.edu
http://www.hampshire.edu

Massachusetts College of Arts
Avenue of the Arts
621 Huntington Avenue
Boston, MA 02115
Phone: (617) 879-7000
Fax: (617) 879-7250
http://www.massart.edu

Montserrat College of Art
23 Essex Street
P.O. Box 26
Beverly, MA 01915

Phone: (978) 921-4242
Fax: (978) 921-4241
http://www.montserrat.edu

Pine Manor College
400 Heath Street
Chestnut Hill, MA 02467
Phone: (617) 731-7000 or (800) 762-1357
Fax: (617) 731-7199
http://www.pmc.edu

**School of the Museum of Fine
    Arts–Boston**
230 The Fenway
Boston, MA 02115
Phone: (617) 267-6100 or (800) 643-6078
Fax: (617) 424-6271
E-mail: academicaffairs@smfa.edu
http://www.smfa.edu

University of Massachusetts–Dartmouth
285 Old Westport Road
North Dartmouth, MA 02747-2300
Phone: (508) 999-8000
Fax: (508) 999-8901
http://www.umassd.edu

MICHIGAN

College for Creative Studies
201 East Kirby
Detroit, MI 48202-4034
Phone: (313) 664-7400 or
        (800) 952-ARTS
Fax: (313) 872-2739
E-mail: admissions@ccscad.edu
http://www.ccscad.edu

Ferris State University
1201 South State Street
Big Rapids, MI 49307
Phone: (231) 591-2000 or (800) 4FERRIS
Fax: (231) 591-3944
http://www.ferris.edu

Kendall College of Art and Design
17 Fountain Street
Grand Rapids, MI 49503-3102
Phone: (616) 451-2787 or (800) 676-2787
Fax: (616) 831-9689
http://www.kcad.edu

Northern Michigan University
1401 Presque Isle Avenue
Marquette, MI 49855
Phone: (800) 682-9797
Fax: (906) 227-2276
E-mail: admiss@nmu.edu
http://www.nmu.edu

Siena Heights University
1247 East Siena Heights Drive
Adrian, MI 49221
Phone: (517) 263-0731
http://www.sienahts.edu

University of Michigan–Ann Arbor
Ann Arbor, MI 48109
Phone: (734) 764-1817
http://www.umich.edu

Western Michigan University
1903 West Michigan Avenue
Kalamazoo, MI 49008-5201
Phone: (269) 387-1000
http://www.wmich.edu

MINNESOTA

**The Art Institutes International
    Minnesota**
15 South 9th Street
Minneapolis, MN 55402-3137
Phone: (612) 332-3361 or (800) 777-
        3643
E-mail: aimadm@aii.edu
http://www.aim.artinstitutes.edu

Brown College
1440 Northland Drive
Mendota Heights, MN 55120
Phone: (800) 766-2040
http://www.browncollege.edu

College of Visual Arts
344 Summit Avenue
St. Paul, MN 55102
Phone: (651) 224-3416 or (800) 224-1536
Fax: (651) 224-8854
E-mail: info@cva.edu
http://www.cva.edu

Minneapolis College of Art & Design
2501 Stevens Avenue South
Minneapolis, MN 55404
Phone: (612) 874-3760 or (800) 874-6223
E-mail: admissions@mcad.edu
http://www.mcad.edu

Minnesota State University–Moorhead
1104 Seventh Avenue South
Moorhead, MN 56563
Phone: (800) 593-7246
http://www.mnstate.edu

Saint Cloud State University
720 Fourth Avenue South
Saint Cloud, MN 56301-4498
Phone: (320) 308-0121

E-mail: scsu4u@stcloudstate.edu
http://www.stcloudstate.edu

MISSISSIPPI

Delta State University
1003 West Sunflower
Cleveland, MS 38732
Phone: (662) 846-3000 or
     (800) GOTODSU
http://www.deltastate.edu

Mississippi State University
Mississippi State, MS 39762
Phone: (662) 325-2323
http://www.msstate.edu

MISSOURI

Fontbonne University
6800 Wydown Boulevard
St. Louis, MO 63108
Phone: (314) 862-3456
http://www.fontbonne.edu

Kansas City Art Institute
4415 Warwick Boulevard
Kansas City, MO 64111
Phone: (816) 474-5224 or (800) 522-5224
Fax: (816) 802-3309
E-mail: admiss@kcai.edu
http://www.kcai.edu

Washington University in Saint Louis
One Brookings Drive
Saint Louis, MO 63130-4899
Phone: (314) 935-5000
E-mail: admissions@wustl.edu
http://www.wustl.edu

MONTANA

University of Montana
32 Campus Drive
Missoula, MT 59812
Phone: (406) 243-0211
http://www.umt.edu

NEBRASKA

Nebraska Wesleyan University
5000 St. Paul Avenue
Lincoln, NE 68504-2794
Phone: (402) 466-2371 or (800) 541-3818
E-mail: admissions@nebrwesleyan.edu
http://www.nebrwesleyan.edu

University of Nebraska–Lincoln
Lincoln, NE 68588
Phone: (402) 472-7211
http://www.unl.edu

NEVADA

Sierra Nevada College
999 Tahoe Boulevard
Incline Village, NV 89451
Phone: (775) 831-1314
Fax: (775) 832-1727
http://www.sierranevada.edu

University of Nevada–Las Vegas
4505 Maryland Parkway
Las Vegas, NV 89154
Phone: (702) 895-3011
E-mail: undergraduate.recruitment@
     ccmail.nevada.edu
http://www.unlv.edu

NEW HAMPSHIRE

Chester College of New England
40 Chester Street
Chester, NH 03036
Phone: (603) 887-4401 or (800) 974-6372
Fax: (603) 887-1777
E-mail: admissions@chestercollege.edu
http://www.chestercollege.edu

New Hampshire Institute of Art
148 Concord Street
Manchester, NH 03104
Phone: (603) 623-0313
E-mail: aabbott@nhia.edu
http://www.nhia.edu

Rivier College
420 South Main Street
Nashua, NH 03060
Phone: (603) 888-1311 or
     (800) 44-RIVIER
E-mail: admissions@rivier.edu
http://www.rivier.edu

NEW JERSEY

Kean University
Morris Avenue
Union, NJ 07083
Phone: (908) 737-KEAN
E-mail: admitme@kean.edu
http://www.kean.edu

Montclair State University
1 Normal Avenue
Upper Montclair, NJ 07043
Phone: (973) 655-4000
E-mail: undergraduate.admissions@
     montclair.edu
http://www.montclair.edu

New Jersey City University
2039 Kennedy Memorial Boulevard
Jersey City, NJ 07305-1597
Phone: (201) 200-3241 or
     (888) 441-NJCU (toll-free)
http://www.njcu.edu

NEW MEXICO

Institute of American Indian Arts
83 A Van Nu Po Road
Santa Fe, NM 87508
Phone: (505) 424-2300
http://www.iaiancad.org

NEW YORK

**Alfred School of Art and Design at
     Alfred University**
2 Pine Street
Alfred, NY 14802
Phone: (607) 871-2441
Fax: (607) 871-2490
http://art.alfred.edu

Briarcliffe College–Patchogue
225 West Main Street
Patchogue, NY 11772
Phone: (631) 654-5300 or
     (866) 235-5207 (toll-free)
http://www.bcpat.com

Buffalo State College
1300 Elmwood Avenue
Buffalo, NY 14222
Phone: (716) 878-4000
Fax: (716) 878-6697
http://www.buffalostate.edu

Cazenovia College
22 Sullivan Street
Cazenovia, NY 13035
Phone: (800) 654-3210
http://www.cazenovia.edu

College of Saint Rose
432 Western Avenue
Albany, NY 12203
Phone: (518) 485-3900 or (800) 637-8556
http://www.strose.edu

College of Staten Island
2800 Victory Boulevard
Staten Island, NY 10314
Phone: (718) 982-2000
http://www.csi.cuny.edu

**The Cooper Union for the
     Advancement of Science & Art**
30 Cooper Square
New York, NY 10003

Phone: (212) 353-4120
E-mail: admissions@cooper.edu
http://www.cooper.edu

Hartwick College
One Hartwick Drive
Oneonta, NY 13820-4020
Phone: (607) 431-4150 or (888)
HARTWICK (toll-free)
Fax: (607) 431-4102
E-mail: admissions@hartwick.edu
http://www.hartwick.edu

Hobart and William Smith Colleges
629 South Main Street
Geneva, NY 14456
Phone: (800) 852-2256
E-mail: admissions@hws.edu
http://www.hws.edu

Hofstra University
Hempstead, NY 11549
Phone: (800) HOFSTRA
http://www.hofstra.edu

Ithaca College
953 Danby Road
Ithaca, NY 14850
Phone: (607) 274-3011
Fax: (607) 274-1900
E-mail: admission@ithaca.edu
http://www.ithaca.edu

Long Island University–C.W. Post Campus
720 Northern Boulevard
Brookville, NY 11548
Phone: (516) 299-2000
Fax: (516) 299-3829
E-mail: cwpost@liu.edu
http://www.liu.edu

Marist College
3399 North Road
Poughkeepsie, NY 12601
Phone: (845) 575-3000
E-mail: admissions@marist.edu
http://www.marist.edu

Parsons School of Design
66 Fifth Avenue
New York, NY 10011
Phone: (212) 229-5150 or
(877) 528-332 (toll-free)
Fax: (212) 229-8975
E-mail: studentinfo@newschool.edu
http://www.parsons.edu

Rochester Institute of Technology
One Lomb Memorial Drive
Rochester, NY 14623-5603

Phone: (585) 475-2411
Fax: (585) 475-7279
http://www.rit.edu

Sage College of Albany
140 New Scotland Avenue
Albany, NY 12208
Phone: (518) 445-1778 or
(888) VERY-SAGE (toll-free)
http://www.sage.edu/sca

School of Visual Arts
209 East 23rd Street
New York, NY 10010
Phone: (212) 592-2000 or (888) 220-5782 (toll-free)
Fax: (212) 725-3587
E-mail: admissions@sva.edu
http://www.schoolofvisualarts.edu

State University of New York–New Paltz
75 South Manheim Boulevard
New Paltz, NY 12561-2443
Phone: (845) 257-2121
E-mail: admissions@newpaltz.edu
http://www.newpaltz.edu

SUNY Purchase College
735 Anderson Hill Road
Purchase, NY 10577
Phone: (914) 251-6300
E-mail: admissions@purchase.edu
http://www.purchase.edu

Syracuse University
Syracuse, NY 13244
Phone: (315) 443-1870
E-mail: orange@syr.edu
http://www.syr.edu

Tisch School of the Arts, New York University
721 Broadway
New York, NY 10003
Phone: (212) 998-1930
E-mail: photo.tsoa@nyu.edu
http://www.tisch.nyu.edu

NORTH CAROLINA

East Carolina University
East Fifth Street
Greenville, NC 27858-4353
Phone: (252) 328-6131
http://www.ecu.edu

University of North Carolina–Charlotte
9201 University City Boulevard
Charlotte, NC 28223-0001

Phone: (704) 687-2000
http://www.uncc.edu

Western Carolina University
242 H.F. Robinson Administration Building
Cullowhee, NC 28723
Phone: (877) WCU4YOU
Fax: (828) 227-7505
E-mail: admiss@wcu.edu
http://www.wcu.edu

NORTH DAKOTA

University of North Dakota
Grand Forks, ND 58202
Phone: (701) 777-2011 or
(800) CALL-UND
E-mail: enroll@mail.und.nodak.edu
http://www.und.edu

OHIO

The Cleveland Institute of Art
11141 East Boulevard
Cleveland, OH 44106-1710
Phone: (216) 421-7000 or (800) 223-4700
Fax: (216) 421-7438
E-mail: admiss@gate.cia.edu
http://www.cia.edu

Columbus College of Art & Design
107 North Ninth Street
Columbus, OH 43215
Phone: (614) 224-9101 or
(877) 997-CCAD (toll-free)
Fax: (614) 222-4040
http://www.ccad.edu

Miami University
501 East High Street
Oxford, OH 45056
Phone: (513) 529-1809
E-mail: admission@muohio.edu
http://www.miami.muohio.edu

Ohio State University–Columbus
154 West 12th Avenue
Columbus, OH 43210
Phone: (614) 292-3980
http://www.osu.edu

Ohio University
Athens, OH 45701
Phone: (740) 593-1000
http://www.ohio.edu

Otterbein College
One Otterbein College
Westerville, OH 43081

Phone: (614) 890-3000 or (800) 488-8144
http://www.otterbein.edu

University of Akron
277 East Buchtel Avenue
Akron, OH 44325-2001
Phone: (330) 972-7077 or (800) 655-4884
E-mail: admissions@uakron.edu
http://www.uakron.edu

University of Cincinnati
2600 Clifton Avenue
Cincinnati, OH 45221-0016
Phone: (513) 556-1100
http://www.uc.edu

University of Dayton
300 College Park
Dayton, OH 45469
Phone: (937) 229-1000 or (800) 837-7433
E-mail: admission@udayton.edu
http://www.udayton.edu

Youngstown State University
One University Plaza
Youngstown, OH 44555
Phone: (330) 941-2000 or
    (877) GO-TO-YSU (toll-free)
E-mail: enroll@ysu.edu
http://www.ysu.edu

OKLAHOMA

University of Central Oklahoma
100 North University Drive
Edmond, OK 73034
Phone: (405) 974-2000
http://www.ucok.edu

OREGON

Marylhurst University
17600 Pacific Highway
P.O. Box 261
Marylhurst, OR 97036-0261
Phone: (503) 636-8141 or (800) 634-9982
Fax: (503) 636-9526
E-mail: admissions@marylhurst.edu
http://www.marylhurst.edu

Oregon College of Art & Craft
8245 Southwest Barnes Road
Portland, OR 97225
Phone: (503) 297-5544 or (800) 390-0632
E-mail: admissions@ocac.edu
http://www.ocac.edu

Pacific Northwest College of Art
1241 Northwest Johnson Street
Portland, OR 97209

Phone: (503) 226-4391
Fax: (503) 226-3587
E-mail: admissions@pnca.edu
http://www.pnca.edu

University of Oregon
1217 University of Oregon
Eugene, OR 97403-1217
Phone: (541) 346-3201 or
    (800) BE-A-DUCK
http://www.uoregon.edu

PENNSYLVANIA

Arcadia University
450 South Easton Road
Glenside, PA 19038
Phone: (215) 572-2995 or
    (877) ARCADIA (toll-free)
E-mail: admiss@arcadia.edu
http://www.arcadia.edu

Cabrini College
610 King of Prussia Road
Radnor, PA 19087-3698
Phone: (610) 902-8100 or (800) 848-1003
http://www.cabrini.edu

Drexel University
3141 Chestnut Street
Philadelphia, PA 19104
Phone: (215) 895-2400 or
    (800) 2-DREXEL
http://www.drexel.edu

Kutztown University
P.O. Box 730
Kutztown, PA 19530
Phone: (610) 683-4000 or (877) 628-
    1915 (toll-free)
E-mail: admission@kutztown.edu
http://www.kutztown.edu

Marywood University
2300 Adams Avenue
Scranton, PA 18509
Phone: (570) 348-6211 or TO-
    MARYWOOD (toll-free)
Fax: (570) 340-6023
http://www.marywood.edu

Penn State Altoona
3000 Ivyside Park
Altoona, PA 16601
Phone: (814) 949-5000 or (800) 848-9843
Fax: (814) 949-5564
E-mail: aaadmit@psu.edu
http://www.aa.psu.edu

Pennsylvania College of Art and Design
204 North Prince Street
P.O. Box 59
Lancaster, PA 17608-0059
Phone: (717) 396-7833
Fax: (717) 396-1339
E-mail: admissions@pcad.edu
http://www.pcad.edu

Pennsylvania State University
201 Shields Building
P.O. Box 3000
University Park, PA 16804-3000
Phone: (814) 865-5471
Fax: (814) 863-7590
http://www.psu.edu

Temple University
1801 North Broad Street
Philadelphia, PA 19122
Phone: (215) 204-7000
E-mail: info@temple.edu
http://www.temple.edu

The University of the Arts
320 South Broad Street
Philadelphia, PA 19102
Phone: (800) 616-ARTS
http://www.uarts.edu

RHODE ISLAND

Rhode Island College
600 Mount Pleasant Avenue
Providence, RI 02908-1991
Phone: (401) 456-8000
E-mail: theweb@ric.edu
http://www.ric.edu

Rhode Island School of Design
Two College Street
Providence, RI 02903
Phone: (401) 454-6300 or
    (800) 364-RISD
E-mail: admissions@risd.edu
http://www.risd.edu

SOUTH CAROLINA

Coker College, Department of Art
300 East College Avenue
Hartsville, SC 29550
Phone: (843) 383-8000
Fax: (843) 383-8056
E-mail: admissions@coker.edu
http://www.coker.edu

Winthrop University
Rock Hill, SC 29733
Phone: (803) 323-2211

Fax: (803) 323-2137
E-mail: admissions@winthrop.edu
http://www.winthrop.edu

SOUTH DAKOTA

University of South Dakota
414 East Clark Street
Vermillion, SD 57069
Phone: (605) 677-5637
E-mail: admissions@usd.edu
http://www.usd.edu

TENNESSEE

Austin Peay State University
Ellington Building
Room 117
P.O. Box 4548
Clarksville, TN 37044
Phone: (931) 221-7661
E-mail: admissions@apsu.edu
http://www.apsu.edu

Carson-Newman College
2130 Branner Avenue
Jefferson City, TN 37760
Phone: (865) 471-2000
http://www.cn.edu

East Tennessee State University
P.O. Box 70267
Johnson City, TN 37614-1700
Phone: (423) 439-1000
http://www.etsu.edu

Memphis College of Art
1930 Poplar Avenue
Overton Park
Memphis, TN 38104-2764
Phone: (901) 272-5100 or (800) 727-1088
http://www.mca.edu

University of Memphis
Memphis, TN 38152-3380
Phone: (901) 678-2169 or (800) 669-2678
E-mail: recruitment@memphis.edu
http://www.memphis.edu

Watkins College of Art and Design
2298 MetroCenter Boulevard
Nashville, TN 37228
Phone: (615) 383-4848
Fax: (615) 383-4849
http://www.watkins.edu

TEXAS

Baylor University
Waco, TX 76798
Phone: (800) BAYLOR-U
http://www.baylor.edu

Midwestern State University
3410 Taft Boulevard
Wichita Falls, TX 76308
Phone: (940) 397-4000
Fax: (940) 397-4369
E-mail: information@mwsu.edu
http://www.mwsu.edu

Rice University
6100 Main Street
Houston, TX 77005
Phone: (713) 348-0000
Fax: (713) 348-5910
http://www.rice.edu

Texas Tech University
2500 Broadway
Lubbock, TX 79409-2081
Phone: (806) 742-2011
http://www.ttu.edu

University of Texas at San Antonio
6900 North Loop 1604 West
San Antonio, TX 78249
Phone: (210) 458-4011
http://www.utsa.edu

UTAH

Brigham Young University
Provo, UT 84602
Phone: (801) 422-4429
Fax: (801) 422-0005
E-mail: admissions@byu.edu
http://www.byu.edu

University of Utah
201 South Presidents Circle
Room 201
Salt Lake City, UT 84112
Phone: (801) 581-7200
Fax: (801) 585-6171
E-mail: admissions@sa.utah.edu
http://www.utah.edu

VERMONT

Bennington College
One College Drive
Bennington, VT 05201
Phone: (802) 442-5401
http://www.bennington.edu

VIRGINIA

Longwood University
201 High Street
Farmville, VA 23909
Phone: (434) 395-2000
Fax: (434) 395-2775

E-mail: lcadmit@longwood.edu
http://www.longwood.edu

Lynchburg College
1501 Lakeside Drive
Lynchburg, VA 24501
Phone: (434) 544-8100
http://www.lynchburg.edu

Old Dominion University
108 Alfred B. Rollins Jr. Hall
Norfolk, VA 23529-0050
Phone: (757) 683-3685
Fax: (757) 683-5923
http://www.odu.edu

Virginia Commonwealth University
Richmond, VA 23284
Phone: (804) 828-0100
E-mail: ugrad@vcu.edu
http://www.vcu.edu

Virginia Intermont College
1013 Moore Street
Bristol, VA 24201
Phone: (800) 451-1-VIC
http://www.vic.edu

WASHINGTON

Cornish College of the Arts
1000 Lenora Street
Seattle, WA 98121
Phone: (206) 726-5016 or
     (800) 726-ARTS
E-mail: admissions@cornish.edu
http://www.cornish.edu

Henry Cogswell College
3002 Colby Avenue
Everett, WA 98201
Phone: (425) 258-3351
E-mail: admissions@henrycogswell.edu
http://www.henrycogswell.edu

Washington State University
Lighty 370
Pullman, WA 99164-1067
Phone: (509) 335-5586 or
     (888) GO-TO-WSU (toll-free)
Fax: (509) 335-7742
E-mail: admiss2@wsu.edu
http://www.wsu.edu

WEST VIRGINIA

Marshall University
One John Marshall Drive
Huntington, WV 25755

Phone: (304) 696-3170 or (800) 642-3463
E-mail: admissions@marshall.edu
http://www.marshall.edu

WISCONSIN

Cardinal Stritch University
6801 North Yates Road
Milwaukee, WI 53217
Phone: (414) 410-4040 or (800) 347-8822

E-mail: admityou@stritch.edu
http://www.stritch.edu

Carroll College Academy
100 North East Avenue
Waukesha, WI 53186
Phone: (262) 547-1211 or
    (800) CARROLL
Fax: (262) 524-7139
http://www.cc.edu

Milwaukee Institute of Art & Design
273 East Erie Street
Milwaukee, WI 53202
Phone: (414) 291-8070 or
    (888) 749-MIAD (toll-free)
Fax: (414) 291-8077
http://www.miad.edu

APPENDIX III
FOUR-YEAR UNDERGRADUATE
COMMERCIAL PHOTOGRAPHY PROGRAMS

ALABAMA

Jacksonville State University
700 Pelham Road North
Jacksonville, AL 36265-9982
Phone: (800) 231-5291
http://www.jsu.edu

CALIFORNIA

Art Center College of Design
1700 Lida Street
Pasadena, CA 91103-1999
Phone: (626) 396-2373
Fax: (626) 405-9104
http://www.artcenter.edu

**Brooks Institute of Photography–Santa
  Barbara**
801 Alston Road
Santa Barbara, CA 93108
Phone: (805) 966-3888 or
  (888) 304-3456 (toll-free)
http://www.brooks.edu

California Polytechnic State University
San Luis Obispo, CA 93407
Phone: (805) 756-111
Fax: (805) 756-6321
http://www.calpoly.edu

California State University–East Bay
25800 Carlos Bee Boulevard
Hayward, CA 94542
Phone: (510) 885-3000
E-mail: adminfo@csuhayward.edu
http://www.csuhayward.edu

California State University–Fullerton
P.O. Box 34080
Fullerton, CA 92834
Phone: (714) 278-2011
http://www.fullerton.edu

**California State University–San
  Bernardino**
5500 University Parkway
San Bernardino, CA 92407
Phone: (909) 880-5000
http://www.csusb.edu

Chapman University
One University Drive
Orange, CA 92866
Phone: (714) 997-6815
http://www.chapman.edu

Sonoma State University
1801 East Cotati Avenue
Rohnert Park, CA 94928
Phone: (707) 664-2880
http://www.sonoma.edu

COLORADO

The Art Institute of Colorado
1200 Lincoln Street
Denver, CO 80203
Phone: (303) 837-0825 or (800) 275-2420
http://www.aic.artinstitutes.edu

University of Colorado–Denver
Campus Box 167
P.O. Box 173364
Denver, CO 80217-3364
Phone: (303) 556-5600
E-mail: admissions@cudenver.edu
http://www.cudenver.edu

DISTRICT OF COLUMBIA

Corcoran College of Art and Design
500 17th Street NW
Washington, DC 20006
Phone: (202) 639-1801, ext. 1800
http://www.corcoran.edu

Howard University
2400 Sixth Street NW
Washington, DC 20059
Phone: (202) 806-6100
Fax: (202) 806-9258
http://www.howard.edu

FLORIDA

Barry University
11300 Northeast Second Avenue
Miami Shores, FL 33161-6695
Phone: (305) 899-3100 or (800) 695-2279
E-mail: admissions@mail.barry.edu
http://www.barry.edu

Florida State University
Tallahassee, FL 32306-1170
Phone: (850) 644-6200
Fax: (850) 644-0197
E-mail: admissions@admin.fsu.edu
http://www.fsu.edu

GEORGIA

**American InterContinental University–
  Atlanta (Buckhead)**
3330 Peachtree Road NE
Buckhead, GA 30326
Phone: (800) 846-1994
http://www.aiuniv.edu

**American InterContinental University–
  Atlanta (Dunwoody)**
6600 Peachtree-Dunwoody Road
Dunwoody, GA 30328
Phone: (800) 846-1994
http://www.aiuniv.edu

Atlanta College of Art
Woodruff Arts Center
1280 Peachtree Street NE
Atlanta, GA 30309
Phone: (404) 733-5100 or (800) 832-2104
E-mail: acainfo@woodruffcenter.org
http://www.aca.edu

Georgia Southern University
P.O. Box 8024
Statesboro, GA 30460
Phone: (912) 681-5391
Fax: (912) 871-1156
E-mail: admissions@georgiasouthern.edu
http://www.georgiasouthern.edu

ILLINOIS

Illinois State University
Normal, IL 61790-5620
Phone: (309) 438-2181 or (800) 366-2478
E-mail: admissions@ilstu.edu
http://www.ilstu.edu

**Southern Illinois University
  Carbondale**
Carbondale, IL 62901-4301

Phone: (618) 453-4315
http://www.siuc.edu

INDIANA

Ball State University
2000 University
Muncie, IN 47306
Phone: (765) 285-8300 or
    (800) 482-4BSU
E-mail: askus@bsu.edu
http://www.bsu.edu

Indiana State University
200 North Seventh Street
Terre Haute, IN 47809-9989
Phone: (800) GO-TO-ISU
http://www.indstate.edu

Saint Mary's College
Notre Dame, IN 46556-5001
Phone: (574) 284-4000
E-mail: admission@saintmarys.edu
http://www.saintmarys.edu

IOWA

University of Northern Iowa
1227 West 27th Street
Cedar Falls, IA 50614
Phone: (319) 273-2311
E-mail: admissions@uni.edu
http://www.uni.edu

MASSACHUSETTS

Pine Manor College
400 Heath Street
Chestnut Hill, MA 02467
Phone: (617) 731-7000 or (800) 762-1357
Fax: (617) 731-7199
http://www.pmc.edu

MICHIGAN

Grand Valley State University
1 Campus Drive
Allendale, MI 49401
Phone: (616) 331-5000
http://www.gvsu.edu

Hope College
Holland, MI 49422
Phone: (616) 395-7000
E-mail: admissions@hope.edu
http://www.hope.edu

MINNESOTA

Brown College
1440 Northland Drive
Mendota Heights, MN 55120

Phone: (800) 766-2040
http://www.browncollege.edu

Minnesota State University Moorhead
1104 Seventh Avenue South
Moorhead, MN 56563
Phone: (800) 593.7246
http://www.mnstate.edu

MONTANA

Montana State University
Bozeman, MT 59717-0368
Phone: (406) 994-4501
http://www.montana.edu

NEW MEXICO

Institute of American Indian Arts
83 A Van Nu Po Road
Santa Fe, NM 87508
Phone: (505) 424-2300
http://www.iaiancad.org

NEW YORK

Parsons School of Design
66 Fifth Avenue
New York, NY 10011
Phone: (212) 229-5150 or
    (877) 528-332 (toll-free)
Fax: (212) 229-8975
E-mail:studentinfo@newschool.edu
http://www.parsons.edu

Rochester Institute of Technology
One Lomb Memorial Drive
Rochester, NY 14623-5603
Phone: (585) 475-2411
Fax: (585) 475-7279
http://www.rit.edu

SUNY Fredonia
280 Central Avenue
Fredonia, NY 14063
Phone: (716) 673-3111 or (800) 252-1212
Fax: (716) 673-3249
http://www.fredonia.edu

University at Buffalo
17 Capen Hall
Buffalo, NY 14260-1660
Phone: (716) 645-6878 or
    (888) UB-ADMIT (toll-free)
E-mail: ubadmit@buffalo.edu
http://www.buffalo.edu

NORTH CAROLINA

East Carolina University
East Fifth Street
Greenville, NC 27858-4353

Phone: (252) 328-6131
http://www.ecu.edu

North Carolina State University
Raleigh, NC 27695
Phone: (919) 515-2011
http://www.ncsu.edu

OHIO

University of Akron
277 East Buchtel Avenue
Akron, OH 44325-2001
Phone: (330) 972-7077 or (800) 655-4884
E-mail: admissions@uakron.edu
http://www.uakron.edu

OREGON

Eastern Oregon University
One University Boulevard
La Grand, OR 97850-2899
Phone: (541) 962-3672, ext. 23635
E-mail: webmaster@eou.edu
http://www.eou.edu

Pennsylvania
Drexel University
3141 Chestnut Street
Philadelphia, PA 19104
Phone: (215) 895-2400 or
    (800) 2-DREXEL
http://www.drexel.edu

Messiah College
One College Avenue
Grantham, PA 17027
Phone: (717) 766-2511 or (800) 233-4220
http://www.messiah.edu

Pennsylvania State University
201 Shields Building
P.O. Box 3000
University Park, PA 16804-3000
Phone: (814) 865-5471
Fax: (814) 863-7590
http://www.psu.edu

RHODE ISLAND

Rhode Island College
600 Mount Pleasant Avenue
Providence, RI 02908-1991
Phone: (401) 456-8000
E-mail: theweb@ric.edu
http://www.ric.edu

Salve Regina University
100 Ochre Point Avenue
Newport, RI 02840-4192

Phone: (401) 847-6650
http://www.salve.edu

SOUTH CAROLINA

Francis Marion University
P.O. Box 100547
Florence, SC 29501
Phone: (843) 661-1362
http://www.fmarion.edu

Furman University
3300 Poinsett Highway
Greenville, SC 29613
Phone: (864) 294-2000
http://www.furman.edu

TENNESSEE

Carson-Newman College
2130 Branner Avenue

Jefferson City, TN 37760
Phone: (865) 471-2000
http://www.cn.edu

Union University
1050 Union University Drive
Jackson, TN 38305
Phone: (731) 668-1818
E-mail: info@uu.edu
http://www.uu.edu

APPENDIX IV
CINEMATOGRAPHY AND
VIDEOGRAPHY PROGRAMS

CALIFORNIA

Art Center College of Design
1700 Lida Street
Pasadena, CA 91103-1999
Phone: (626) 396-2373
Fax: (626) 405-9104
http://www.artcenter.edu

Brooks Institute of Photography–Santa Barbara
801 Alston Road
Santa Barbara, CA 93108
Phone: (805) 966-3888 or
     (888) 304-3456 (toll-free)
http://www.brooks.edu

California College of the Arts
1111 Eighth Street
San Francisco, CA 94107-2247
Phone: (415) 703-9500 or
     (800) 447-1ART
E-mail: enroll@cca.edu
http://www.cca.edu

California Institute of the Arts
24700 McBean Parkway
Valencia, CA 91355
Phone: (661) 255-1050
E-mail: admiss@calarts.edu
http://www.calarts.edu

Cogswell College
1175 Bordeaux Drive
Sunnyvale, CA 94089-9772
Phone: (408) 541-0100 or (800)
     COGSWLL
Fax: (408) 747-0764
E-mail: info@cogswell.edu
http://www.cogswell.edu

Columbia College Hollywood
18618 Oxnard Street
Tarzana, CA 91356-1411
Phone: (818) 345-8414 or (800) 785-0585
Fax: (818) 345-9053
E-mail: info@columbiacollege.edu
http://www.columbiacollege.edu

De Anza College
21250 Stevens Creek Boulevard
Cupertino, CA 95014
Phone: (408) 864-5678
http://www.deanza.fhda.edu

Miami Ad School San Francisco
415 Jackson Street
Suite B
San Francisco, CA 94111
Phone: (415) 837-0966
Fax: (415) 837-0967
http://www.miamiadschool.com

New York Film Academy–Universal Studios Location
Hollywood, CA
Phone: (818) 733-2600
Fax: (818) 733-4074
E-mail: studios@nyfa.com
http://www.nyfa.com

COLORADO

Rocky Mountain College of Art & Design
1600 Pierce Street
Lakewood, CO 80214
Phone: (800) 888-ARTS
E-mail: admission@rmcad.net
http://www.rmcad.edu

FLORIDA

Florida Metropolitan University– Melbourne Campus
2401 North Harbor City Boulevard
Melbourne, FL 32935
Phone: (321) 253-2929
http://www.fmu.edu

Florida Metropolitan University–North Orlando Campus
5421 Diplomat Circle
Orlando, FL 32810
Phone: (407) 628-5870
http://www.fmu.edu

Florida State University
Tallahassee, FL 32306-1170
Phone: (850) 644-6200
Fax: (850) 644-0197
E-mail: admissions@admin.fsu.edu
http://www.fsu.edu

Miami International University of Art & Design
1501 Biscayne Boulevard
Suite 100
Miami, FL 33132-1418
Phone: (800) 225-9023
Fax: (305) 374-5933
http://www.ifac.edu

GEORGIA

Savannah College of Art and Design
P.O. Box 2072
Savannah, GA 31402-2072
Phone: (912) 525-5100 or
     (800) 869-7223
Fax: (912) 525-5986
E-mail: admission@scad.edu
http://www.scad.edu

IOWA

Maharishi University of Management
1000 North Fourth Street
Fairfield, IA 52557
Phone: (800) 369-6480
Fax: (641) 472-1179
E-mail: admissions@mum.edu
http://mum.edu

KENTUCKY

Kentucky State University
400 East Main Street
Frankfort, KY 40601
Phone: (502) 597-6000
Fax: (502) 597-6409
http://www.kysu.edu

MASSACHUSETTS

Emerson College
120 Boylston Street
Boston, MA 02116-4624
Phone: (617) 824-8500
http://www.emerson.edu

Hampshire College
893 West Street
Amherst, MA 01002
Phone: (413) 559-5471
E-mail: admissions@hampshire.edu
http://www.hampshire.edu

The New England Institute of Art
10 Brookline Place West
Brookline, MA 02445
Phone: (800) 903-4425
Fax: (617) 582-4500
http://www.neia.aii.edu

School of the Museum of Fine Arts, Boston
230 The Fenway
Boston, MA 02115
Phone: (617) 267-6100 or (800) 643-6078
Fax: (617) 424-6271
E-mail: academicaffairs@smfa.edu
http://www.smfa.edu

MICHIGAN

Northern Michigan University
1401 Presque Isle Avenue
Marquette, MI 49855
Phone: (800) 682-9797
Fax: (906) 227-2276
E-mail: admiss@nmu.edu
http://www.nmu.edu

MINNESOTA

Minneapolis College of Art & Design
2501 Stevens Avenue South
Minneapolis, MN 55404
Phone: (612) 874-3760 or (800) 874-6223
E-mail: admissions@mcad.edu
http://www.mcad.edu

MISSOURI

Kansas City Art Institute
4415 Warwick Boulevard
Kansas City, MO 64111
Phone: (816) 474-5224 or (800) 522-5224
Fax: (816) 802-3309
E-mail: admiss@kcai.edu
http://www.kcai.edu

NEW JERSEY

Kean University
Morris Avenue
Union, NJ 07083
Phone: (908) 737-KEAN
E-mail: admitme@kean.edu
http://www.kean.edu

NEW MEXICO

College of Santa Fe
1600 St. Michael's Drive
Santa Fe, NM 87505
Phone: (505) 473-6133 or (800) 456-2673
Fax: (505) 473-6127
E-mail: admissions@csf.edu
http://www.csf.edu

NEW YORK

Alfred School of Art and Design at Alfred University
2 Pine Street
Alfred, NY 14802
Phone: (607) 871-2441
Fax: (607) 871-2490
http://art.alfred.edu

Columbia University
2960 Broadway
New York, NY 10027-6902
Phone: (212) 854-1754
http://www.columbia.edu

New York Film Academy–New York City Location
100 East 17th Street
New York, NY 10003
Phone: (212) 674-4300
Fax: (212) 477-1414
E-mail: film@nyfa.com
http://www.nyfa.com

Rochester Institute of Technology
One Lomb Memorial Drive
Rochester, NY 14623-5603
Phone: (585) 475-2411
Fax: (585) 475-7279
http://www.rit.edu

School of Visual Arts
209 East 23rd Street
New York, NY 10010
Phone: (212) 592-2000 or
    (888) 220-5782 (toll-free)
Fax: (212) 725-3587
E-mail: admissions@sva.edu
http://www.schoolofvisualarts.edu

Syracuse University
Syracuse, NY 13244
Phone: (315) 443-1870
E-mail: orange@syr.edu
http://www.syr.edu

Tisch School of the Arts, New York University
721 Broadway
New York, NY 10003
Phone: (212) 998-1930
E-mail: photo.tsoa@nyu.edu
http://www.tisch.nyu.edu

NORTH CAROLINA

North Carolina School of the Arts
1533 South Main Street
Winston-Salem, NC 27127-2188
Phone: (336) 770-3399
Fax: (336) 770-3370
E-mail: admissions@ncarts.edu
http://www.ncarts.edu

PENNSYLVANIA

Drexel University
3141 Chestnut Street
Philadelphia, PA 19104
Phone: (215) 895-2400 or
    (800) 2-DREXEL
http://www.drexel.edu

Pittsburgh Filmmakers, Inc.
477 Melwood Avenue
Pittsburgh, PA 15213
Phone: (412) 681-5449
http://www.pghfilmmakers.org

TENNESSEE

Southern Adventist University
School of Visual Art & Design
P.O. Box 370
Collegedale, TN 37315
Phone: (423) 236-2732 or
    (800) SOUTHERN
E-mail: art@southern.edu
http://art.southern.edu

Watkins College of Art and Design
2298 MetroCenter Boulevard
Nashville, TN 37228
Phone: (615) 383-4848
Fax: (615) 383-4849
http://www.watkins.edu

TEXAS

Rice University
6100 Main Street
Houston, TX 77005

Phone: (713) 348-0000
Fax: (713) 348-5910
http://www.rice.edu

University of Texas at Austin
1 University Station
Austin, TX 78712
Phone: (512) 475-7348
Fax: (512) 471-7801
http://www.utexas.edu

VIRGINIA

Virginia Commonwealth University
Richmond, VA 23284
Phone: (804) 828-0100

E-mail: ugrad@vcu.edu
http://www.vcu.edu

WASHINGTON

Cornish College of the Arts
1000 Lenora Street
Seattle, WA 98121
Phone: (206) 726-5016 or
    (800) 726-ARTS
E-mail: admissions@cornish.edu
http://www.cornish.edu

Henry Cogswell College
3002 Colby Avenue
Everett, WA 98201

Phone: (425) 258-3351
E-mail: admissions@henrycogswell.edu
http://www.henrycogswell.edu

APPENDIX V
GRADUATE PROGRAMS IN PHOTOGRAPHY

ALABAMA

University of Alabama
Tuscaloosa, AL 35487-0270
Phone: (205) 348-6010
E-mail: admissions@ua.edu
http://www.ua.edu

ARIZONA

Arizona State University
P.O. Box 870112
Tempe, AZ 85287-0112
Phone: (480) 965-3468
Fax: (480) 965-8338
http://www.asu.edu

University of Arizona
Tucson, AZ 85721-0002
Phone: (520) 621-2211
http://www.arizona.edu

CALIFORNIA

Academy of Art University
79 New Montgomery Street
San Francisco, CA 94105
Phone: (415) 274-2200 or
  (800) 544-ARTS
E-mail: admissions@academyart.edu
http://www.academyart.edu

**Brooks Institute of Photography–Santa
  Barbara**
801 Alston Road
Santa Barbara, CA 93108
Phone: (805) 966-3888 or
  (888) 304-3456 (toll-free)
http://www.brooks.edu

California State University–Fullerton
P.O. Box 34080
Fullerton, CA 92834
Phone: (714) 278-2011
http://www.fullerton.edu

California State University–Long Beach
1250 Bellflower Boulevard
Long Beach, CA 90840-3501
Phone: (562) 985-4111
http://www.csulb.edu

Otis College of Art and Design
9045 Lincoln Boulevard
Los Angeles, CA 90045
Phone: (310) 665-6800 or (800) 527-OTIS
Fax: (310) 665-6821
E-mail: admissions@otis.edu
http://www.otis.edu

San Jose State University
One Washington Square
San Jose, CA 95192-0089
Phone: (408) 924-1000
Fax: (408) 924-4326
http://www.sjsu.edu

University of California–Los Angeles
1147 Murphy Hall, Box 951436
Los Angeles, CA 90095-1436
Phone: (310) 825-3101
Fax: (310) 206-1206
E-mail: ugadm@saonet.ucla.edu
http://www.ucla.edu

CONNECTICUT

University of Connecticut
875 Coventry Road
Storrs, CT 06269-1099
Phone: (860) 486-2000
http://www.uconn.edu

University of Hartford
200 Bloomfield Avenue
West Hartford, CT 06117
Phone: (860) 768-4100
http://www.hartford.edu

DISTRICT OF COLUMBIA

Howard University
2400 Sixth Street NW
Washington, DC 20059
Phone: (202) 806-6100
Fax: (202) 806-9258
http://www.howard.edu

FLORIDA

Barry University
11300 Northeast Second Avenue
Miami Shores, FL 33161-6695

Phone: (305) 899-3100 or (800) 695-2279
E-mail: admissions@mail.barry.edu
http://www.barry.edu

University of Florida
Gainesville, FL 32611
Phone: (352) 392-3261
http://www.ufl.edu

GEORGIA

Georgia State University
P.O. Box 3965
Atlanta, GA 30302-3965
Phone: (404) 651-2000
http://www.gsu.edu

Savannah College of Art and Design
P.O. Box 2072
Savannah, GA 31402-2072
Phone: (912) 525-5100 or (800) 869-7223
Fax: (912) 525-5986
E-mail: admission@scad.edu
http://www.scad.edu

University of Georgia
Athens, GA 30602-7287
Phone: (706) 542-3000
E-mail: undergrad@admissions.uga.edu
http://www.uga.edu

ILLINOIS

Bradley University
1501 West Bradley Avenue
Peoria, IL 61625
Phone: (309) 677-2967
E-mail: admissions@bradley.edu
http://www.bradley.edu

Governors State University
1 University Parkway
University Park, IL 60466-0975
Phone: (708) 534-5000
E-mail: gsunow@govst.edu
http://www.govst.edu

Illinois State University
Normal, IL 61790-5620
Phone: (309) 438-2181 or (800) 366-2478
E-mail: admissions@ilstu.edu
http://www.ilstu.edu

Northern Illinois University
DeKalb, IL 60115
Phone: (815) 753-1000
http://www.niu.edu

Southern Illinois University Carbondale
Carbondale, IL 62901-4301
Phone: (618) 453-4315
http://www.siuc.edu

University of Illinois–Chicago
Chicago, IL 60612
Phone: (312) 996-7000
http://www.uic.edu

**University of Illinois at Urbana–
    Champaign**
901 West Illinois Street
Urbana, IL 61801
Phone: (217) 333-0302
Fax: (217) 333-0035
E-mail: iuinfo@uiuc.edu
http://www.uiuc.edu

INDIANA

Indiana State University
200 North Seventh Street
Terre Haute, IN 47809-9989
Phone: (800) GO-TO-ISU
http://www.indstate.edu

Indiana University
107 South Indiana Avenue
Bloomington, IN 47405
Phone: (812) 855-4848
E-mail: iuadmit@indiana.edu
http://www.indiana.edu

KANSAS

Kansas State University
Manhattan, KS 66506
Phone: (785) 532-6250
Fax: (785) 532-6393
E-mail: kstate@k-state.edu
http://www.ksu.edu

KENTUCKY

University of Louisville
Louisville, KY 40292
Phone: (502) 852-5555 or (800) 334-UofL
Fax: (502) 852-6791
http://www.louisville.edu

LOUISIANA

Louisiana State University
110 Thomas Boyd Hall
Baton Rouge, LA 70803

Phone: (225) 578-1175
E-mail: admissions@lsu.edu
http://www.lsu.edu

Louisiana Tech University
P.O. Box 3178
Ruston, LA 71272
Phone: (318) 257-3036 or (800)
    LATECH-1
http://www.latech.edu

MARYLAND

Maryland Institute College of Art
1300 Mount Royal Avenue
Baltimore, MD 21217
Phone: (410) 669-9200
http://www.mica.edu

MASSACHUSETTS

Massachusetts College of Arts
Avenue of the Arts
621 Huntington Avenue
Boston, MA 02115
Phone: (617) 879-7000
Fax: (617) 879-7250
http://www.massart.edu

**School of the Museum of Fine Arts,
    Boston**
230 The Fenway
Boston, MA 02115
Phone: (617) 267-6100 or (800) 643-
    6078
Fax: (617) 424-6271
E-mail: academicaffairs@smfa.edu
http://www.smfa.edu

**University of Massachusetts–
    Dartmouth**
285 Old Westport Road
North Dartmouth, MA 02747-2300
Phone: (508) 999-8000
Fax: (508) 999-8901
http://www.umassd.edu

MICHIGAN

Cranbrook Academy of Art
39221 Woodward Avenue
P.O. Box 801
Bloomfield Hills, MI 48303-0801
Phone: (248) 645-3301 or (877) GO-
    CRANBrook (toll-free)
http://www.cranbrook.edu

Kendall College of Art and Design
17 Fountain Street

Grand Rapids, Kent, MI 49503-3102
Phone: (616) 451-2787 or (800) 676-2787
Fax: (616) 831-9689
http://www.kcad.edu

University of Michigan–Ann Arbor
Ann Arbor, MI 48109
Phone: (734) 764-1817
http://www.umich.edu

Western Michigan University
1903 West Michigan Avenue
Kalamazoo, MI 49008-5201
Phone: (269) 387-1000
http://www.wmich.edu

MINNESOTA

Minneapolis College of Art & Design
2501 Stevens Avenue South
Minneapolis, MN 55404
Phone: (612) 874-3760 or (800) 874-6223
E-mail: admissions@mcad.edu
http://www.mcad.edu

MISSOURI

Washington University in Saint Louis
One Brookings Drive
Saint Louis, MO 63130-4899
Phone: (314) 935-5000
E-mail: admissions@wustl.edu
http://www.wustl.edu

MONTANA

University of Montana
32 Campus Drive
Missoula, MT 59812
Phone: (406) 243-0211
http://www.umt.edu

NEBRASKA

University of Nebraska–Lincoln
Lincoln, NE 68588
Phone: (402) 472-7211
http://www.unl.edu

NEVADA

University of Nevada–Las Vegas
4505 Maryland Parkway
Las Vegas, NV 89154
Phone: (702) 895-3011
E-mail: undergraduate.recruitment@
    ccmail.nevada.edu
http://www.unlv.edu

NEW JERSEY

Montclair State University
1 Normal Avenue
Upper Montclair, NJ 07043
Phone: (973) 655-4000
E-mail: undergraduate.admissions@
  montclair.edu
http://www.montclair.edu

New Jersey City University
2039 Kennedy Memorial Boulevard
Jersey City, NJ 07305-1597
Phone: (201) 200-3241 or
  (888) 441-NJCU (toll-free)
http://www.njcu.edu

NEW YORK

**Alfred School of Art and Design at
  Alfred University**
2 Pine Street
Alfred, NY 14802
Phone: (607) 871-2441
Fax: (607) 871-2490
http://art.alfred.edu

Bard College
**Milton Avery Graduate School of the
  Arts**
P.O. Box 5000
Annandale-on-Hudson, NY 12504-5000
Phone: (845) 758-6822
Fax: (845) 758-7507
E-mail: admission@bard.edu
http://www.bard.edu

Parsons School of Design
66 Fifth Avenue
New York, NY 10011
Phone: (212) 229-5150 or
  (877) 528-332 (toll-free)
Fax: (212) 229-8975
E-mail: studentinfo@newschool.edu
http://www.parsons.edu

Rochester Institute of Technology
One Lomb Memorial Drive
Rochester, NY 14623-5603
Phone: (585) 475-2411
Fax: (585) 475-7279
http://www.rit.edu

School of Visual Arts
209 East 23rd Street
New York, NY 10010
Phone: (212) 592-2000 or
  (888) 220-5782 (toll-free)
Fax: (212) 725-3587

E-mail: admissions@sva.edu
http://www.schoolofvisualarts.edu

Syracuse University
Syracuse, NY 13244
Phone: (315) 443-1870
E-mail: orange@syr.edu
http://www.syr.edu

NORTH CAROLINA

East Carolina University
East Fifth Street
Greenville, NC 27858-4353
Phone: (252) 328-6131
http://www.ecu.edu

OHIO

Bowling Green State University
Bowling Green, OH 43403
Phone: (419) 372-2531
http://www.bgsu.edu

Ohio State University at Columbus
154 West 12th Avenue
Columbus, OH 43210
Phone: (614) 292-3980
http://www.osu.edu

Ohio University
Athens, OH 45701
Phone: (740) 593-1000
http://www.ohio.edu

University of Cincinnati
2600 Clifton Avenue
Cincinnati, OH 45221-0016
Phone: (513) 556-1100
http://www.uc.edu

PENNSYLVANIA

Marywood University
2300 Adams Avenue
Scranton, PA 18509
Phone: (570) 348-6211 or TO-
  MARYWOOD (toll-free)
Fax: (570) 340-6023
http://www.marywood.edu

Pennsylvania State University
201 Shields Building
P.O. Box 3000
University Park, PA 16804-3000
Phone: (814) 865-5471
Fax: (814) 863-7590
http://www.psu.edu

Temple University
1801 North Broad Street
Philadelphia, PA 19122
Phone: (215) 204-7000
E-mail: info@temple.edu
http://www.temple.edu

RHODE ISLAND

Rhode Island School of Design
Two College Street
Providence, RI 02903
Phone: (401) 454-6300 or
  (800) 364-RISD
E-mail: admissions@risd.edu
http://www.risd.edu

SOUTH CAROLINA

Clemson University
Clemson, SC 29634-0001
Phone: (864) 656-3311
http://www.clemson.edu

TENNESSEE

East Tennessee State University
P.O. Box 70267
Johnson City, TN 37614-1700
Phone: (423) 439-1000
http://www.etsu.edu

Memphis College of Art
1930 Poplar Avenue
Overton Park
Memphis, TN 38104-2764
Phone: (901) 272-5100 or (800) 727-1088
http://www.mca.edu

University of Memphis
Memphis, TN 38152-3380
Phone: (901) 678-2169 or (800) 669-2678
E-mail: recruitment@memphis.edu
http://www.memphis.edu

TEXAS

Texas Tech University
2500 Broadway
Lubbock, TX 79409-2081
Phone: (806) 742-2011
http://www.ttu.edu

University of Texas–Austin
1 University Station
Austin, TX 78712
Phone: (512) 475-7348
Fax: (512) 471-7801
http://www.utexas.edu

University of Texas–San Antonio
6900 North Loop 1604 West
San Antonio, TX 78249
Phone: (210) 458-4011
http://www.utsa.edu

UTAH

University of Utah
201 South Presidents Circle
Room 201
Salt Lake City, UT 84112
Phone: (801) 581-7200
Fax: (801) 585-6171
E-mail: admissions@sa.utah.edu
http://www.utah.edu

VERMONT

Bennington College
One College Drive
Bennington, VT 05201

Phone: (802) 442-5401
http://www.bennington.edu

VIRGINIA

James Madison University
800 South Main Street
Harrisonburg, VA 22807
Phone: (540) 568-6211
http://www.jmu.edu

Virginia Commonwealth University
Richmond, VA 23284
Phone: (804) 828-0100
E-mail: ugrad@vcu.edu
http://www.vcu.edu

WASHINGTON

Central Washington University,
Department of Art
400 East University Way

Ellensburg, WA 98926-7564
Phone: (509) 963-1111
Fax: (509) 963-1918
http://www.cwu.edu

Washington State University
Lighty 370
Pullman, WA 99164-1067
Phone: (509) 335-5586 or
    (888) GO-TO-WSU (toll-free)
Fax: (509) 335-7742
E-mail: admiss2@wsu.edu
http://www.wsu.edu

APPENDIX VI
ASSOCIATIONS AND ORGANIZATIONS

Advertising Photographers of America
28 East Jackson Building, #10-A855
Chicago, IL 60604-2263
Phone: (800) 272-6264
Fax: (888) 889-7190
http://www.apanational.com

American Film Institute
2021 North Western Avenue
Los Angeles, CA 90027-1657
Phone: (323) 856-7600
Fax: (323) 467-4578
http://afionline.org

American Society of Media
  Photographers, Inc.
150 North Second Street
Philadelphia, PA 19106
Phone: (215) 451-ASMP
Fax: (215) 451-0880
http://www.asmp.org

The American Society of Picture
  Professionals
409 South Washington Street
Alexandria, VA 22314
Phone: (703) 299-0219
Fax: (703) 299-0219
http://www.aspp.com

Aperture Foundation
547 West 27th Street
4th floor
New York, NY 10001
E-mail: info@aperture.org
Phone: (212) 505-5555
Fax: (212) 598-4015
http://www.aperture.org

Blue Earth Alliance
P.O. Box 94388
Seattle, WA 98124-6688
http://www.blueearth.org

The Center for Photography at
  Woodstock
59 Tinker Street
Woodstock, NY 12498
Phone: (845) 679-9957
Fax: (845) 679-6337
http://www.cpw.org

FiftyCrows
5214-F Diamond Heights Boulevard,
  #615
San Francisco, CA 94131-2118
Phone: (415) 647-1100
http://www.fiftycrows.org

Graphic Artists Guild
90 John Street
Suite 403
New York, NY 10038-3202
(212) 791-3400
http://www.gag.org

Houston Center for Photography
1441 West Alabama
Houston, TX 77006-4103
Phone: (713) 529-4755
Fax: (713) 529-9248
http://www.hcponline.org

International Center of Photography
1114 Avenue of the Americas
New York, NY 10036
Phone: (212) 857-0001
Fax: (212) 857-0090
http://www.icp.org

International Freelance Photographers
  Organization
P.O. Box 777
Lewisville, NC 27023-0777
Phone: (336) 945-9867
Fax: (336) 945-3711
http://www.aipress.com

International Institute of Photographic
  Arts
1690 Frontage Road
Chula Vista, CA 91911
Phone: (866) IAM-FOTO
Fax: (619) 423-1818
http://www.iipa.org

The Light Factory
345 North College Street
Charlotte, NC 28202
Phone: (704) 333-9755
http://www.lightfactory.org

National Press Photographers
  Association
3200 Croasdaile Drive
Suite 306
Durham, NC 27705
Phone: (919) 383-7246
Fax: (919) 383-7261
http://www.nppa.org

New York Institute of Photography
211 East 43rd Street
Suite 2402
New York, NY 10017
Phone: (212) 867-8260
http://www.nyip.com

North American Nature Photography
  Association
10200 West 44th Avenue
Suite 304
Wheat Ridge, CO 80033-2840
Phone: (303) 422-8527
Fax: (303) 422-8894
http://www.nanpa.org

Photographic Resource Center at
  Boston University
832 Commonwealth Avenue
Boston, MA 02215
Phone: (617) 975-0600
Fax: (617) 975-0606
http://www.prcboston.org;
  http://www.bu.edu/prc

Photographic Society of America,
  Inc.
3000 United Founders Boulevard
Suite 103
Oklahoma City, OK 73112-3940
Phone: (405) 843-1437
Fax: (405) 843-1438
http://www.psa-photo.org

Professional Photographers of
  America, Inc.
229 Peachtree Street NE
Suite 2200
Atlanta, GA 30303
Phone: (800) 786-6277
http://www.ppa.com

Society for Photographic Education
SPE National Office
110 Art Building
Department of Art
Miami University
Oxford, OH 45056-2486
Phone: (513) 529-8328
Fax: (513) 529-9301

Student Photographic Society
229 Peachtree Street NE
Suite 2200
Atlanta, GA 30303
Phone: (866) 886-5325
http://www.studentphoto.com

Texas Photographic Society
6338 North New Braunfels
Suite 174
San Antonio, TX 78209
Phone: (210) 824-4123
Fax: (210) 822-8910
http://www.texasphoto.org

HISTORICAL

The Daguerreian Society
3043 West Liberty Avenue

Pittsburgh, PA 15216-2460
Phone: (412) 343-5525
Fax: (412) 207-9119
http://www.daguerre.org

WORKSHOPS

Great American Photography Workshops
902 Broyles Avenue
Maryville, TN 37801
Phone: (866) 747-GAPW
Fax: (865) 981-3234
http://www.gapweb.com

Pictures of the Year International
109 Lee Hills Hall
Columbia, Missouri 65211
Phone: (573) 882-4882
Fax: (573) 884-4999
http://www.poy.org

Santa Fe Workshops
P.O. Box 9916
Santa Fe, NM 87504-5916
Phone: (505) 983-1400
Fax: (505) 989-8604
http://www.sfworkshop.com

The Workshops
P.O. Box 200
2 Central Street
Rockport, ME 04856
Phone: (207) 236-8581 or
    (877) 577-7700 (toll-free)
Fax: (207) 236-2558
http://www.theworkshops.com

Youth Outlook Photography Workshop
YO! (Youth Outlook)
660 Market Street
Room 210
San Francisco, CA 94104
Phone: (415) 438-4755
http://www.pacificnews.org/yo

APPENDIX VII
WEB SITES

EQUIPMENT MANUFACTURERS, RETAILERS, AND TECHNICAL SITES

Canon U.S.A., Inc.
http://www.canonusa.com

Nikon Inc.
http://www.nikonusa.com

Olympus
http://www.olympusamerica.com

Kodak
http://www.kodak.com

B&H Photo-Video-Pro Audio
http://www.bhphotovideo.com

The Analog Photography Users Group
http://www.apug.org

CLUBS AND SOCIETIES

Royal Photographic Society
http://www.rps.org

Wellington Photographic Society
http://photosoc.wellington.net.nz

New Hampshire Society of Photographic Artists
http://www.nhspa.org

Northern California Council of Camera Clubs
http://www.n4c.org

Twin Cities Area Council of Camera Clubs
http://www.cameracouncil.org

The Photographic Federation of Long Island
http://www.pflionline.org

Nevada Camera Club
http://nevadacc.org

New Jersey Federation of Camera Clubs
http://www.njfcc.org

South Bay Camera Club
http://www.sbccphoto.org

Palo Alto Camera Club
http://www.pacamera.com

Vienna Photographic Society
http://www.safeport.com/vps

Greater New Orleans Photographic Society
http://www.gnocc.org

Women in Photography International
http://www.womeninphotography.com

Stock Artists Alliance
http://www.stockartistsalliance.org

Leica Historical Society of America
http://www.lhsa.org

Toscana Photographic Workshop
http://www.tpw.it

The Camera Club of New York
http://www.cameraclubofnewyork.org

ONLINE PUBLICATIONS

Photo Traveler
http://phototravel.com

Apogee Photo
http://www.apogeephoto.com

Double Exposure
http://www.photoworkshop.com/double_exposure/publish

COLLECTIONS AND GALLERIES

American Museum of Photography
http://www.photography-museum.com

New York Public Library Photography Collection
http://www.nypl.org/research/chss/spe/art/photo/photo.html

Western History Photos
http://www.photoswest.org

University of California, Riverside / California Museum of Photography
http://www.cmp.ucr.edu

Smithsonian American Art Museum
http://americanart.si.edu/art_info/photoarchives.cfm

National Museum of Photography, Film & Television
http://www.nmsi.ac.uk/nmpft

HISTORICAL FIGURES AND PHOTOGRAPHIC HISTORY

Henri Cartier-Bresson Foundation
http://www.henricartierbresson.org

The Robert Mapplethorpe Foundation, Inc.
http://www.mapplethorpe.org

The Ansel Adams Gallery
http://www.anseladams.com

BoxCameras.com
http://www.boxcameras.com

Midley History of Photography
http://www.midleykent.fsnet.co.uk

The Magic Mirror of Life: An Appreciation of the Camera Obscura
http://brightbytes.com/cosite/cohome.html

Get the Picture: Thinking about Photographs
http://www.artsmia.org/get-the-picture

Digital Video Professionals Association
http://www.dvpa.com

BetterPhoto
http://www.betterphoto.com

PhotographyTips
http://photographytips.com

WORKSHOPS

Alexia Foundation for World Peace, Inc.
http://www.alexiafoundation.org

College Photographer of the Year
http://www.cpoy.org

Midwest Photographic Workshops
http://www.mpw.com

APPENDIX VIII
PERIODICALS

American Photo
1633 Broadway
43rd Floor
New York, NY 10019
Phone: (212) 767-6203
Fax: (212) 489-4217
http://www.americanphotomag.com

Black & White **Magazine**
1789 Lyn Road
Arroyo Grande, CA 93420
Phone: (805) 967-8161
http://www.bandwmag.com

Blind Spot **Magazine**
210 11 Avenue
New York, NY 10001
Phone: (212) 633-1317
Fax: (212) 627-9364
http://www.blindspot.com

Digital Imaging Techniques
445 Broad Hollow Road
Suite 21
Melville, NY 11747
Phone: (631) 845-2700
Fax: (631) 845-7109
http://www.imaginginfo.com/di

Digital Photographer
290 Maple Court
Suite 232
Ventura, CA 93003
Phone: (805) 644-3824
http://www.digiphotomag.com

Imaging Business
3 Huntington Quadrangle
Suite 301N
Melville, NY 11747
Phone: (631) 845-2700
Fax: (631) 845-7109
http://www.imaginginfo.com/pgp

Nature Photographer Magazine
P.O. Box 220
Lubec, ME 04652
Phone: (617) 847-0091
http://www.naturephotographermag.com

News Photographer **Magazine**
6677 Whitemarsh Valley Walk
Austin, TX 78746-6367
Phone: (419) 352-8175
http://www.nppa.org/news_and_events/
  magazine

Outdoor Photographer
Werner Publishing Corporation
12121 Wilshire Boulevard
12th floor
Los Angeles, CA 90025-1176
Phone: (310) 820-1500
Fax: (310) 826-5008
http://www.outdoorphotographer.com

PCPhoto **Magazine**
Werner Publishing Corporation
12121 Wilshire Boulevard
12th floor
Los Angeles, CA 90025
Phone: (310) 820-1500
Fax: (310) 826-5008
http://www.pcphotomag.com

Photo District News
770 Broadway
7th floor
New York, NY 10003
Phone: (646) 654-5780
Fax: (646) 654-5813
http://www.pdnonline.com

The Photo Review
140 East Richardson Avenue
Suite 301
Langhorne, PA 19047-2824
Phone: (215) 891-0214
http://www.photoreview.org

Photo Techniques
Preston Publications
6600 West Touhy Avenue
Niles, IL 60714
Phone: (847) 647-2900
Fax: (847) 647-1155
http://www.phototechmag.com

Photo Trade News
445 Broad Hollow Road
Suite 21
Melville, NY 11747
Phone: (631) 845-2700
Fax: (631) 845-7109
http://www.imaginginfo.com/ptn

Photograph America
P.O. Box 86
Novato, CA
Phone: (415) 898-3736
http://photographamerica.com

Photographic
P.O. Box 420235
Palm Coast, FL 32142-0235
Phone: (800) 800-3686
E-mail: photographic@palmcoastd.com
http://www.photographic.com

Photoshop User
333 Douglas Road East
Oldsmar, FL 34677
Phone: (813) 433-5006
Fax: (813) 433-5015
http://www.photoshopuser.com

Picture
41 Union Square West, #504
New York, NY 10003
Phone: (212) 352-2700
Fax: (212) 352-2155
http://www.picturemagazine.com

Popular Photography & Imaging
1633 Broadway
New York, NY 10019
Phone: (212) 767-6000
Fax: (212) 767-5602
http://www.popphoto.com

Professional Photographer **Magazine**
229 Peachtree Street NE
Suite 2200
International Tower
Atlanta, GA 30303
Phone: (404) 522-8600
http://www.ppmag.com

Shutterbug
1419 Chaffee Drive
Suite #1
Titusville, FL 32780
Phone: (321) 269-3212
http://www.shutterbug.net

Studio Photography & Design
445 Broad Hollow Road
Suite 21
Melville, NY 11747
Phone: (631) 845-2700
Fax: (631) 845-7109
http://www.imaginginfo.com/spd

Today's Photographer **Magazine**
P.O. Box 777
Lewisville, NC 27023-0777
Phone: (336) 945-9867
Fax: (336) 945-3711
http://www.aipress.com/tpmag.html

BIBLIOGRAPHY

GENERAL PHOTOGRAPHY

Adams, Ansel, and Robert Baker. *The Camera.* Reprint ed. New York: Bulfinch Press, 1995.

————. *The Negative.* Reprint ed. New York: Bulfinch Press, 1995.

————. *The Print.* Reprint ed. New York: Bulfinch Press, 1995.

Bervin, Johnson, Robert E. Mayer, and Fred Schmidt. *Opportunities in Photography Careers.* Chicago: VGM Career Horizons, 1999.

Frost, Lee. *The A–Z of Creative Photography: Over 70 Techniques Explained in Full.* New York: Watson-Guptill Publications, 1998.

Graphic Artists Guild. *Graphic Artists Guild Handbook of Pricing and Ethical Guidelines.* 11th ed. New York: Graphic Artists Guild, 2003.

Grimm, Tom, and Michele. *The Basic Book of Photography.* 5th ed. New York: Plume, 2003.

Horenstein, Henry. *Black and White Photography: A Basic Manual.* 3d. edition, rev. New York: Little, Brown and Company, 2004.

Horenstein, Henry, and Russell Hart. *Photography.* Rev. ed. Upper Saddle River, N.J.: Prentice Hall, 2003.

Horenstein, Henry. *Beyond Basic Photography: A Technical Manual.* New York: Little, Brown and Company, 1977.

Langford, Michael. *Basic Photography.* 7th ed. Burlington, Mass.: Focal Press, 2000.

London, Barbara, and John Upton. *Photography.* 7th ed. Upper Saddle River, N.J.: Prentice Hall, 2001.

McLean, Cheryl. *Careers for Shutter Bugs & Other Candid Types.* New York: McGraw-Hill, 2003.

Oberrecht, Ken. *How to Start a Home-Based Photography Business.* 5th ed. Guilford, Conn.: Globe Pequot, 2005.

Peterson, Bryan. *Learning to See Creatively: Design, Color & Composition in Photography.* Revised Edition. New York: Amphoto Books, 2003.

Peterson, Bryan. *Understanding Exposure: How to Shoot Great Photographs with a Film or Digital Camera.* Revised Edition. New York: Amphoto Books, 2004.

Piscopo, Maria. *The Photographer's Guide to Marketing & Self-Promotion.* New York: Allworth Press, 2001.

Poehler, Donna. *2006 Photographer's Market.* Cincinnati, Ohio: Writer's Digest Books, 2005.

Heron, Michael, and David MacTavish. *Pricing Photography: The Complete Guide to Assignment & Stock Prices.* 3rd ed. New York: Watson-Guptill Publications, 2002.

Zimberoff, Tom. *Photography: Focus on Profit.* New York: Watson-Guptill Publications, 2002.

BUSINESS AND INDUSTRIAL PHOTOGRAPHY

Hawkes, Jason, and Adele McConnel. *Aerial: The Art of Photography from the Sky.* East Sussex, U.K.: RotoVision, 2003.

Roth, Eric. *Interior Photography: Lighting and Other Professional Techniques with Style.* New York: Amphoto Books, 2004.

Shulman, Julius. *Photographing Architecture and Interiors.* New York: Princeton Architectural Press, 2000.

CINEMATOGRAPHY AND VIDEOGRAPHY

Alton, John. *Painting with Light.* Berkeley, Calif.: University of California Press, 1995.

Brown, Blain. *Cinematography: Image Making for Cinematographers, Directors, and Videographers.* Burlington, Mass.: Focal Press, 2002.

Mascelli, Joseph V. *The Five C's of Cinematography: Motion Picture Filming Techniques.* Los Angeles: Silman-James Press, 1998.

Rogers, Pauline B. *Contemporary Cinematographers on Their Art.* Burlington, Mass.: Focal Press, 1998.

Samuelson, David. *Hands-on Manual for Cinematographers.* 2d. ed. Burlington, Mass.: Focal Press, 1998.

COMMERCIAL PHOTOGRAPHY, ADVERTISING, AND PUBLICITY

Engh, Rohn. *Sell & Resell Your Photos: Learn How to Sell Your Pictures Worldwide.* 5th ed. Cincinnati, Ohio: Writer's Digest Books, 2003.

————. *SellPhotos.Com: Your Guide to Establishing a Successful Stock Photography Business on the Internet.* Cincinnati, Ohio: Writer's Digest Books, 2000.

Heron, Michael. *How to Shoot Stock Photos That Sell.* 3d ed. New York: Allworth Press, 2001.

Jacobs, Lou. *The Big Picture: The Professional Photographer's Guide to Rights, Rates & Negotiation.* Cincinnati, Ohio: Writer's Digest Books, 2000.

Weisgrau, Richard. *Real Business of Photography.* New York: Allworth Press, 2004.

Zuckerman, Jim. *Shooting & Selling Your Photos: The Complete Guide to Making Money With Your Photography.* Cincinnati, Ohio: Writer's Digest Books, 2003.

EVENT AND TRAVEL PHOTOGRAPHY

Arndt, David Neil. *How to Shoot and Sell Sports Photography.* Buffalo, N.Y.: Amherst Media, 1999.

Cantrell, Bambi, and Skip Cohen. *The Art of Wedding Photography: Professional Techniques with Style.* New York: Watson-Guptill Publications, 2000.

Gero, Paul. *Digital Wedding Photography.* Muska & Lippman, 2004.

McCartney, Susan. *Travel Photography: A Complete Guide to How to Shoot and Sell.* 2d ed. New York: Allworth Press, 1999.

FINE ARTS AND EDUCATION

Editors of Phaidon Press. *The Photo Book.* Boston: Phaidon Press, 1997.

Hope, Terry. *Fine Art Photography: Creating Beautiful Images for Sale and Display.* East Sussex, U.K.: RotoVision, 2003.

Long, Ben. *Complete Digital Photography.* 3rd ed. Hingham, Mass.: Charles River Media, 2004.

Peterson, Bryan. *Understanding Digital Photography: Techniques For Getting Great Pictures.* New York: Amphoto Books, 2005.

MEDICAL AND SCIENTIFIC PHOTOGRAPHY

Howell, Carol, and Warren Blanc. *A Practical Guide to Archaeological Photography.* Los Angeles: UCLA Institute of Archaeology, 1995.

Ray, Sidney F. *Scientific Photography and Applied Imaging.* Burlington, Mass.: Focal Press, 1999.

Stack, Lawrence B. *Handbook of Medical Photography.* Philadelphia: Hanley & Belfus, 2001.

NEWS MEDIA AND ENTERTAINMENT PHOTOGRAPHY

American Society of Media Photographers. *ASMP Professional Business Practices in Photography.* 6th ed. New York: Watson-Guptill Publications, 2001.

Evans, Duncan. *A Comprehensive Guide to Digital Glamour Photography.* Lausanne, Switzerland: AVA Publishing, 2005.

Gray, Jon. *Complete Guide to Beauty & Glamour Photography.* Devon, U.K.: David & Charles Publishers, 2003.

Horton, Brian. *Associated Press Guide to Photojournalism.* 2d. ed. New York: McGraw-Hill, 2000.

Kobre, Kenneth. *Photojournalism: The Professional's Approach.* 5th ed. Burlington, Mass.: Focal Press, 2004.

Sedge, Michael. *The Photojournalist's Guide to Making Money.* New York: Allworth Press, 2000.

PHOTOGRAPHY BUSINESS AND RELATED JOBS

Crawford, Tad. *Business and Legal Forms for Photographers.* 3d. edition. New York: Watson-Guptill Publications, 2002.

Orenstein, Vik. *Photographer's Market Guide to Building Your Photography Business.* Cincinnati, Ohio: Writer's Digest Books, 2004.

PORTRAIT PHOTOGRAPHY

Buselle, Michael. *Better Picture Guide to Photographing People.* East Sussex, U.K.: RotoVision, 1999.

Cleghorn, Mark. *Portrait Photography: Secrets of Posing & Lighting.* Asheville, N.C.: Lark Books, 2004.

Lilley, Edward R. *The Business of Studio Photography: How to Start and Run a Successful Photography Studio.* New York: Allworth Press, 2002.

Muska, Debra H. *Professional Techniques for Pet and Animal Photography.* Buffalo, N.Y.: Amherst Media, 2003.

Sholin, Marilyn. *Studio Portrait Photography of Children and Babies.* Buffalo, N.Y.: Amherst Media, 2002.

INDEX